BROKE OF THE SHANNON

The Glorious Victory
of the

SHANNON over the CHESAPEAKE,

A Descriptive

BATTLE PIECE,

for the

Piano Forte,

Composed & Most Respectfully Dedicated to

Capt.ⁿ Broke, his Officers & Crew,

BY

T. HOWELL.

Price 3

London, Printed by J & G. BALLS, Music Warehouse, 408, Oxford Street.

BROKE OF THE SHANNON

and the War of 1812

Edited by Tim Voelcker

Seaforth
PUBLISHING

[Frontispiece]

The title page of 'The Glorious Victory of the Shannon over the Chesapeake' by Thomas Howell, London, 1813.

Text copyright © Individual contributors 2013

First published in Great Britain in 2013 by
Seaforth Publishing,
Pen & Sword Books Ltd,
47 Church Street,
Barnsley S70 2AS

www.seaforthpublishing.com

British Library Cataloguing in Publication Data
A catalogue record for this book is available
from the British Library

ISBN 978 184832 179 3

Typeset and designed by M.A.T.S. Leigh-on-Sea, Essex
Printed and bound by CPI Group (UK) Ltd, Croydon, CR0 4YY

Contents

Illustrations and Maps

Black and White Plates (between pages 102 and 103)

11 HMS *Shannon* under sail, by Admiral King. (Brighton, *Memoir of Admiral Broke*, London 1866)
12 Broke as a young captain by F Blood.
13 Broke in old age, by Sir William Ross in 1833. (Brighton, *Memoir of Admiral Broke*, London 1866)
14 Photograph of the breech of a Blomefield cannon. (Martin Bibbings)
15 A replica of one of Broke's designs for a tangent sight fitted to the breech of a cannon behind the gunlock. (Martin Bibbings)
16 Quarterdeck of HMS *Trincomalee*. (Martin Bibbings)
17 Gun drill. (Martin Bibbings)
18 A romantic vision of the death of Lawrence. (Suffolk Record Office, Ipswich, HA93/13/21)
19 *Peace of Ghent 1814 and Triumph of America*. (Library of Congress, Washington DC, USA)
20 *PREPARING* JOHN BULL for GENERAL CONGRESS, by George Cruikshank, 1813. (© Trustees of the British Museum, British Museum Satires 12077)
21 *THE FALL OF WASHINGTON – or Maddy in full flight*. (© Trustees of the British Museum, British Museum Satires 12311)
22 *Bruin become MEDIATOR or Negotiation for PEACE*, by William Charles. (Courtesy The Lily Library, Indiana University, Bloomington, Indiana)
23 *Trincomalee* – a sister-ship restored. (Image courtesy of Nick Servian/Robert Harding World Imagery)

Illustrations

Page
Frontispiece 'The Glorious Victory of the Shannon over the Chesapeake'. (© British Library Board, h.1480.w.(12.)1813)
xvii Maps of the naval battleground. (Peter Wilkinson)
58 Portrait of Captain James Lawrence, by William Rollinson. (Library of Congress, Washington DC, USA)
106 The parts of a cannon. (Martin Bibbings)
112 The manning and layout for firing an 18pdr gun, from Captain

Preface and Acknowledgements

For reasons that you can read in the Introduction, this book is an anthology of works that selected historians have been asked to write against a tight deadline to celebrate the bicentenary of the finest frigate action in the era of wooden sailing men-of-war. The one exception is the first contribution, the 'Historical Note' of the Revd Brighton, dated 1866, which is included out of sentiment for Broke's first memorialist and for its historic value in recording the events he considered important. The Editor is most grateful to all contributors for the time and trouble they have taken and the enthusiasm they have shown despite the pressure put on them. They range in age from under 30 to over 90, and so include both some of the leading names in this field and those who will doubtless go on to succeed them. Thanks are also due to Seaforth Publishing and the Naval Institute Press, Annapolis, for their readiness to commit to a print-run that allows the finished volume to be sold at under £20. Without the support of the Ipswich Maritime Trust and the new University Campus Suffolk it would have been impossible to hold the Symposium to launch the book; and without the editorial assistance of Colin Reid, who is also the final contributor, the task of gently trimming or drastically pruning (according to one's viewpoint) contributions from sixteen different writers would never have been completed in time. Thanks must also go to Martin Bibbings for his endless labour of love and discoveries, to Stuart Grimwade for stepping in at the last minute to help with the illustrations and to Mary Murphy for her speedy and helpful copy-editing.

Academics may regret the thinness of references. The policy has been that as a general rule we should include references only for straight quotations of some substance; that where possible the three facts of 'who said it', 'when', and 'where it can be found' should be covered; that these should be worked into the text if this could be done comfortably but otherwise as a footnote; and that further reference details could then be found in the bibliography which would include a wide range of secondary sources. Most of the Broke letters are in the Suffolk Record Office, Gatacre Road, Ipswich IP1 2LQ, tel: 01473 263910 (shortened to SRO in footnotes).

Variations in the spelling of English between Britain, Canada and the USA have been left in the original tongue in direct quotations, but otherwise are normally in the UK version since that is where the book is printed. Words such as 'honour/honor' are confusing since both forms were used in Britain in Broke's day. Errors of spelling, punctuation or grammar have normally been left as in the original. It was decided not to include a nautical glossary as alternative sources and the internet are readily available.

Notes on Contributors

Captain Michael Barritt was Hydrographer of the Navy from 2001 to 2003. During his naval career he served in both north and south polar areas, and visited Spitsbergen during subsequent work for the International Hydrographic Organisation. He is President of the Hakluyt Society and a director of the Nautical Institute. In 2008 he published *Eyes of the Admiralty*, a study in front-line hydrographic data collection in the French Revolutionary War, and is currently writing an account of the emergence of the RN Surveying Service in the period 1793–1823.

Martin Bibbings worked as one of the principal historical advisers for the Oscar-winning 2003 film *Master and Commander: Far Side of the World* based on Patrick O'Brian's novels, providing technical expertise and gunnery training. He worked in a similar capacity for the television dramatisation of the C S Forester *Hornblower* series and he has undertaken extensive research into naval gunnery in the smooth-bore era, including detailed examination of the Broke archives in Ipswich. He is also a practical gunner and has used his own collection of cannons for displays around the country and abroad. In 2005, he recreated a 52-gun broadside from HMS *Victory* to celebrate the bicentenary of the Battle of Trafalgar.

Dr John Blatchly first came to Suffolk in 1955 to teach boy seamen at HMS *Ganges*, returning in 1972 as headmaster of Ipswich School. Since retiring in 1993, he has governed and inspected schools, written for the *Oxford Dictionary of National Biography*, worked with the Heritage Lottery Fund in the East of England and published more than a dozen books. For nearly eight years he published a full-page article on Suffolk history in the *East Anglian Daily Times* every Saturday; he continues to do so once a month.

Dr James Davey is Curator of Naval History at the National Maritime Museum and a Visiting Lecturer at the University of Greenwich. He holds degrees from King's College London, and the University of Oxford, and completed his PhD at the University of Greenwich in 2010. His publications include *Broadsides: Caricature and the Navy, 1756–1815* (with Richard Johns), *The Transformation of British Naval Strategy: Supply and Seapower* *in Northern Europe, 1808–1812*, and *Nelson, Navy & Nation* (edited with Quintin Colville). He is currently editing a volume of Admiral Saumarez's correspondence with Tim Voelcker.

Dr Gabriela A Frei has recently finished her DPhil in History at Merton College, Oxford, examining the role of international law in the making of British maritime strategy prior to the First World War. She earned a Master of Studies in Historical Research from the University of Oxford and a Licentiata Philosophiae (History, Constitutional Law and English Literature) from the University of Berne. In 2013, she was awarded a Brandon Research Fellowship at the Lauterpacht Centre for International Law at the University of Cambridge.

Dr Ellen Gill recently completed her PhD thesis at the University of Sydney, Australia, which focused on the correspondence of naval families, including Philip Broke, between 1740 and 1820. Her research examines the effects of war on the family and considers the themes of familial relationships, duty, love, patronage and networks. She moved to England in 2011, where she now lives in Kent, and is married to Martin Salmon, another contributor to this book.

Dr Julian Gwyn is Professor Emeritus, University of Ottawa. He edited *The Royal Navy and North America: The Warren Papers, 1736–1752* for the Navy Records Society and has written a number of other books on North American history, including *Ashore and Afloat: The British Navy and the Halifax Naval Yard before 1820*; *Frigates and Foremasts: The North American Squadron in Nova Scotia Waters, 1745–1815*; and *Maritime Commerce & the Economic Development of Nova Scotia, 1740–1870*.

Dr John B Hattendorf is the Ernest J King Professor of Maritime History at the US Naval War College in Newport, Rhode Island. A former officer in the US Navy, he holds degrees in history from Kenyon College and Brown University, with his DPhil from the University of Oxford, where he studied at Pembroke College. He is the author or editor of more than forty books, including being editor-in-chief of *The Oxford Encyclopedia of Maritime History* (2007). He has received many awards, including the Caird Medal of the National Maritime Museum, Greenwich, and an honorary doctorate.

Dr Andrew Lambert is Laughton Professor of History in the Department of War Studies at King's College London. His work has addressed technology, policy-making, regional security, deterrence, historiography, crisis management and conflict. He presented the acclaimed television series *War at Sea* for BBC2 in 2004. His latest book, *The Challenge: Britain versus America in the Naval War of 1812*, was published by Faber in 2012.

Dr Chris Madsen is Professor in the Department of Defence Studies at the Royal Military College of Canada and Canadian Forces College in Toronto, where he teaches senior and mid-rank officers in various professional military education programmes and conducts staff rides related to the War of 1812. He holds a BA Honors in history from Simon Fraser University, an MA in history from the University of Western Ontario, and a PhD from the University of Victoria. He has published widely in military, naval, legal, and business history in the research fields of shipbuilding, military law, and operational planning. Professor Madsen is currently First Vice President of the Canadian Nautical Research Society.

Colin Reid read history at Corpus Christi College, Cambridge, and later returned as a Schoolteacher Fellow Commoner to Clare College. He was Head of History at the United World College of the Atlantic when it pioneered the International Baccalaureate. He has directed a Peace Education project funded by the Leverhulme Trust and edited a series of teaching books and some colonial memoirs. After twenty-three years as Head of St Christopher School in Letchworth he retired to Suffolk, but spends a large part of each summer cruising in the Hebrides.

Martin Salmon grew up in Chatham and developed an interest in the Royal Navy from an early age. He works as an archivist in the Manuscripts Department of the National Maritime Museum, Greenwich, where he has been for the past seven years. He has always had an interest in maritime history, Anglo-American relations and especially the War of 1812. He is married to Dr Ellen Gill and lives near the river Medway, a stone's throw from where HMS *Shannon* was built.

Peter Schurr CBE MA FRCS, Professor Emeritus of Guy's Hospital, studied medicine at Cambridge and University College Hospital, London. He joined the Royal Army Medical Corps in 1943 and served in Egypt and Greece. In 1949, he trained in neurosurgery at Oxford and became a surgical research fellow at Harvard. In 1955, he became consultant neurosurgeon at Guy's and the Maudsley Hospitals, London, and held honorary appointments in Britain and the USA, including at the Queen Elizabeth Military Hospital in Woolwich. He has been visiting professor at medical schools in the USA, Canada and Egypt, and an officer of numerous medical societies. As an author he has written numerous papers and two biographies of distinguished surgeons.

Dr Tim Voelcker did National Service in the Royal Navy, continuing for thirty-five years in the RNR. He bought his first sailing dinghy at the age of 13 and is a member of the Ocean Cruising Club. He read history at Peterhouse, Cambridge. After various educational jobs, he moved into the drinks trade, later setting up a wine business in Ipswich. He sold this in 2000 to study for a PhD at Exeter. His thesis on Admiral Saumarez was published in 2008. This led him to Captain Broke, since the two families became joined by marriage and share the same Suffolk archive. With James Davey, he is currently editing the Saumarez correspondence for the Navy Records Society.

John Wain at age 15 built a Canadian canoe to explore the River Thames. It taught him about wooden boats and their handling characteristics before a science career in the NHS got in the way. Dealing with his father's estate which included ship models and a nautical library, he discovered that naval history could be interpreted via its historic artefacts, turning a passion for collecting into a business as a maritime antiques dealer. In 2002, he co-founded the Oxford-based Britannia Naval Research Association, presenting and publishing naval history via monthly meetings, a bi-annual journal and a naval history conference now in its eleventh year.

Richard Wilson, like Philip Vere Broke, was educated at Ipswich School. He then read history at Cambridge University before pursuing a career as a tenor soloist in classical music (with the professional name Richard Edgar-Wilson). He has worked with many of the world's leading conductors and orchestras in more than thirty countries, made more than fifty solo recordings and sung on two Oscar-winning films. Richard has also written and edited a number of articles and books on music, history and wildlife.

The Naval Battlegrounds

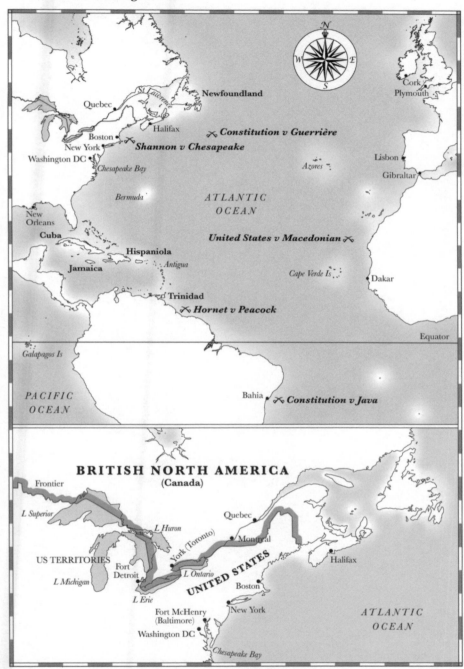

xvii

Introduction

Tim Voelcker

Three nations – one new, one yet to be formally created and one long-established – faced each other in the War of 1812. It is a war that is little-known outside the academic world and could be said to have had little impact at the time since the treaty that brought it to an end had a negative result in its restoration of the status quo. That negativity is far from the truth. Each of the three nations – the United States, Canada and Great Britain – maintained both then and to this day that it won, or at least did not lose. If 'beauty is in the eye of the beholder', that is equally true of victory. The reports of combatants may be sincerely believed by those writing them but how often does hindsight show them to be highly glossed.

In the belief that there is some truth in each country's claim, this book does not seek to draw conclusions but to present alternative views, leaving it to the reader to make his or her own judgement. There is much more to war than military success. It was inevitable, short of gross incompetence, that, in what was inherently a naval war, the fledgling US Navy would be overwhelmed by the world's most powerful navy of its time, when it could abstract itself from the pressures of the world's most powerful armies and their leader Napoleon. What mattered in the long term were the varying impacts of that war on the countries involved and their future relations. These will be covered by the international trio of professors and in the final selection of quotations from distinguished commentators.

Turning to detail, Ipswich, the county town of Suffolk, historically a predominantly agricultural area, is not noted for famous names despite the maritime heritage it also possesses. That of Cardinal Wolsey, chief adviser to King Henry VIII, seems to appear everywhere for want of any other. More recently, Sir Alf Ramsey and Sir Bobby Robson are names that football followers will enthuse over and the cartoonist Giles has been commemorated by a splendid statue of his much-loved character Grandma. But after that one hesitates. The names are indeed there, but they need to be hunted out. One such is Admiral Philip Broke from the nearby village of Nacton. Two hundred years ago he was a national hero, yet today, even locally, there is only a scattering of people who actually recognise his name. And they may not know much more – why, for instance, the pub in the next village, Bucklesham, is called the Shannon, or anything about the War of 1812 in which he became the toast of the nation: 'To an Irish river and an English brook' (for that is how the family and their friends have always pronounced it). This book's first purpose was to try to remedy this in the bicentenary year of the battle that brought fame to both the man and the ship.

From this grew a second objective. There is a great gulf between the heavy monograph of the academic world of naval history, often a doctoral thesis, that sells in small numbers at a high price, and the popular tales of naval fiction that are printed in thousands. At an Oxford conference, Professor Andrew Lambert of King's College London, urged naval historians present to reach out to a wider audience in this island whose history is so closely bound to the sea. *Broke of the Shannon* is a response; an anthology of many voices, seeking to combine good scholarship with a more appealing presentation. A friend politely criticised a previous book for having 'too much detail' at the same time that a scholastic review condemned it for failing to cover important aspects. The present work is therefore a compromise which it is hoped will encourage the passage of more readers across the divide.

The first part covers the setting for the battle, the War of 1812, when the young USA declared war, fed up with what it saw as Britain's arrogant harassment of its growing merchant fleet. At the same time, it invaded Canada, seizing the opportunity offered by Britain's preoccupation with the conflict against Napoleon, which President Madison judged her likely to lose. Leading professors from each of the three countries give their own independent assessments. The war was complex and the distances in North America are enormous. On land, the action stretched from New Orleans to the Great Lakes and from Maine down the long eastern seaboard in what today might be called commando raids, including the burning of the White House. At sea, warships girdled the world. The North Atlantic from Halifax to Bergen and from Jamaica to the Cape Verdes was the chief hunting ground, but the Pacific and even the Indian Ocean came into play.

Rather than attempt to cover all this, the second part concentrates on Broke and the less controversial battle between HMS *Shannon* and USS *Chesapeake*, though there are still arguments about how Broke won and why so quickly. There has not been a biography since the excellent *Broke and the Shannon* of 1968 by Peter Padfield, another Suffolk man. The original *Memoir* of 1866 by Revd J G Brighton is slightly suspect, though full of useful information. Brighton firmly asserts that 'the main end of a biography is less the laudation of the dead than the advantage of the living' but goes on to say that his main source materials are Broke's journals and private log-books, regretting that 'Broke was profoundly averse to all mention of himself or his feelings',[1] and noting that he records his greatest event with just two words: 'Took *Chesapeake*'. Brighton's other source is the invaluable *Naval History of Great Britain* by W M James. James had an axe to grind against American writing on the naval War, claiming that 'official letter-writing, so far from being a fair representation of facts, was a political engine made use of by the government . . . to render the war popular throughout the union',[2] but he did largely confine himself to well-researched facts rather than opinions. However, Brighton's transcription is not always accurate. In one case he has misled painters of the action, who show the captured *Chesapeake* flying a white ensign as she approaches Halifax rather than the blue ensign of the admiral under whose command Broke then was (see Plate 4). Writing in 1866, two years after the white ensign was ordered to be virtually uniquely flown by Royal Naval ships, Brighton had substituted 'white' for 'English' in following James's account.

In this work, contributors from a variety of fields look at the man himself from different angles. Especially important are the letters Broke wrote to his much-loved wife Louisa or, as he called her, Loo. Letters were the vital link that took a warship's captain out of the enclosed world of his 'wooden wife' and kept him in touch with his home and family. A substantial chapter deals with naval gunnery, for Broke's contribution to that field had greater long-term effect on British seapower in the nineteenth century than the single battle for which he

1 Brighton, *Broke Memoir*, pp 9–10.
2 James, *Naval History*, vol I, p i.

is renowned. That battle, however, was the event that brought his inventive skills to public notice although, ironically, circumstances prevented him from using many of his innovations in the action itself. Moreover, its impact on the morale and strategies of the two rival navies made it a turning point in the war. The suggestion is made that the initial run of American victories in single-ship actions had the reverse effect of what was believed at the time and that this was accentuated by Broke's victory. Similarly, the apparent success of Admiral Cockburn's commando-like raids on the USA's eastern sea-board, intended to make the Americans sue for peace, instead heightened their anger and antagonism, and strengthened their will to fight on, even when it was evident to their political leaders that national bankruptcy must follow.

The book delves briefly into a number of what might be called side-lines which nonetheless help to make up a fuller picture – Broke's youth and education, Prize Law, the Royal Navy's base at Halifax, convoy duties off Spitsbergen, a medical opinion on his recovery from near death, the *Shannon*'s later history and the *Chesapeake*'s transformation into a Hampshire watermill. Scattered through the book the Editor has inserted boxes of details intended to illuminate particular facets. More importantly, there are chapters on public opinion about the war, the Navy and the battle expressed in popular art, ballads and poetry, before it ends with a collection of often contradictory comments from politicians and historians. Put all together, the contributions gathered here confirm a view that Broke was a talented, determined and likeable man who deserves to be better known and that the war was not just a 'tiresome irritant' as it was considered in Britain at the time,[3] but an important episode in the development of the Western world.

Further General Reading
James, William, *The Naval History of Great Britain*, vols 1 & 6 (1837; reprinted 2002).
Padfield, Peter, *Broke and the Shannon* (1968).

---

3 Rodger, *The Command of the Ocean*, p 571.

Historical Note

From *Admiral Sir P B V Broke: A Memoir*, by Revd J G Brighton (1866), pp ix–xi. This note has been transcribed as originally printed except for font and punctuation.

The following were the principal events preceding and occurring in the second war with the *United States*:–

1806

April 25   *John Pierce*, an American citizen, accidentally killed by a shot fired from the *British* ship *Leander*, Captain *H Whitby*.

May   The *British* Government captures many *American* vessels for a breach of the paper blockade.[1]

May 3   President *Jefferson* issues a proclamation forbidding certain *British* armed vessels to enter the ports of the *United States* and interdicting supplies to them.

November   The Emperor *Napoleon* issues a decree at *Berlin* declaring the *British Islands* in a state of blockade.

A Treaty concluded with *England* by Messrs *Monroe* and *Pinkney*, but rejected by President *Jefferson*.

1807

June 22   The *American* frigate *Chesapeake* brought-to by the *British* ship *Leopard*, and several *English* deserters captured.

President *Jefferson* issues a proclamation forbidding *British* vessels of war to enter the ports of the *United States*.

The *British* Government issues Orders in Council, prohibiting to neutral nations the trade with *France*.

The Emperor *Napoleon* issues a decree at *Milan* affecting neutrals.

Congress passes an Act laying a general embargo on vessels of the *United States*.

---

[1] One which has been promulgated but is not enforced by actual men-of-war on station.

1808

January 1   Commodore *Barron* of the *Chesapeake* tried by a court-martial at *Norfolk* and sentenced to be suspended for five years. Congress authorizes the President to suspend the embargo in favour of that Power which should repeal its decrees.

One of the seamen taken from the *Chesapeake* executed at Halifax.

1809

March 4   *James Madison* inaugurated President and *George Clinton* Vice President.

The *British* Government refuses to ratify the Treaty concluded with the *United States*.

The Non-Intercourse Law renewed against *Great Britain*.

Mr *Erskine*, the *British* Minister, recalled.

November   Mr *Jackson*, the *British* Minister,[2] dismissed by the President for offensive expressions in his correspondence with the Government.

1811

May 16   Gallant defence of HM sloop *Little Belt* when attacked by Commodore *Rodgers* in the *President*.

1812

June 18   War declared against *Great Britain* by the *United States*.

July 12   General *Hull* invades *Canada*.

August 13   *British* sloop *Alert* taken by US frigate *Essex*.

   16   General *Hull* capitulates.

   19   *British* frigate Guerriere taken by US frigate *Constitution*.

October 17   *British* ship *Frolic* taken by US *Wasp*; both vessels afterwards captured by *British Poictiers* (seventy-four).

   25   *British* frigate *Macedonian* taken by US frigate *United States*.

December 29   *British* frigate *Java* taken by US frigate *Constitution*.

---

[2] Jackson was Foreign Secretary George Canning's special envoy to Denmark in 1807 who had so antagonised Crown Prince Frederik, leading to Britain's second attack on Copenhagen (see Voelcker, *Admiral Saumarez*, pp 11–12).

1813

February 23   *British* sloop *Peacock* taken by US *Hornet*.
June 1   US frigate *Chesapeake* taken by HMS *Shannon*.
August 14   US brig *Argus* taken by HMS *Pelican*.
September 4   HMS *Boxer* taken by US *Enterprise*.

1814

March 20   US frigate *Essex* taken by HM [*sic*] *Phoebe*.
April   21   US *Frolic* taken by HMS *Orpheus*.
         29   HMS *Epervier* taken by US *Peacock*.
June 28   HMS *Reindeer* taken by US *Wasp*.
August 24   City of *Washington* taken by *British* forces.
September 1   HMS *Avon* taken by US *Wasp*.
The *Avon* was retaken by HMS *Castilian* and the *Wasp* shortly after
    foundered at sea.

1815

January 15   USS *President* taken by HMS *Endymion*.
February 20   Two small ships, the *Cyane* and the *Levant*, taken by
    the *American* frigate *Constitution*; but the *Levant* was recaptured
    by Sir *G Collier*.
March 23   HMS *Penguin* taken by US *Hornet*.
Several of these actions occurred subsequently to the Treaty of Peace,
    signed at *Ghent, December* 24th 1814.

BRIEF BROKE FAMILY TREE

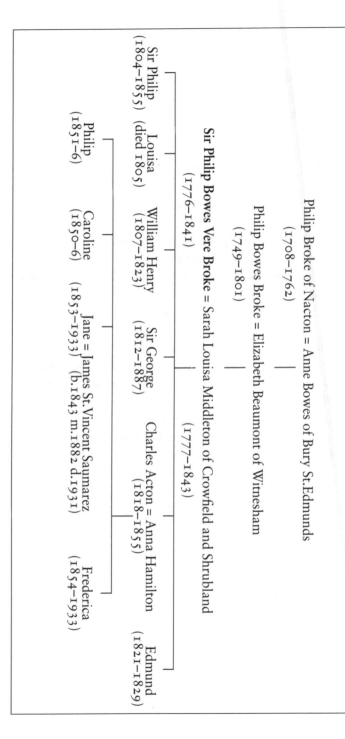

Philip Broke of Nacton = Anne Bowes of Bury St.Edmunds
(1708–1762)

Philip Bowes Broke = Elizabeth Beaumont of Witnesham
(1749–1801)

Sir Philip Bowes Vere Broke = Sarah Louisa Middleton of Crowfield and Shrubland
(1776–1841)   (1777–1843)

Sir Philip   Louisa   William Henry   Sir George   Charles Acton = Anna Hamilton   Edmund
(1804–1855) (died 1805)   (1807–1823)   (1812–1887)   (1818–1855)   (1821–1829)

Philip   Caroline   Jane = James St.Vincent Saumarez   Frederica
(1851–6)   (1850–6)   (1853–1933) (b.1843 m.1882 d.1931)   (1854–1933)

I

The War of 1812:
A Perspective from the United States*

John B Hattendorf

Over the past two centuries, the War of 1812 has been interpreted in a variety of ways in the United States. In the passions of that time – the echoes of which can still be heard in some historical interpretations – a segment of Americans viewed it as a second war for independence that was being fought to consolidate what had been started in 1775. By the late nineteenth century, many forgot what the war had been about. They forgot American defeats on land and at sea. They forgot how closely the country had come to financial ruin at the hands of the Royal Navy's blockade. Instead, the American public retained a vague memory of only selected events, but not the context in which they occurred. They still remember Andrew Jackson's victory at New Orleans in 1815, the frigate victories early in the war, the burning of Washington, 'the rockets' red glare' that showed that the flag was still there at Baltimore. And they still remember the ringing phrase 'Don't give up the ship!'

Among naval victories, the American public put relatively little emphasis on Macdonough's victory off Plattsburg on Lake Champlain in September 1814 that had resulted in halting the British Army's invasion from Canada. Instead, they remember more vividly Oliver Hazard Perry's victory a year earlier on Lake Erie, an important victory for Americans that cut British supply lines on the Great Lakes, but one of lesser strategic importance than Lake Champlain. Nevertheless, one of the most famous and enduring images of the war is William Henry Powell's historical painting of this event that was placed in the Ohio

---

* The views expressed in this paper are the academic judgements of the author alone and do not reflect any current official policy of the Naval War College, US Navy, US Department of Defense, or any other entity.

State Capitol in Columbus in 1865 and his second version placed in the National Capitol in Washington DC, in 1873. More recently, it has been reproduced on a US postage stamp issued for the bicentenary of that battle on 10 September 2013. This iconic image shows Perry making his way through heavy British fire in a ship's boat from his severely damaged flagship, the US brig *Lawrence* – a vessel that Perry had built and named in honour of his friend and professional colleague, Captain James Lawrence – to its sister-ship and his relief flagship, *Niagara*. Although not shown in Powell's painting, the most widely known and venerated relic from the war is Perry's battle flag with the paraphrase of James Lawrence's dying words: 'Don't give up the ship'. Ever since, American naval officers – apparently forgetting about the circumstances and the fact that Lawrence's *Chesapeake* was captured – have seen that battle flag as a patriotic invocation. Recently, it has been carefully conserved for permanent display in the US Naval Academy Museum. Facsimiles of the flag are widely available and often seen today flying from flagpoles or in naval buildings in the United States. In naval museum shops in America, one can even find the phrase used as a motto on men's neckties and women's scarves.

In twentieth-century American historical writing, the subject of the war has been somewhat confusing with a variety of interpretive emphases. On the one hand, it was seen attached to the rise of America as a world power, while others interpreted it in the light of the dynamics of internal American regional politics and political interest groups in the expansion of the United States across the continent. Some interesting new work has been done on the cultural history and the role of the war in American society. An interminable debate has looked at the priority of internal versus external causes for the war. This was then replaced by a series of historical debates that placed the war in the context of the rise and preservation of republicanism, the assertion of individualism, liberalism and domestic political extremism.

Alongside this changing debate about the general nature and character of the war among American historians, there has been a more consistent debate among naval historians. This discussion falls into several national categories and perspectives. The longest and most persistent tradition in American naval historical writing is a biographical one. Starting with the work of the American writer Washington Irving and his biographical sketch of Captain James

Lawrence published in the *Analectic Magazine* in 1813, there have been a large number of biographies about the heroic exploits of naval captains such as Lawrence, Stephen Decatur, John Rodgers and Isaac Hull, as well as biographies of the American commanders in the battles on Lake Erie and Lake Champlain, Oliver Hazard Perry and Thomas Macdonough. This category has also included general studies of the frigates, either collectively or individually.

A complementary American line of naval interpretation has been called the 'navalist school' in which those who were arguing for the development of a strong US Navy between 1882 and 1905 reinterpreted the naval side of the War of 1812 as a cautionary tale that demonstrated the dire straits that the nation fell into with inadequate naval preparation and an inadequate naval force. Among a number of writers, the most prominent authors in this school were future president of the United States Theodore Roosevelt, who in 1882 published *The Naval War of 1812*, and the naval historian and theorist Alfred Thayer Mahan, whose *Sea Power in its Relation to the War of 1812* appeared in 1905. This late nineteenth- and early twentieth-century navalist school of interpretation argued that the lack of naval preparation before the war had crippled the United States, but despite this serious handicap, the more extreme interpreters claimed that American sailors had heroically won glorious victories and had obtained an acceptable end to the war. The navalists concluded that the War of 1812 showed future generations the futility of land warfare and demonstrated the strategic imperative of having a strong navy for national defence. While still using the War of 1812 as an instructive example for current policy, Captain Mahan was more insightful. 'Not by rambling operations, or naval duels, are wars decided, but by force massed, and handled in skillful combination,' Mahan advised. 'It matters not that the particular force be small. The art of war is the same throughout; and may be illustrated as readily, though less conspicuously, by a flotilla as by an armada.'[1]

This American naval tradition of using the War of 1812 as an exemplar for the naval profession continues today. During the past thirty years, the Naval History and Heritage Command (and its predecessor organisations) have rendered valuable service by publishing

---

1 Mahan, *Sea Power in its Relations to the War of 1812*, vol I, p v.

a multi-volume edition of naval documents on the war. In the preface to the US Navy's recently published illustrated history of the war, the current Secretary of the Navy, Ray Mabus, wrote, 'The lessons that the Navy and Marine Corps learned during the War of 1812 continue to shape our history. Our earliest heroes – Decatur, Hull, Perry, Macdonough, Porter, and others – set the standard for leadership, courage, seamanship, and innovation that our modern leaders strive to emulate.'[2] In the June 2012 issue of *Naval History* magazine, the current Chief of Naval Operations Admiral Jonathan Greenert, USN, drew 'three key lessons from the US Navy's first sustained trial by fire: Warfighting First. Operate Forward. Be Ready'.

The US Navy's experience in the War of 1812 had indeed shown that the shortfalls in naval preparation before the war had hurt the country. At the same time, tactical proficiency, forward operations and readiness have become the key hallmarks of the US Navy today. For this reason, the US Navy has used these same values in promoting public memory of selected naval events that occurred during the War of 1812, while also fostering these values as continuing elements of professional naval heritage.

Both the use of history for professional heritage purposes and the debates among American historians reveal the broad diversity of interpretation about the war in the United States, something which is expanded exponentially when the views from other countries are added to the mix. Despite the recent outpouring of books and articles on the subject during these bicentenary years, there are many questions that still need to be clarified. It is difficult to understand, from the perspective of either twenty-first-century great power America or early nineteenth-century great power Britain, why the War of 1812 occurred or what was in the minds of the American leaders who undertook the war. Clearly, the American leaders of the day did not use a cold, rational analysis of international power politics to calculate its military and naval strength to gauge what could realistically be achieved through the use of armed force. Nor were American leaders of the day guided by an interconnected policy and strategy to achieve their political purposes with measured force, undergirded by effective logistical and financial support. To be fair, such thinking is rare enough

---

2 Jenkins and Taylor, *Yardarm to Yardarm*, p vii.

in history. In 1812, thinkers like Antoine-Henri Jomini and Carl von Clausewitz, who both became famous for fostering this sort of thinking, were only just experiencing the Napoleonic style of warfare that eventually gave rise to their reflections. Today in the twenty-first century, it has become a familiar phenomenon to see rash and idealistic leaders of small and relatively new states making what may be seen as irrational challenges to the established military and naval powers of the day. It behoves us to try to understand this phenomenon more clearly and the United States in the War of 1812 can provide an interesting historical case study of the problem.

In 1812, the American republic was not yet forty years old and its government had only been settled with its written constitution twenty-three years earlier in 1789. Colonial America had been a deeply divided society when seen across its thirteen separate colonies, and so was the new republic. The American historian Jack P Greene has pointed out that in these early days the strong continuity with the colonial past was maintained.[3] On the far side of the Atlantic, 'a weak American state' had replaced 'a weak British state'. Local interests dominated and cut across national interests. George Washington lamented to Henry Laurens in the last stages of the war for independence in July 1782, 'The spirit of freedom which at the commencement of this contest would have gladly sacrificed everything to the attainment of its object has long since subsided and every selfish passion has taken its place.' Narrow sectional and local interests prevailed, creating a rising lack of national consensus. As the British historian P J Marshall has pointed out for this early period, 'Common transatlantic values survived the sundering of imperial links'.[4] Americans still sought British goods, read British books, aspired to British models and sought recognition in Britain, yet at the same time, Americans were 'a world within themselves'.

The war of 1775–83 had brought independence, but it did not bring an integrated national identity or shared social values in America. Diametrically opposed views about why the war had been fought and what it achieved formed the basis for the first two political parties that emerged there after the war: the Federalists and the Republicans. The

---

3 Green, 'Colonial History and National History', p 246.
4 Marshall, *Remaking the British Atlantic*, p 314.

broader international scene that the new American republic entered was very quickly dominated by the series of wars that surrounded the French Revolution and Empire. In the decade before the French Revolution had created its own threat to European monarchies, the creation of the United States had already placed a republic on the international scene. Its very existence presented an implicit challenge to Britain's imperial authority and momentarily raised the stakes in the political discussion that ensued throughout the British Empire about the legitimacy of British claims to be a model of liberty and the universal rights of humanity.

At the outset, Americans sought to stand aside from such issues in international politics, using the protection and isolation that three thousand miles of ocean and a vast continent could provide. This proved difficult to achieve as the war and war-related issues came to dominate global international relations after the rise of Napoleon. American merchants quickly made substantial fortunes on profits earned in neutral trade with the opposing European states. Unknowingly or insensitively, they placed themselves at increasing risk as their successful commercial enterprise created a jealousy that each European belligerent saw as assisting its enemies. Yet neither of the major powers took the United States seriously. For Britain, the Americans were a nuisance. For Napoleon, the fledgling country was no major threat to his ambitions. He predicted that America would not become a threat to anyone for another two or three centuries. Americans, however, were living in their own world. As historian Gordon Wood characterised the situation in his history of the early American republic, Americans 'had an extraordinary emotional need to exaggerate their importance in the world – a need that lay behind their efforts to turn their diplomacy into a major means of defining their national identity'.[5] In 1801, President Thomas Jefferson defeated his Federalist opponents and carried the Republican Party to power for the first time, bringing with it a distinctive set of ideas about the United States and its foreign policy roles.

The Republicans shared with the Federalists the desire to be neutral in European power politics and conflict, but in opposition to the Federalists they believed that Americans had the right to trade with all

<hr>

5 Wood, *Empire of Liberty*, p 622.

belligerents and they would go to war to protect that right. At the same time, they demanded a narrow definition of contraband to promote this trade. Curiously, the Republicans who supported these policies represented areas that were not engaged in maritime commerce. They were from the agrarian South or from inland areas, not the north-eastern New England states which depended on this trade for its livelihood. Maritime New England was predominantly Federalist in its political inclinations and opposed the Republicans on these policies. The Federalists envisioned a diversified American manufacturing economy with urban growth, but the Republicans opposed this. Instead, they sought an idyllic agrarian democracy and economy that spread westward across the continent without major urban centres. To their way of thinking, maritime commerce was not really something to be liked for its own sake. Republicans encouraged maritime trade because they thought it an effective way of keeping America a rural agrarian culture and preventing large urban growth at home. They intended to use commerce as a means to discourage urban industrial development by sending agricultural goods to distant urban manu-facturing centres in Europe instead of developing them locally. They specifically wanted to keep America from becoming a corrupt, luxury-loving, sophisticated country such as they thought the European countries had become.

The Republicans had similar radical ideas about the role of maritime commerce in international affairs. In their thinking, maritime commerce was a weapon that could be used against Britain. They believed that Britain was dependent on American markets for their exports. If Americans coercively restricted their purchases, Britain would have no other effective markets. As a result, British workers would be thrown out of work, start riots and force the British government to change its policies. Republicans thought that they held a dagger that could strike at Britain's heart. Unlike the Federalists, whose policies Republicans considered were pro-British, the Republicans had political as well as economic motives. At the bottom of it, Republicans resented European, and particularly British, attitudes of superiority and disdain for the new American republic. They wanted the United States to be taken seriously and not be regarded as a minor nation under the thumb of British commercial and political dominance. In the midst of the Napoleonic wars, Republicans dreamt of a world without war. Most importantly, they wanted a world in which the United States took its place as an internationally respected, independent, sovereign country respected for its own separate national identity.

The Republican ideas championed by President Thomas Jefferson and his secretary of state and successor, James Madison, threw the country into a deep economic depression and almost destroyed the United States in a war. Under Jefferson, and for most of Madison's first term of office from 1809 onwards, the policies were focused on peaceful means to put a stop to Britain impressing American seamen and to British interference with American neutral trade. On both issues, the American government justified its positions in its own political and national terms that reflected Republican principles, not the terms of accepted international law and practice. While political slogans such as 'Free Trade and Sailor Rights' became the common battle cry, these were just the issues of the day that symbolised in a few words a range of more complex ideas. At the heart of it, what the Republicans desperately wanted was Britain's recognition of the United States as an equal, sovereign and independent nation with its own distinctive identity.

Behind the political rhetoric, Madison was deeply concerned about America's future. He saw his own party splintering into factions in Congress and the country as a whole largely devoid of a national spirit. As the 'Father of the American Constitution' and key promoter of its Bill of Rights a quarter-century earlier, Madison had deeply held opinions about the country, although his political views had matured and changed somewhat with his experience over time. As he saw it, the lack of a national spirit and of a clear national identity that was recognised by the outside world was not just a matter of abstract principles; they were also issues that reflected whether or not he could garner enough votes to be re-elected president for a second term in November 1812.

When James Madison asked Congress to declare war against Britain in June of 1812, the opposing political party, the Federalists, made it clear that they did not think that any of the issues were worth fighting a war with Britain. Not a single Federalist voted in favour of it. Despite this, Republicans found the votes among themselves to approve the declaration of war that Madison requested. It was very clearly a war that reflected party political principles and party objectives. One of the leading theorists of Jefferson's agrarian Republicanism, John Taylor of

Caroline County, Virginia, wrote that this war was a 'metaphysical war, a war not for conquest, not for defence, not for sport', but rather 'a war for honour like that of the Greeks against Troy'. But, he warned, that it was also a war that 'might terminate in the destruction of the last experiment in . . . free government'.[6]

President Madison exuded confidence in America's eventual victory but, by the standards of other countries and other wars, the United States was singularly unprepared to instigate a war and to engage in serious offensive operations against one of the world's great powers. As a minor and insignificant naval and military power in the global perspective of that time, the United States could not hope to win a direct power struggle by armed force with Britain. In practical military terms, the United States could only do what minor powers can always attempt to do with their small military forces in a war:

a. irritate and embarrass the major power by the occasional local victory with regular forces,
b. use unconventional weapons,
c. challenge local control in distant areas where a major power is momentarily weak,
d. engage in a propaganda campaign,
e. attack enemy trade and logistics as a means to increase enemy costs, and
f. try to create in the enemy country public opposition to the expense of the war as a means to pressure the enemy government to come to acceptable terms during peace negotiations.

The United States had very restricted geo-strategic options to fight Britain: its armed forces did not have the logistical capability to reach across the Atlantic to launch a major attack and its small navy could not match the Royal Navy massed in fleet battle formation. The US Navy did not even have the resources and capabilities needed to launch a major amphibious landing on British possessions as close as Bermuda, the Bahamas or the West Indies. What was within the realm of practical possibility was to attack British forces across the land border with Canada, to send American naval frigates out to attack or capture

---

6 Wood, *Empire of Liberty*, p 659.

smaller British warships, and to release a horde of privateers to attack British trade in a manner that put pressure on the British economy at home by raising maritime shipping insurance rates and by lost cargoes.

Even this was difficult for the United States to achieve; it lacked the elements of the fiscal-bureaucratic state that had developed over several centuries in Europe and allowed those governments to maintain effective armies and navies. This absence was deliberate. The Republicans, in particular, did not believe that the United States should have a large central government establishment. They did not want to have a standing army and they certainly did not want a large navy. They believed in the effectiveness of what they thought had won the American War for Independence: the rural militiaman with his right to carry his own gun and defend the country on a moment's notice. For them, privateers at sea were the maritime equivalents of militiamen. A navy was the worst thing in the world. It not only needed an expensive bureaucratic establishment to support it, but it was so expensive to build and to maintain that it would create a permanent national debt and be the cause of ever-rising taxes. As Republican representatives in Congress pointed out, a navy would only increase the number of paupers in the country and bankrupt the nation. While more 'war hawks' were elected to Congress in the 1810 election, who throughout the next two years increasingly promoted the idea of going to war, they refused to accept the logical consequence of their views. They consistently voted against all attempts to arm and prepare the navy for war, opposed nearly all attempts to increase the size of the War Department, rejected all tax increases, and then voted to go to war. Congress did take some steps to increase the army by 35,000 men, but, reflecting Republican Party views, it relied mainly on raising another 50,000 volunteers for one year at the expense of the states, rather than to add that cost to those of the national government.

Despite these internal naval and military issues, Madison confidently led the country into war. The global strategic situation provided some hope. Once again the United States placed its bet on France as it had in 1778. While Americans did not expect or even desire direct military and naval assistance from Napoleon (as they had needed from Louis XVI), Napoleon was at the height of his power in early 1812. Going into the war, Madison's government, in so far as it calculated strategic issues at all, had the general idea that Napoleon's challenge to Britain could at least present an opportunity for the United States to make a successful case to be recognised as a nation that could stand entirely independent from the British sphere of influence. The Republicans were badly mistaken in this assessment. Not only were they wrong about Napoleon, they were wrong in thinking that the British government in power would give them the satisfaction they so ardently desired.

The course of the Anglo-American conflict that followed demonstrated this error in American thinking. Between 1812 and 1814, every major American attempt to attack Canada offensively on land was turned back by an effective British defence. Britain's remarkable ability to marshal her scarce resources to defeat Napoleon became the wonder of the age, a process that historians are still learning about through current scholarship. While concentrating on Napoleon as the first priority, Britain was also incrementally increasing her military manpower and naval strength in North America to create a punishing economic blockade that nearly destroyed the American economy. The Royal Navy slowly and effectively immobilised and gradually eliminated the US Navy as an effective force. At the same time, Britain made retaliatory raids as warnings of her capability to make more serious attacks.

Oddly, the Madison government in its persistence seemed to be as oblivious to these strategic, military and economic realities as it had been to the lack of logical practicality in its war preparations. Nevertheless, the experience of war gradually did bring home to the administration and to Congress the need to take some steps to strengthen the Navy and to organise the War Department better. During the course of the war and afterwards, Americans made much of their six victories in the single-ship actions during the first period of the war. A turning point came at sea on 1 June 1813 with the British victory over *Chesapeake* and the blockade of Decatur's squadron at New London, removing nearly half of the US Navy's operational force in a single day. Certainly, this was a pair of British successes with cumulative strategic consequences, while, in contrast, the earlier single-ship actions were displays of American tactical prowess in battles that brought little strategic advantage to the American side. Yet, these frigate actions have outweighed other aspects in the politics of the time as well as in the public and professional naval memory of the war. In some important respects, among Americans the memory of James

Lawrence's death in *Chesapeake* has outstripped that of the frigate actions.

One is left to wonder: 'Why?' None of these frigate actions was a Trafalgar and Lawrence was no Nelson. To the rational mind, the American viewpoint initially appears to make no sense beyond nationalistic bombast. Yet, a closer examination suggests that there is something much more substantial here. One might begin to seek an answer by reflecting on the War of 1812 in the light of Carl von Clausewitz's famous dialectical supposition that 'War is simply a continuation of political intercourse, with the addition of other means'. As discussed above, Madison's aim in going to war was not to achieve any particular tangible military or naval gain. For much of the war, the American government had no clear idea how to use its navy. Madison was focused on the intangible political results of the war rather than the practical means of warfare. In effect, he used the war for his party political objectives. His ultimate goal was to contribute to developing a distinctive national identity that separated the American people from their significant and innate political sympathies for Britain. At the same time, he also wanted Britain's recognition of that identity confirmed by a change in British attitudes. The successes of the American Navy were ultimately significant contributions to Madison's first political goal in developing a sense of national honour, pride and achievement. The frigate actions were remarkable in showing to the American people that the tiny United States Navy could dare to challenge the Royal Navy and even have some success against it. It is this basic sense of unspoken wonderment that contemporary newspapers built upon in the hype that they generated in reporting naval actions. For example, when Captain Stephen Decatur, commanding the American frigate *United States*, sent in HMS *Macedonian* as a prize to Newport, Rhode Island, the local newspaper, *The Newport Mercury* of 12 December, welcomed the news with the headline 'Another Brilliant Naval Victory'. The editor noted that 'with emotions of heartfelt pride and pleasure, we place before our readers another proof of the superior skill and bravery of our officers, seamen, and marines which will secure to them the unanimous applause of a grateful country'. Such patriotic sentiments were exactly the type of attitude that Madison wanted to hear.

The death of Captain James Lawrence provided a martyr for the cause, making him an even more important figure. In 1813, Washington

Irving wrote one of the first biographies of American naval figures and it was devoted to the life of Lawrence.[7] In his concluding paragraphs of reflection on Lawrence in *The Analectic Magazine*, he writes:

> For our part, we conceive that the great purpose of our navy is accomplished. It was not to be expected that with so inconsiderable a force, we should make any impression on British power, or materially affect British commerce. We fought, not to take their ships and plunder their wealth, but to pluck some of their laurels wherewith to grace our own brows. In this we have succeeded; and thus the great mischief that our little navy was capable of doing to Great Britain, in showing that her maritime power was vulnerable, has been effected, and is irretrievable.

Irving was quick to point out how very difficult it is 'to speak feelingly, yet temperately, of the merits of those who have bravely fought and gloriously fallen in the service of their country'. Lawrence already had a reputation within the naval service as a successful leader, officer and family man, but as Irving noted:

> the popular career of this youthful hero has been so transient, yet dazzling, as almost to prevent sober investigation. Scarcely had we ceased to rejoice in his victory [over *Peacock* on 24 February 1813] before we are called on to deplore his loss. He passed before the public eye like a star, just beaming on it for a moment, and falling in the midst of his brightness.

Emphasising his point, Irving concluded:

> He who falls a martyr to his country's cause excites the fullness of public sympathy. Envy cannot repine at laurels so dearly purchased, and gratitude feels that he is beyond the reach of such rewards.

Appealing to the youth of a young country, the romantic Irving exhorted, 'where is the son of honour, panting for distinction, who would not like Lawrence, be snatched away in the brightness of youth

---

7 Irving, *The Analectic Magazine*, II (1813), pp 137–242.

and glory, than dwindle down to what is termed a good old age, wearing his reputation to the shreds, and leave behind him nothing but the remembrance of decrepitude and imbecility'. Not everyone agreed, particularly in Federalist New England. In the issue of 15 July 1815, the *Concord Gazette*, a New Hampshire newspaper publishing the report of the court martial that cleared the officers and men of *Chesapeake* from any wrongdoing, there also appeared a piece entitled 'Madison's Glory War'. Its author acidly remarked: 'we are paid in buckets full of glory, such as it is! A kind of drab coloured, linsey-woolsey glory . . .' Going on to complain about the increase in taxes and the growth of the national debt, he asked: 'Does anybody think you the better for what Jackson and Brown and Hull and Decatur have accomplished? Not a whit. They are glorious; and you must rejoice – and PAY!' Exasperated by the Madison administration's viewpoint, he exclaimed 'They do not pretend that anything has been procured – but *glory*!'

In August 1814, peace negotiations opened between the British and American representatives at Ghent. For several months, there was little common ground upon which to agree to end the war. The negotiators saw no decisive military or naval action that swayed a mutual decision one way or the other to break what turned out to be a stalemate. The operational history of the war illustrates Clausewitz's thought that defence is the stronger form of war. On both sides, defence was more effective than the offence. The burning of York and Washington had balanced one another, while attacking British forces had been repulsed at Plattsburg and Baltimore. Despite Britain's military and naval defeat of the entire range of American offensives, despite the British stranglehold on the American economy, Britain's armed forces had been unable to persuade Madison's government to capitulate. Madison was heartened by the fact that American forces had held their ground and maintained a reasonably effective defence.

British military forces were certainly very close to achieving their objectives, but it would require many more ships, thousands of men and massive additional funding for the British Army and Royal Navy to impose an effective peace on the reluctant Americans. In the end, Lord Liverpool's government backed away from the harsh peace terms it had been proposing and accepted American intransigence by agreeing to settle on the basis of the status quo ante. They did so not because of any American military or naval victory, but rather because of issues far beyond American control. The strategic stalemate in America was resolved through internal British politics in the light of the continuing cost of prosecuting war and the broader international issues that Britain faced. The British electorate opposed the high cost and taxes involved in continuing the war, while there was significant public opinion in Britain that continuation of the war only increased taxes that benefited the war contractors, not the wider British economy. In international politics, Britain's continuation of the war in America indirectly threatened the establishment of a balance of power for Europe in the delicate negotiations at the Congress of Vienna.

As many great powers in history have found, there are limits to how far to push a war and how much the cost and effort is worth. In the end, the Treaty of Ghent did not resolve the specific issues of free trade, impressment and sailors' rights that the Americans had stated as their chief complaints at the outset of the war, but the effect of its provisions was to acknowledge indirectly the intangible object that Madison had sought all along. As the American delegation at Ghent had stated early on in the negotiations on 14 September 1814, that object was to establish relations between the countries on the basis of 'a mutual respect for the rights of each other, and in the cultivation of friendly understanding between them'.

In fighting the Royal Navy, American seamen showed that they could make a decent showing against overwhelming odds that exemplified courage, honour and commitment. Because of this, Captain Philip Broke's skilful defeat of *Chesapeake* turned his opponent, James Lawrence, into a martyr for the American cause and his dying words into a rallying cry still cherished after two centuries. Fighting against such huge odds, men such as Lawrence bequeathed a patriotic example that showed to Americans the potential value of an effective navy.

Suggested Further Reading

Eustace, N, *1812: War and the Passions of Patriotism* (2012).

Gilje, Paul A, *Free Trade and Sailors' Rights in the War of 1812* (2013).

Hattendorf, John B, 'The Naval War of 1812 in International Perspective' (2013).

Stagg, J C A, *The War of 1812: Conflict for a Continent* (Cambridge, 2012).

FEDS AND DEMMIES

'From papers up to last week it appears that their government is determined to make a war with us, but the people in general are equally determined they will have peace . . . but there's a great discordancy of opinion between the Feds and the Demmies (as the Federalists and the Democrats call each other) tho' neither party seem yet to have looked beyond their own immediate interests in trade and agriculture and never with a generous impartiality to have considered which nation of the two they are jarring with is engaged in the most moral and honorable course – and to which they owe their boasted freedom and their corn laws and every virtue which they have retained. I am really ashamed of the narrow, selfish light in which they have regarded the last struggle for liberty and morality in Europe – but our cousin Jonathan has no romantic fits of energy and acts only upon cool, solid calculation of a good market for rice or tobacco!'

Broke to his wife Loo (20 October 1811)

2

Sideshow? British Grand Strategy and the War of 1812

Andrew Lambert

News of the American declaration of war in June 1812 prompted a brief outburst of patriotic anger in London, where most had expected a peaceful outcome. *The Times* regretted the need to carry 'the flame and devastation of war' to America, but did so without fear of the outcome. Even America's friends were convinced the matter would blow over once news that the Orders in Council had been repealed reached Washington. It would take six months of war, and a number of naval defeats, to make the British take the Americans seriously enough to hate them.

President Madison had declared war in the expectation that Napoleon would defeat Russia, reimpose his 'Continental System' of economic war against Britain and force the islanders to make peace. After nine years of Anglo-French total war the conflict was reaching a crisis; one side would be destroyed. With the main British army engaged in Spain, and the Royal Navy spread around the globe securing trade, blockading Europe and seizing French islands, the war could not have come at a worse time for Britain. Madison was banking on Britain being unable to respond to his opportunistic attack. Throughout the War of 1812 this lack of resources restricted British strategy to the defensive, reacting to American initiatives. The invasion of Canada determined the main theatre of the conflict, forcing the British to deploy all available military resources to defend the provinces. The navy sustained the strategic link between Britain and Canada, defending troopships and oceanic commerce, and slowly built up effective naval and economic blockades. Only the last was a truly offensive, coercive measure, and its application was greatly delayed by lack of resources. Although he shared the widespread hope that the

Americans would negotiate, Lord Melville, the First Lord of the Admiralty, summoned Vice Admiral Sir John Borlase Warren to London on 30 July offering him command of the combined North American and West Indies squadrons. In a career stretching back to the previous American war, Warren had been an enterprising frigate commander, an effective diplomat and a loyal Parliamentary supporter of the Pitt/Grenville government. He had been Ambassador to Russia between 1802 and 1804 and later Commander-in-Chief on the North American Station between 1808 and 1810, specifically chosen to reduce tensions after *Leopard* had fired on the American ship *Chesapeake* and seized four of her crew in 1807. Above all, Warren had considerable experience of America and Americans. Most commentators dismiss him with faint praise, greatly underestimating the profound problems of controlling a war that stretched from Newfoundland to Mexico with inadequate means and poor communications, while his political masters back in London maintained a very different view of the conflict. London only decided to take the conflict seriously some months after war began, the build-up of resources was slow, while endless demands to protect West Indian trade, which had high-level support in Parliament, compromised theatre strategy. The Government and the Admiralty consistently underestimated the scale of the American threat to maritime trade: Warren did not. Once appointed, he received a rich haul of intelligence, records, charts, drawings, statistics and other data to inform the development of strategy. Throughout the conflict he collected and processed every scrap of human, cartographic and technical intelligence he could acquire; soon his files bulged with American coastal charts, captured orders and signal logs.

With Napoleon's 650,000-man Grande Armée advancing towards Russia the Government was desperate to avoid an awkward distraction. Foreign Secretary Lord Castlereagh ordered Warren to offer the Americans a ceasefire and authorised him to negotiate, within limits. Warren's primary role was to restore peace. By contrast, Lord Melville spent more time and effort managing his extensive patronage interests, providing Warren with a list of promotion candidates on all three American stations, and the precise order in which they should be promoted. This was not untypical; Melville's political power in Scotland depended on the effective use of patronage. More worryingly, the First Lord of the Admiralty normally maintained a confidential private correspondence with senior officers holding important commands. This allowed both men the freedom to express opinions and requests that could not be entrusted to anodyne public dispatches. When the relationship was based on trust and confidence the First Lord's private letters could explain the political and diplomatic basis of official orders, discuss strategy and reflect on the merits of subordinate officers. Because Warren and Melville were never close their letters remained guarded, and rather stiff. Melville's subtext was clear: the American war was an awkward embarrassment for the Government, and he blamed Warren for not making it go away.

On 3 August, Warren received orders to unite the three American stations under his command, so as to ensure the most efficient use of resources. On the same day Rear Admirals Sawyer and Laforey and Vice Admiral Stirling, respectively commanders of the Halifax, Leeward Islands and Jamaica stations, were directed to place themselves under his orders. To provide a suitable fleet the Admiralty added several ships just coming out of refit to his command. Desperate for additional frigates and smaller cruisers to defend trade against American privateers, Melville could only pray for peace in a trying autumn. He waited anxiously for the returning Baltic fleet to provide ships and men. He sent two 74s and 'nine of our heaviest frigates' to prevent the American Navy 'making any very formidable efforts by sea. If the war continues however, we must expect considerable annoyance from their Privateers, as soon as they are able to fit out vessels of that description to any extent.' This had an immediate impact on other fleets. The Commander-in-Chief in the Mediterranean learnt that his time-expired battleships would not be relieved until Warren had enough frigates. The Admiralty also picked out some of the Navy's best senior officers, including Rear Admiral George Cockburn and Captain Robert Dudley Oliver, who were directed to leave the Cadiz station and join Warren. Combat veterans like these would translate strategy into operational effect. Melville looked to Cockburn, an expert in amphibious warfare, to take the offensive onto the American coast to 'accelerate the return of peace'.[1]

However, the opening moves of the naval war would be dominated

---

1 Melville to Sir Edward Pellew, 10 August and 10 November 1812: Melville MS at the Clements Library.

by diplomacy and the defence of trade. Urgent reinforcements were invariably delayed by the need to escort convoys, while Warren was ordered to base himself at Halifax, the best location to wait for a diplomatic response from the American Government. A week later he was directed to convoy valuable merchant shipping, along with vital naval and military store-ships heading for Halifax, Bermuda and Jamaica. His subordinates in American waters were directed to station cruisers in the key choke points and dispersal areas where merchant shipping would be especially vulnerable to American cruisers.[2] After the early and complete failure of the American offensive into Canada the Madison administration's only offensive strategy was the campaign against British floating commerce, largely conducted by privateers, licensed predators using private ships, money and manpower.

Before sailing Warren reflected on his twin-track mission: although his primary role was to secure peace he needed to prepare for war. He recognised that the war had assumed a 'more active and inveterate aspect than heretofore', and addressed the threat posed by American sloops, brigs and privateers. His limited resources were already spread thin by convoys and cruising, and he had nothing left to meet the challenge. Short of resources, and hamstrung by restrictive rules of engagement designed to facilitate peace, Warren faced a near impossible task with little help from home. Fortunately, just as the American war added a significant new demand for ships and men, the decline of the French threat released the means without a significant increase in cost. The 1813 Naval Estimates were £20 million, only £700,000 more than in 1812. Little wonder the Admiralty clung to the hope that 'there was some appearance at one time of the American Government being inclined to return to a state of peace' for as long as possible. Warren accepted that defensive tasks must take priority, and at this late season the majority of merchant shipping would be coming from the West Indies, not Canada. Once the Americans had responded to the peace initiative he would head south to Bermuda, the central point of his vast command, and take the 74s with him, leaving a frigate squadron to protect Nova Scotia during the winter. While he waited for an American answer, Warren put the Halifax station on a war footing, inspecting the dockyard, meeting his officers and developing the

2 Admiralty Board Minute 15 December 1812 and Special Minute 10 and 11 August 1812: ADM 3/259.

intelligence picture. His ships began the basic wartime task of sweeping up the American privateers. Such successes kept insurance rates low, a critical indicator of effective sea control, while the prizes could be used to reinforce the British cruiser fleet, or sold to local privateers. The crew would be locked up for the duration: as British prisons filled with prime American seamen, the American war effort began to falter.

In mid-November, Warren learnt that the diplomatic mission had failed. The American privateer effort had been highly successful in the first few months when the convoy system in American waters remained embryonic. At least 150 British ships had been taken, and more privateers were fitting out. To meet the combined challenge of privateers and frigates he needed reinforcements, a theme that would dominate his command. The Admiralty response was distinctly unsympathetic. In November the Board declared that, as he faced only a handful of warships, and had a clear superiority in all classes, he should 'quickly and completely' dispose of the enemy. Such nonsense reflected growing demands from well-connected Liverpool merchants like John Gladstone and local MP, former Foreign Secretary George Canning, for increased naval protection. Without more ships and men Warren could do little to meet such demands. The key to success was to control the Atlantic coast of America through an effective naval blockade, to prevent hostile shipping putting to sea. More than 2,000 miles long, with numerous harbours and inlets the American coast posed a formidable challenge for Warren's pitifully small force; he stressed it would 'require twice my numbers' to produce the desired effect.

The British Government remained understandably anxious to limit the American conflict. Having repealed the Orders in Council, the Cabinet expected Washington to negotiate, restricting military action to an active defence to avoid exacerbating the situation. Everything depended on Napoleon. Once the French began the retreat from Moscow the Americans would have to fight their own war, on land and sea, while Britain would be able to send more ships and a few more men. President Madison opened the New Year by signing into law the naval programme of four 74-gun ships of the line and six 44-gun frigates, marking the collapse of his hopes and a dawning realisation that, having taken his country to war utterly unprepared, he, as Chief Magistrate, was responsible for a looming catastrophe.

Contrary to all expectation the American naval campaign of 1812 had been successful, at one level. In reality, winning six single-ship actions wrecked the naval attack on British commerce. The only national cruisers to achieve any success were those, like Rodgers' *President*, that failed to find and fight British warships. In the autumn of 1812, the Royal Navy lost three frigates in single-ship actions with American ships that were one-third larger, and more heavily armed and manned. The loss of *Macedonian* on 25 October reflected badly on her captain, John Carden, who sacrificed his speed advantage to fight a long-range battle with the far heavier *United States*. He was never employed again. In comparison, the Royal Navy's loss of *Guerrière* and *Java* to the equally powerful *Constitution* (19 August and 29 November) was neither dishonourable nor especially disadvantageous. The British got the precious crews back within weeks, and on all three occasions the big American ships headed home to replace their masts – leaving the seas open for British commerce. Isaac Hull, Stephen Decatur and William Bainbridge had sacrificed their mission of commerce-raiding for a shot at glory. That said, these victories, however unexpected, and strategically irrelevant, provided potent, if undeserved, propaganda for Madison's anti-navalist Republican government.

Throughout the first month of his command Warren's main focus had been to defend critical convoys while refitting and maintaining his scant, worn squadron. The small dockyard at Halifax was struggling to meet wartime demands and harsh winter weather.[3] To impose an effective economic blockade, the strategic measure he knew would 'produce a great change in the people of the Country', Warren needed enough battleships and frigates to cover all the key American ports. The latest intelligence downplayed the much anticipated fracturing of the United States: the southern states might have been composed of 'the most vile materials', but the Union would hold. When fresh forces finally arrived, Warren faced incessant demands to protect Caribbean islands and their shipping, and subordinate flag officers who viewed the war as an opportunity for personal advantage. The political influence of West Indian planters in Westminster remained a powerful distraction throughout his command.

---

3 See Chapter 13.

Blockade

On 16 November, news that the British Government had finally ordered general reprisals against America reached Warren, just as he learnt the Americans had rejected an armistice. In economic terms the first six months of war had been wasted. On 21 November 1812, Earl Bathurst, Secretary of State for War and the Colonies, ordered the Admiralty to impose 'a strict and rigorous Blockade', on Chesapeake Bay and Delaware River.[4] This blockade, overtly targeting the Republican decision-makers who voted for the war, was finally established on 21 February 1813. Believing the Republican Mid Atlantic and Southern states, where the slave plantations of the governing class, who were responsible for the war, produced cotton, tobacco and rice, Bathurst advised finding other sources of supply, and destroying these trades. Prime Minister Lord Liverpool agreed. The British had excluded Federalist New England, well aware that the American declaration of war had been partisan; the Republicans voted for war, the Federalists voted against. By leaving the Federalist northeast states relatively unscathed, the British could harness their resources, weaken the American war effort and promote secession, or civil war.

With an effective blockade in place and duly notified, Warren could stop neutral ships entering American harbours. The blockade had been designed to achieve maximum impact at the least cost. To maintain the supply of grain to the army in the Peninsula, provide shipbuilding stores and food for the West Indies and Canada, and exploit internal factional divisions, the British issued hundreds of trading licences. Licensed trade also kept skilled seamen away from warships and privateers. American owners trusted British paperwork and kept on trading, widening the divisions between maritime and inland states, and weakening the war effort. American merchants happily forged suitable licences to widen their access to other markets. By controlling the sea Britain could protect and promote any trade it chose to sanction; and it could stop the trade of the United States at will. As a result, Britain could borrow and tax to fund an effective war, while the United States could not.[5] The American Atlantic coast had to be blockaded both to protect British West Indian commerce and impose

---

4 Bathurst to Admiralty, 21 November 1812: National Archives Colonial Office (CO) 43/49, pp 153–4.
5 See Arthur, *How Britain Won the War of 1812*, for discussion of the two economies.

economic hardship on America. This presented a formidable challenge for Warren's force, and it proved impossible to achieve absolute control despite a major expansion of the squadron. The Atlantic theatre tested the fabric of his ships and the mettle of his men, leaving around one-fifth of his force in harbour under repair at any one time.

Warren's naval blockade began to take effect in the spring of 1813 when additional ships and better weather enabled him to keep the American fleet largely confined to Boston and New York. This reduced the threat to convoys, releasing ships to impose the economic blockade. Furthermore, fundamental strategic changes in Europe, especially opening the Baltic for large-scale trade in grain and timber in the summer of 1812, had ended British dependence on American supplies. In consequence the British could adopt more stringent measures. New York, the largest American port, producing approximately one-quarter of national revenue from customs dues, was effectively closed for business by May 1813. Despite doubling the rate of customs, American revenues fell to catastrophic levels, making it impossible to fund the war. Philadelphia suffered a 90 per cent fall in revenue. American Government stock failed to sell at sustainable rates, while the economic impact of war made it increasingly unpopular with many sections of society. The British had carefully targeted specific sections of American society, hoping to exacerbate internal divisions. The American administration reinforced the British blockade by stopping 'illegal' imports of British goods on American vessels, further cutting customs revenue. As Henry Adams noted, 'the pressure of the blockades was immediately felt'.[6]

Shooting the messenger

The first six months of war proved curious and troubling for the British. While the naval defeats had been embarrassing, the war on land had been unexpectedly successful. Against all the odds the British had held the Canadian frontier, and by the close of the year the first flush of American success at sea had begun to ebb. In Europe the news had been bigger, and better. Napoleon's catastrophic defeat in Russia transformed Britain's position from strategic stalemate to expanding success. From Salamanca to Smolensk, the French were in retreat. By

---

6 Adams, *The Writings of Albert Gallatin*, vol VII, pp 262–4.

December, Napoleon's fleet was visibly shrinking as men and material were diverted to the army, allowing the British to redeploy naval power to the New World.

The war at sea turned decisively in Britain's favour on 1 June 1813 when three American frigates were effectively lost. The *United States* and the refitted prize, now USS *Macedonian*, were driven into New London by the Royal Navy line-of-battle ship *Valiant* and the frigate *Acasta*. Then the *Chesapeake* was taken by *Shannon* in an action of unparalleled speed, ferocity and skill. Many years later American diplomat Richard Rush recorded how news of this battle had stunned his country. Only twelve months before no one would have been surprised by a British victory, but a year of success had turned so many heads that American despair exceeded British exultation. The actions of 1 June 1813 broke the back of the American naval threat, allowing the Royal Navy to focus on the privateer threat. Privateering was dealt with by escorted convoys and the incarceration of increasing numbers of American sailors at Dartmoor Prison. By late 1814, 6,500 American privateersmen had been detained for the duration. It only remained for the United States to acknowledge the futility of the war: a process delayed by two more chaotic, unsuccessful attempts to invade Canada.

In 1812, the British Government had taken several months to accept that the Americans would not give way without a serious war. Not only did this policy cripple Warren's attempt to impose an economic blockade, but the timing of every subsequent British policy shift would be driven by the same overriding imperative – Europe. In 1813, most cabinet ministers effectively ignored the American war, leaving a profoundly unenthusiastic Melville to conduct a secondary naval war, under the overall direction of Earl Bathurst, another minister with more pressing duties, in his case supporting Wellington in Spain. Although the brilliance of the *Shannon–Chesapeake* action briefly shifted attention westward, 1813 would be dominated by the crisis and collapse of Napoleon's German empire. The sheer scale and significance of the battles fought at Lutzen, Bautzen and Dresden, the critical role of Austria's accession to the Russian, Prussian, Swedish and British coalition, and the final titanic battle of Leipzig, where Napoleon lost 73,000 men from an army of 250,000, simply dwarfed the American war. It was no more than a trifling, tedious distraction. Instead, Britain was pouring money and munitions into Europe to help her allies defeat Napoleon. Little wonder ministers had no time for North America. It is worthy of note that the critical turning point for the direction of British strategy against America was the collapse of Napoleonic Spain. The battle of Vitoria on 21 June 1813 enhanced British diplomatic leverage with other European powers, and ended the need for American grain and flour; soon Wellington's troops would dine in France.

At any stage before spring 1814 the British Government would have made peace on status quo ante terms that stopped America invading Canada, and ended the US pretension to lecture London on the definition of maritime belligerent rights and the services owed the Crown by British seamen. To secure this end ministers adopted a strategy conditioned by the desperate lack of military resources. Canada would be defended on the frontiers, but the army would fall back to the major fortresses of Quebec and Halifax in the event of defeat, relying on impregnable fortifications and seaborne supply to hold these bastions, and recapturing lost ground later. Governor General Sir George Prevost proved an adept player of this limited/ defensive posture, carefully husbanding resources at Quebec to avoid the danger of a sudden reversal of fortune, doling out troops to the porous borders with an economy that suited his Swiss ancestry. The comprehensive failure of every American invasion has obscured the very real danger that the British faced. With the benefit of hindsight some suggest that Prevost might have been more aggressive, but he rightly looked to the other arm of British strategy, the naval and economic offensive, to save Canada. Canada would be defended on the shores of Chesapeake and in the counting houses of American cities.

With this strategy in place, the government could ignore the American war because the convoy system reduced commercial risk and loss to manageable levels, while intelligence-sharing between Lloyds and the Admiralty ensured there were no unpleasant surprises. In 1813, Rear Admiral Sir George Cockburn's Chesapeake raids began the process of taking the initiative on the littoral, and closing the American cruiser ports. By late 1813 it was clear that the strategy of isolating and targeting the Southern and Mid Atlantic states by economic blockade and coastal raids had not broken the Union. Consequently, Ministers stepped up pressure on Washington, translating the vital naval blockade of New England into an economic offensive, and increasing the scale and tempo of coastal raids. Even so, British options were limited. While Napoleon remained in power few British soldiers could be spared for America; none were sent from Europe. Wellington was always looking for more manpower, while 1813 opened fresh theatres in northern Europe that only served to emphasise the limits of British power.

As Napoleon retreated westward the British saw an opportunity to destroy his naval arsenal and fleet at Antwerp. This was the overriding British strategic aim – in comparison, reinforcing Canada or attacking America was insignificant. Antwerp, the *casus belli* in 1793, had become a major French naval base and the fixed point around which successive Tory ministries of Pitt, Portland, Perceval and now Liverpool developed their war aims. Yet the Cabinet could only find a paltry 11,000 men for General Lord Lynedoch's army, a stark illustration of British military limitations. An attack on Antwerp in February 1814 and an assault on the fortress at Bergen op Zoom in March both failed. Lynedoch had too few men and they were second-class units. The point is telling. If Britain lacked the military force to secure its fundamental war aim in nearby Belgium, there was no prospect that troops could be found to pursue altogether less important aims in America.

In 1813, British strategists had few options. They had to maintain the naval and economic blockades, to deny the American cruisers and privateers access to the sea, and ruin the American treasury; but limited military manpower meant that anything beyond holding the Canadian frontier, the dominant military effort, and Admiral Cockburn's brilliant, small-scale, high-tempo raiding on the Chesapeake was simply impossible. Too many troops were tied down in West Indies garrisons, ostensibly against the improbable risk of an American attack, but in reality to calm the nerves of politically powerful planters, fearful of slave uprisings.

The political weight of the West Indies remained strong: the Ministry depended on the planters' votes, and their profits, remitted in specie, to retain political power and fund the European war until Napoleon had been defeated. Strategy to fight America was bound by chains of sugar and gold to the defence of West Indian commercial and territorial power. West Indian complaints prompted Melville to remove Warren and replace him with Vice Admiral Sir Alexander

Cochrane, the Governor of Guadeloupe. The change of command occurred in April 1814. The British would not risk the sugar islands for some fleeting advantage on the mainland. This severely limited the scale of operations in Canada and on the American coast until Europe was at peace.

Over the autumn and winter of 1813 Foreign Secretary Castlereagh had spent every waking moment trying to sustain the European coalition, seeing the American war as both a distraction and a weakness that Russia and France could exploit to limit British influence. Castlereagh's diplomacy was dominated by Britain's refusal to compromise on the issue of maritime belligerent rights, which was at once the core of the American challenge, and a long-term aim of Russia and France. He made the British position very clear, and did not hesitate to issue a scarcely veiled threat to Russia: 'Great Britain may be driven out of a Congress but not out of her maritime rights, and if the continental Powers know their own interests they will not hazard this.' There would be no Congress at Vienna until the subject had been taken off the agenda, nor could the American war be discussed there. Britain used naval power to isolate the wider world from European interference. The British could wait for Madison to recognise the inevitable. American obduracy meant negotiations only began after Napoleon had abdicated. The British diplomatic network picked up the American envoys when they arrived at Gothenburg, from whence the British vice consul forwarded the American mail bag to London. Here it was opened and deciphered by the Post Office's secret 'Black Chamber', a dedicated code-breaking unit. Reading enemy mail helped ensure diplomatic success. Although Castlereagh spent much of this period moving round Europe, the Foreign Office kept him up to date with American issues. Face-to-face discussions in London with two American peace delegates, former Treasury Secretary Albert Gallatin and Congressman James Bayard, revealed 'very amicable dispositions', suggesting the Americans hoped to get out of the war 'with a safe conscience, by saying that, the war in Europe having ceased, the causes of their quarrel with us have ceased also'.[7] In effect, the Americans conceded Britain's core war aims, maritime belligerent rights and impressment, at the outset. This was logical: having failed to conquer

---

7 *Castlereagh* II, pp 471–2.

Canada, the Americans had nothing to trade. The only question for the British was how far the blockade and coastal operations could be translated into more positive outcomes. The inner Cabinet showed little interest in anything more, which explains why they only sent a small military reinforcement, despite initially planning a far more ambitious programme. Placing the peace negotiations in Ghent enabled the British to exploit both the close proximity to London and their military occupation of the Austrian Netherlands (modern Belgium), allowed by Austria which had no interest in America or maritime rights.

Napoleon's abdication on 6 April 1814 changed everything, and nothing. Three weeks after the end of the European conflict Melville advised Castlereagh that the Admiralty was short of troop ships; Britain's ability to repatriate French prisoners of war had been compromised by the need to take troops from the Garonne to America, and to repatriate the Portuguese army from the South of France to Lisbon. The dull, prosaic troop ship occupied a central place in British strategy: amphibious operations on the American coast would tie down a large fleet of such ships, because the troops had to be based afloat. British troop numbers in America would be restricted by the logistical demands of a floating army. Armchair generals proposed sending 25,000 troops to conquer Virginia and Maryland, separate them from the United States and emancipate slaves – a strategy to wreck America and ensure peace. The grim realities of shipping and stores left such visionary schemes floating in mid-air. The British army that captured Washington was little more than 4,000 strong.

Peace talks

After Napoleon's abdication the American war became a diplomatic embarrassment for the British Government. The continued drain of troops and money left Britain looking weak and distracted just as her European partners were about to settle the political future of the Continent. Peace with America would allow the British to focus on the big questions that were to be settled at the Vienna Congress, the pan-European conference to redraw the political and strategic map of Europe. Castlereagh kept the two peace processes separate, but his key demand in both reflected the vital role of maritime economic warfare in British strategy. His instructions to the British Commissioners at Ghent focused on maritime rights; the right to search neutral merchant ships on the high seas in wartime 'can never be given up'. To give the Americans an easy way out, he followed the line discussed with Bayard and Gallatin – that peace in Europe had rendered the subject academic and it should be allowed to drop. By contrast, Indian lands, border rectification and the Newfoundland fishery were open for discussion. The British negotiators were to stress that America had started the war, the invasion of Canada being consonant with a 'general system of aggrandisement, in the execution of which they had possessed themselves of Louisiana and a part of the Floridas, in the midst of peace'.[8] Castlereagh refused to discuss blockade, captures made under the Orders in Council and other maritime issues. In this he was entirely successful. The Americans conceded maritime rights and impressment at the outset, even if they had to be reminded of that fact a few months later. Having capitulated on the big issues, as far as Britain was concerned, the American team could be allowed to draw some small comfort from trifling exchanges over Indian lands and the Canadian frontier. Having set the parameters, Castlereagh left day-to-day control of the peace process to Bathurst, the most anti-American cabinet minister.

Recognising the diplomatic utility of bad news, Bathurst linked reports that Washington had fallen with a hint that, despite their triumph, the British 'wish to terminate the present unfortunate contest on principles honourable to both parties', so far as the terms did not risk the security of His Majesty's dominions. This last point was becoming more important. During his lengthy journey across Europe Castlereagh had studied British economic policy toward America, and 'the growing value of Canada': 'I have acquired by these researches a very increased notion of the value of our North American possession to us as a naval power.' As he worked on the shape of a new Europe, Castlereagh recognised that Canadian timber, forest products and grain would reduce British dependence on European produce, especially from the Russian-dominated Baltic.

By 1 September 1814 the British Government knew about the financial failure of the American administration. Rather than press their advantage for territorial gain, or humiliating terms, they wanted to restore the European state system, and rebuild Atlantic trade. Liverpool

---

8 Castlereagh to Commissioners at Ghent, 14 August 1814, *Castlereagh* II, pp 86–91.

observed to Bathurst, on 11 September, 'I cannot believe that, with the prospect of bankruptcy before them, the American Government would not wish to make peace, if they can make terms which would not give a triumph to their enemies.' The enemies he had in mind were the Federalists in New England. With an eye on opinion in Parliament, Lord Liverpool was anxious to ensure the blame for any breakdown fell on the 'impudent' Americans. Anticipating their position would soften as war came home to Washington, he was content to wait out the initial posturing.

The prospect of peace revealed a divergence of opinion in Cabinet. Bathurst, the Colonial Secretary, wanted a buffer state for the Indians, while Liverpool, recognising the impossibility of making terms to cover semi-nomadic tribal peoples, preferred a general understanding. Home Secretary Sidmouth's judgement was clear and correct:

> We could not sustain the claim to the absolute independence of nations or tribes within the frontier of the United States & never thought we could, but an attempt has been made to consider them as subjects, which is quite novel, & must be resisted at all hazards.[9]

Instability in France and uncertainty at Vienna made peace imperative.

In the autumn, American operations briefly returned to centre stage. The capture and destruction of Washington, was followed by British reverses at Baltimore and Plattsburg; these mattered because Britain needed peace with America to secure the benefits of peace in Europe. The death of General Robert Ross outside Baltimore, and the fiasco of the naval battle on Lake Champlain, broke the illusion of triumph, restoring an air of reality to British thinking. Prevost's retreat wasted all the money and effort put into sending 3,000 troops across the Atlantic and, far worse, ended a run of success that was pressurising the Americans into concessions. Victory in Vermont was hardly going to win the war, but it might have been enough to make the Americans concede. Plattsburg cost the British any leverage for border rectification or attempts to create an Indian territory. Strategic choices made in April and May, limiting the military force and retaining Prevost, had produced predictable outcomes. In late October Liverpool accepted the inevitable:

---

9 Sidmouth to Hiley Addington, 7 October 1814: 152M/C1814/OZ 37.

I wish we could get out of this war: but the point upon which I am most anxious is, that we should not get deeper into it, for I fear we shall feel it a most serious embarrassment some months hence; and it is not a contest in which we are likely to obtain any glory or renown at all commensurate to the inconvenience it will occasion.[10]

Fortunately, the Chancellor of the Exchequer reported a dramatic economic upturn and strong revenue streams with Europe open for business. The Plattsburg defeat encouraged Liverpool to move quickly to limit the damage: the Ghent Commissioners must ensure the Americans understood Britain would rectify any such failure and prosecute the war with more vigour. On 21 October he wrote to Henry Goulburn:

we can successfully blockade all their ports, . . . ravage their coasts, ruin their towns, destroy the little commerce which remains to them, and render their agriculture of no profit. They must look, therefore, to the failure of their revenue, to the impoverishment of their country, and probably to a national bankruptcy, from the continuance of the war. Sir A Cochrane has shown that he will not spare them, and, with the additional military force which will be sent to co-operate with him, the Americans may expect greater disasters than even those which they have already encountered.

Continuing the war would cost Britain about £10 million a year but, with trade booming and the economy expanding rapidly as Europe resumed trade, he implied this was not a serious burden

In truth Liverpool was bluffing; he had many reasons to avoid another year of war. He was not optimistic the Americans could be brought to see reason, directing the Cabinet to plan on the basis that the war would continue, and especially anxious that Russia and France might exploit the conflict. Nor was he convinced the country would be happy finding another £10 million for the purpose of securing a better frontier for Canada. The most pressing concern, securing a fresh government loan on suitable terms, would be impossible so long as the American war continued and Europe remained unsettled.

Writing from Vienna, Castlereagh tried to bolster the Prime Minister's morale by stressing that, while the Ghent process was

10 Pellew, *Sidmouth*, vol III, p 121.

unfortunate because it threatened to protract the war, 'it makes little sensation here'. Liverpool's perspective was dominated by the alarming state of France; credible intelligence suggested Bonapartist fanatics planned to assassinate Wellington, the ambassador in Paris. To remove the Duke from Paris without exciting suspicion, Liverpool considered sending him to Vienna, to provide military advice to Castlereagh, or to command in North America, 'with full powers to make peace or to continue the war, if peace should be found impracticable, with renewed vigour'.[11] While ready to do his duty, the Duke was anything but enthusiastic. Fortunately the project was dropped; within months Wellington would be the chief British envoy at Vienna, and then Commander-in-Chief of an allied army at Waterloo.

Crushing the privateers

In attempting to explain the 'victory' of 1812, Garitee[12] and other American authors have argued that a successful privateering effort influenced British decision-making during the peace process. However, this claim finds no support in archives. In reality, it was the complex diplomatic process underway at Vienna and domestic economic concerns that persuaded the British to offer America the status quo ante. British maritime insurance rates had remained stable throughout the war, ministers absorbed pressure from commercial interests and the Cabinet largely ignored privateering. It was not that the problem had gone away; it had never been a significant strategic threat. At the State Opening of Parliament on 8 November 1814, Melville faced serious complaints from commercial houses and colonial planters, who looked to the Navy for protection, assuming the Admiralty would shift warships from European waters to defend the Atlantic sea lanes. Melville was blunt: 'It must inevitably be the case when the whole force of an enemy is devoted to privateers, that our entire fleet, wherever stationed, cannot prevent the capture of some of our merchant vessels.' He also blamed the poor discipline of merchant ships, many of which had been taken after leaving their convoy. The United States Navy took only 172 British merchant ships from an American total of 1,613 captures and this was a mere 7.5 per cent of the British fleet Furthermore, 30 per cent of all American prizes were recaptured before they reached port.

11 *Liverpool* II, pp 56–8.
12 Garitee, *The Republic's Private Navy.*

By contrast, the United States lost 1,407 ships from a fleet of 21,449, less than half the size of the British. The balance of economic effect very much favoured Britain.[13]

The kudos accorded to privateering reflected post-war American political agendas rather than reality. The Republican Party elevated the privateer to join the militiaman as the bedrock of an economic defence. Confused by the nationalistic fervour that has long pervaded the subject, few stop to consider the fundamentally inconclusive nature of commerce-destroying. American historians consciously underplayed the darker aspects of privateering to sustain a useful myth.[14] Many relied on the statistics compiled by Hezekiah Niles, unaware that they were created to serve a Republican agenda.

The War of 1812 confirmed previous experience: commerce raiding has never proved decisive – but defence of trade has never been able to eradicate all threats and stop all losses. The safe and timely arrival of most ships has always been the test of successful trade defence, and in 1812 this was demonstrated by steady insurance rates. The real danger Britain faced was the loss of a major convoy, or the collapse of the convoy system. Commerce-destroying campaigns could never be completely defeated. In both World Wars German U-boats carried on to the bitter end, long after they had been rendered irrelevant. It was no different in 1812. Although the war officially ended on Christmas Eve 1814, American privateers were still putting to sea in February 1815, unaware that events in Belgium had ended their careers. This left Lloyds and the Admiralty to deal with real or rumoured attacks as late as May 1815.

America concedes

The key to British victory lay not in military might, but in the failure of every American offensive and the slow, remorseless pressure of economic blockade. This was a naval victory. After December 1813 American economic warfare, both internal measures to block exports and attacks on British seaborne trade, was simply irrelevant. By contrast, the blockade of New England beginning in the summer of 1814 immediately pushed up commodity prices by 40 per cent,

---

13 Arthur, *How Britain Won the War of 1812*, p 199.
14 For the wider context on smuggling and privateering, see Smith, *Borderland Smuggling*.

devastated national revenue, and sent much of the remaining capital into factories or across the border into British government bonds. Furthermore this was a limited war: Britain had no interest in destroying the United States and compelling it to accept terms after the fashion of Napoleon. By 1814, American commerce warfare was still damaging British economic life, but it was no longer a serious threat and the balance of economic devastation had long since shifted to favour the British. In addition, America was functionally bankrupt, and unable to access European funds after forceful British diplomacy blocked access to Dutch loans.

The capture of Washington and destruction of its public buildings in August 1814 was the final straw, leading to a run on American banks that saw large amounts of specie withdrawn and the collapse of the credit system. Attempts to raise money through internal taxes were hampered by Congress, while the obvious solution of an income tax was rejected. On 4 October the United States Government was insolvent. On 11 November it defaulted on payments due on the National Debt and the Louisiana Purchase. At this stage an individual would have had their affairs wound up, their possessions auctioned off and their family put out on the street. America's credit rating hit an all-time low, the full consequences of which were only avoided by the Treaty of Ghent. With the default rising to $2.8 million by the time news of peace reached Washington in February 1815, and a further $15 million of interest payments falling due, peace was essential for the United States. Little wonder that territorial claims on Canada, demands to end impressment and abrogate maritime belligerent rights were sacrificed to secure the status quo ante. That this decision was due to the British blockade can be seen in post-war measures to improve inland navigation and develop a fleet capable of breaking a blockade.

When the draft Treaty of Ghent reached London a relieved Liverpool explained: 'You know how anxious I was that we should get out of this war as soon as we could do so with honour.' By downplaying the prospects of lasting success, aside from punitive amphibious operations, Wellington had collapsed the logic of continuing the war. Canada could not be defended economically because there were 7.5 million Americans and only 300,000 Canadians. Faced with such numbers, changing the frontier would avail little. Liverpool was satisfied because the Americans had abandoned their maritime challenge, and the British public were content: 'As far as I have any means of judging our decision is generally approved'. More significantly, the future of the strategically vital Low Countries had been settled by a 'secret article in the Treaty of Paris'.[15] It is indicative of the fundamentally maritime nature of British strategy that Liverpool did not feel it necessary to mention the obvious lesson that Canada would be defended by the Royal Navy, not a rectified frontier, fortresses or soldiers.

For the British, the War of 1812 had always been a 'tiresome, pointless distraction, . . . a nuisance, but not a serious threat'.[16] Little wonder public reaction to the Treaty of Ghent was muted; at least the merchant princes of Liverpool and Bristol were content. With the war at an end the Government could focus on Europe and impending domestic battles over taxation and expenditure. The connection between the epic peace process underway at Vienna and the small-scale discussions at Ghent had long been obvious. Castlereagh delightedly observed that news of the Treaty altered the Czar's tone. Once the Treaty had been ratified the British simply forgot the War of 1812 and got back to the business of making money.

The Treaty of Ghent upheld British maritime belligerent rights, the fundamental bedrock of British power. While many have seen the British position as overbearing and dictatorial towards neutrals, there was no room for neutrality in a total war; the alternative would have been Napoleonic domination of the Continent. By keeping the American war isolated from the European conflict, and accepting the status quo ante, British statesmen acted wisely, preserving the legal basis of sea power and reducing the risk of future problems. Ghent established a clear distinction between Europe and the outside world, created by the British using their control of oceanic communications and trade. It helped maintain British global power for two generations at very low cost. Above all, British aims at Ghent and Vienna were clear and consistent: the restoration or recreation of a stable, peaceful world open to trade, one in which the British could prosper while they paid off the mountainous debts incurred waging war with much of the

---

15 *Liverpool* II, pp 88–90.
16 Muir, *Britain and the Defeat of Napoleon*.

very same world between 1793 and 1815. In the process the British forced the Americans to look at their own internal problems, problems that would keep them divided down to 1865.

On 17 January 1815, the *National Intelligencer*, the quasi-official outlet of the Republican administration, effectively admitted that the declaration of war in 1812 had been foolish, and futile. Three years of war proved that Britain had the cash and credit to wage war with America and France, and defeat both. Such insight would inform the way America dealt with Britain for the next century. British strategic leverage against America was a combination of sea control, economic warfare and small scale, targeted coastal offensives. The United States had no answer to those threats, beyond an endless chain of massy stone fortresses. As the maritime belligerent rights regime that won the war of 1812 had not been affected by the Treaty of Ghent, America remained desperately vulnerable after 1815.

The American challenge failed in the counting house: America lacked the military muscle to win a short war, and once the British troops had reinforced Canada the imposition of an effective economic blockade quickly exposed Washington's chronic lack of financial power. America could not pay for a long war, even one conducted on strictly limited terms. The cost of war was a 200 per cent increase in the American national debt, and a decisive shift away from oceanic maritime enterprise.

The sense of relief in Britain was palpable. Finally, twenty-two years of war with most of the modern world had come to an end. It was time to pay off ships and men, cut the estimates and resume business as usual. For the British that meant trade with the world, trade networked through strategic bases like Halifax and Bermuda that enabled the Royal Navy to command great swathes of ocean space, to protect British commerce and to crush that of any hostile power.

Some in Britain greeted peace with little pleasure, because the Treaty did not reflect the reality of British victory. Sir Walter Scott lamented the failure to administer America a stern lesson, but admitted the country was unwilling to wage the war for such a nebulous object. As a world-class creator of fabulous stories he realised the Americans had been given an opportunity to claim victory in print and convince themselves they might try again. Scott understood the enduring legacy of 1812 would not be territory or rights, but a distinct American culture; he expected American pens would create the victory that had eluded their swords and this proved to be the case. The War of 1812 was not a second War of Independence in political terms, but it did mark the decisive parting of two cultures. It drove America to acquire a distinctive identity, one that was truly of the New World, privileging its landscape, scale and opportunities over the narrow confines and dusty histories of Europe.

Suggested Further Reading
Arthur, B, *How Britain Won the War of 1812* (2011).
Bew, John, *Castlereagh*, vol 2 (2011).
Lambert, A, *The Challenge* (2012).

A CANADIAN CONCLUSION

The War of 1812 was not a success for the United States. She had gone to war to oppose Great Britain's policies at sea. In particular she was concerned with the British Orders-in-Council, the impressment of American seamen, British violation of American territorial waters, and the blockade of her sea ports. Despite some naval successes on the Great Lakes, American attempts at invading Canada had been defeated. At sea there had been some outstanding victories against certain of HM ships, but the tide was turned by Captain Broke in HMS *Shannon*.

Rear Admiral H F Pullen RCN,
The Shannon and the Chesapeake, p 106.

1. Captain Philip Bowes Vere Broke RN.

2. USS *Chesapeake* approaching HMS *Shannon*.

3. The melee on the deck of the *Chesapeake*: Captain Broke receiving his wound.

4. *Shannon* and her prize entering Halifax. Note the incorrect white ensign flying as in Brighton's *Memoir*, rather than the blue ensign of Admiral Warren and his squadron.

5 . 2013 US postage stamp celebrating a US victory on the Great Lakes.

6. *British Valour and Yankee Boasting,* a paean of praise for British valour and Shannon's victory (see p 161).

7. *A Sketch for the Regent's Speech*, on the surrender of Detroit to General Brock (see pp 159–60).

8. *The Yankey Torpedo* (see p 164).

9. *Boney and Maddy Gone to Pot*, mocking both Napoleon and Madison (see p 164).

10. *Brother Jonathan Administering a Salutary Cordial to John Bull*, commemorating Captain Perry's US success on the Great Lakes (see p 166).

Unsympathetic Instructions

In reply to the demands for increase of force which you have made, you will observe . . . that their Lordships have, not without inconvenience to other Services, placed under your command a force much greater in proportion than the National Navy of the Enemy opposed to you would seem to warrant . . . In reply to your statement that the Crews of Privateers and letters of Marque which now amount to six hundred, have in several instances landed at the points of Nova Scotia and the Leeward Islands, and cut out Vessels from the Harbours; I am commanded to observe that my Lords never doubted that the Privateers of the Enemy would become extremely numerous, as most if not all, of their commercial Marine would probably be diverted to privateering; but they were convinced of the impracticability of the remedy for this evil which you seem to propose, namely the meeting them with an equal number of ships. The only measures which with any attention to economy, and any reasonable prospect of success can be opposed to the Enemy's privateering system, are those of blockading their Ports, and of not permitting our Trade to proceed without protection; and for the execution of these purposes the force under your command will, no doubt, by judicious arrangement be found adequate. . . . My Lords cannot but hope that the reports which you state of <u>swarms</u> of American Privateers being at Sea, must be, in a great degree exaggerated; as they cannot suppose that you have left the principal Ports of the American Coast so unguarded as to permit such multitudes of Privateers to escape in and out unmolested; and their Lordships are quite sure that by preventing our Merchant Ships from running and by carefully blockading the principal Ports the trade of privateering will be made so hazardous and expensive that it objects will be in most instances frustrated; and that of course the general system will be very considerably checked.

**First Secretary of the Admiralty John Croker
to Admiral Sir John Warren (10 February 1813)**

3

Canada and the War of 1812

Chris Madsen

In August 1812, Thomas Jefferson pronounced, 'The acquisition of Canada this year, as far as the neighborhood of Quebec will be a mere matter of marching, and will give us experience for the attack of Halifax the next, and the final expulsion of England from the American continent.' For the Americans, the remaining British possessions in North America appeared easy pickings. Great Britain was distracted by war in Europe against the French emperor Napoleon, the United States possessed a population of 8 million compared to 300,000 in Upper and Lower Canada combined, Canadians were an assortment of loyalist refugees, economically motivated settlers and conquered peoples without a clear sense of nation or even language, culture and religion, and the military balance on paper clearly favoured the new republic by numbers and geography. The British, however, possessed the advantages of sea power which the pre-eminent navy of the day conferred, an experienced small army with superior training and leadership, and civil administration buttressed by a legal system that instilled the traditions of parliamentary democracy and respect for the monarchy (even for mad King George III).

The American decision to declare war against Great Britain and its holdings in North America on 18 June 1812 owed more to emotion than the product of rational calculation and strategy. Elements within American society, in particular war hawks strong in the northwest territories, pushed armed action to address longstanding grievances, settle the problem of restless first nations peoples purportedly aided by the British, and shamelessly gain space for expansion and further exploitation. President James Madison balanced those desires with sentiment in other established states either moderately supportive of the venture or bordering on outright neutrality. Whereas the United States entered the conflict very divided, by way of endorsement and war aims, Canadians fought a defensive war not of their making. In a contest as much about loyalties as the fortunes of battle, they were forced to choose sides. Several invasion attempts a long distance away from the core strategic positions in Quebec and Halifax were repelled. Consequently, the British remained in charge long enough to maintain the reliability of subordinate allies in local areas, until American unity behind military force of arms eroded and the rush of reinforcements released from Europe and elsewhere in Great Britain's global possessions turned a discretionary war into one directly threatening the American homeland. Canada was always a sideshow, and became increasingly so as the war progressed to culmination. Failure on the part of the Americans to achieve quick, decisive victories early on guaranteed that possessions in British North America survived to form the country known as Canada after Confederation in 1867. If the War of 1812 proved unsatisfactory for both Great Britain and the United States in many ways, Canadians, given their own nation, were arguably the real winners.

Far-flung Canada was a difficult battleground for any military campaign, offensively and defensively. British possessions in North America stretched from the maritime colonies of Nova Scotia, New Brunswick and Newfoundland on the eastern coast, the urban cities of Montreal and Quebec City along the St Lawrence River in Lower Canada (present-day Quebec), the sparsely populated lands on the large, freshwater Great Lakes amenable to farming and livestock in Upper Canada (today part of Ontario), to the relatively untouched westward wilderness areas occupied by first nations peoples and fur traders. Where to concentrate military effort and resources to best effect posed a perennial challenge. The British invested in building up fortresses and garrisons at Halifax, to protect the imperial naval station and deep-sea harbour there, and Quebec City, the important water-access point protecting the approaches to the commercial port and political centre of Montreal and all lands west outside the winter months. The Americans were inclined not to challenge these strong points directly, but instead to seek out places on the periphery where defences were noticeably weaker and superior numbers of troops could be brought to bear.

A significant constraint was logistics. Developed roads and pathways were almost non-existent, and most transportation of goods and people in a timely manner was water-borne by boat and portage canoe. Distance, season and climate together made travel difficult in Canada, particularly in winter, early spring and late autumn. The Canadian winter, characterised by freezing sub-zero temperatures and persistent snowfall, generally brought most activities and military operations to a standstill. Lakes and rivers froze over making travel arduous and dangerous. Those not clothed properly or prepared in advance by way of stored foodstuffs, adequate cut wood for fuel and pre-positioned supply were vulnerable to the harsh climate and occasional enemy action. Death by the elements was not uncommon. Active military campaigning was effectively limited to the months between spring and late autumn when the weather was more amenable and transportation routes passable. The armies and naval forces that fought over the lands of Canada drew sustenance from the people already *in situ*.

Whether Canada was even worth the cost in treasure and lives that a long war involved hardly mattered to most residents of British North America, who were governed by mixed loyalties and motivations for participating in the unwanted conflict. Many had been beaten once before – the loyalists on the losing side of the American Revolution, the French-Canadians at the hands of the British, and the downtrodden first nations peoples by either side and each other. Others came to Canada, including large numbers of Americans, in search of opportunity and sufficient land holdings to raise families and establish themselves for a promised prosperous future. Either way, the threat of war and worse, military occupation and requisitions, imperilled the status quo and whatever gains they had made through hard work and personal sacrifice. Canadians, notoriously adverse to military and defence matters, displayed little enthusiasm for a war on their doorstep.

The invading Americans at first cast themselves as liberators, whose arrival signalled an opportune time for all free persons in Canada to turn against British oppression. Most Canadians, even those with American roots, were unmoved and very practically preferred instead to await the outcome of events. The risk of choosing the wrong side, in terms of property and life, was just too dear. The British, on the other hand, expected allegiance through persuasion, sometimes outright threat, and coercion in the last resort. Occasionally, a few alleged traitors were tried and hanged – notoriously in 1814 at the bloody Ancaster assize – to remind everyone else of the price of disloyalty and treachery. Nevertheless, the nastiness of Canadian Volunteers, those Upper Canada neighbours who chose to join wholeheartedly the American cause led by firebrand Irish immigrant Joseph Willcocks, by burning houses and crops, raping women and destroying livestock, dissipated what little sympathy and support existed amongst a populace seeking a middling peaceful co-existence.

French-Canadians likewise held neither love nor affection for the British and English-speaking brethren, whom they considered alien outsiders. French-speaking Quebec society, at the time, was conservative and insular, far removed from the republican ideals of the French and American revolutions; in turn, British administrators deliberately encouraged traditional institutions like the Catholic Church and preserved the property rights of the landed gentry elite that dominated social and economic relations in Lower Canada. The Canadian *Voltigeurs*, French-Canadian militia raised to train and fight as light infantry, proved a more or less successful experiment to see how far military units drawn from the populace of Lower Canada could be trusted for self-defence against the Americans. Canadian militia, French-speaking and English-speaking, typically fought alongside native warriors in an unconventional fashion. For the British, the first nations peoples were essentially allies of convenience, both those originally residing in Canada and others who had moved north either by choice or having been pushed there by the Americans to escape extermination. Larger groupings, like the Iroquois Grand River six nations and the Mohawk nations, held aspirations to form independent confederacies with autonomy and control over their own affairs without outside interference, a dream that the British quietly broached without actually making any concrete promises. Canadians – English and French, urban and rural, white, native, and mixed – were thrown together in a great conflagration that demanded defence against repeated American attack at numerous points.

From the outset, the initiative belonged to the United States to choose when and where to invade Canada. American ambitions could only be fulfilled militarily by offensive action to seize territory, decisively defeat British armies and permanently occupy key points such as towns and cities. Canadians, like the British, benefited from inaction, hoping the Americans would never come. Calendar time was either neutral or favourable. The defenders prepared and waited for likely avenues of attack from westerly and southerly directions. In fact, some prominent Canadians were far more worried about Great Britain giving away its North America possessions at the negotiating table, once the inevitable peace treaty was signed, in return for other interests and goodwill. The United States would thereby have achieved a bloodless victory and greatly expanded its reach over the large continent. That smarter diplomatic approach, however, was never seriously pursued. The Americans instead embarked on a series of disparate and loosely coordinated military thrusts into the area along the Great Lakes and St Lawrence River, aimed at Upper Canada and thence to Lower Canada, with mixed results. The strategy and military effort behind the enterprise proved deeply flawed in execution. In effect, the Americans chose to go the long way round to reach the final objective, thereby squandering advantages in resources and numbers as well as inviting some really bad command decisions. The British and Canadians exploited to the fullest the forewarning and the golden opportunities so gained.

The Canadians, under overall British command and direction, contributed to the defensive scheme that checked and halted several determined incursions attempted in the initial months and two successive years of military campaigning. In August 1812, the American general and governor of the Michigan Territory William Hull surrendered Detroit, defended by a large army of Ohio and Michigan militia, to a smaller force of British regular troops and native warriors – the greatly exaggerated unseen enemy pouring forth war whoops and yells to hide fewer numbers. American soldiers were absolutely terrorised, with visions of massacre and the trophy scalps native warriors were wont to collect from alive and dead victims. In October 1812, the British defeated an opposed river crossing at Queenston Heights on the Niagara frontier, when the majority of New York militia brought forward for the endeavour decided that their terms of enrolment barred them from leaving the state; but during fighting the commanding British general in Upper Canada, Isaac Brock, was killed. Major General Roger Sheaffe, albeit perhaps not the flamboyant and striking figure of his predecessor, retrieved the situation with a sound knowledge of tactics and made sure the Americans stayed on their side of the river by placing Canadian militia and native warriors at selected points. This new employment was a welcome change from the construction and maintenance of roads that male Canadians subject to call-out for military service usually performed.

The Americans returned in 1813 for more attempts on Lake Ontario and Lake Erie. They undertook an amphibious raid on York (present-day Toronto) where the provincial legislature was torched, assaulted Fort George at the mouth of the Niagara River from the lake, and started a two-brigade advance to the fortified position at Burlington, with plans to march onward thence to York and then east to the advance military and naval base at Kingston. However, a surprise night attack on the American encampment at Stoney Creek, which carried away the two most senior US Army officers and field artillery pieces manhandled from Fort George, foiled the entire endeavour. With more marked success, American general and governor of the Indiana Territory William Harrison landed a menacing force of Kentucky mounted riflemen and militia, with scores to settle against the hated 'Indians', and ran down a retreating British force near Moraviantown in October, killing the inspirational native leader Tecumseh. Instead of reinforcing success, President Madison sidelined Harrison, arguably the best American general by far, for political reasons in favour of the bombastic southern gentleman James Wilkinson, a senior officer with dubious command experience and operational insight, who executed a leisurely descent with 8,000 troops down the St Lawrence River threatening Montreal. The Americans, defiant Kingston still at their backs and meeting the main British military force head-on, were soon stopped by defeat at the Battle of Crysler's Farm on 11 November 1813. Another concurrent advance with 4,000 American troops up the Lake Champlain valley through Vermont, the traditional invasion route toward Quebec, was blocked by French-Canadian militia and Mohawk warriors entrenched behind defensive works in the forests of Chateauguay two weeks earlier. A year that had started so auspiciously for the Americans ended in failure and stalemate.

In 1814, the grandly named Northern Army, commanded by Major General Jacob Brown, which included the efficient and tactically adept Winfield Scott, crossed the Niagara River from the Lake Erie side in force. The Americans captured the half-finished Fort Erie, beat the surprised British and Canadians on the Chippawa River, fought a major engagement battle to a draw at Lundy's Lane near Niagara Falls, and withstood a long siege again at Fort Erie, a place which they enlarged and reinforced. It was their best effort so far, but still not enough to ensure the right results. Each attempted invasion followed a similar pattern, wherein the Americans were unable to capitalise on victory when achieved, and allowed small tactical reverses again and again to upset plans causing near collapse and retreat. Besides obvious failings in political decision-making and higher command on the American side, Canadian assistance proved pivotal. British regulars on the spot with the help of allies kept the Americans forward engaged, far away from the strategic positions in Quebec and Nova Scotia, where the bulk of British troops were held in reserve in case of need. Senior commanders were ever willing to trade ground in Upper Canada, to assure defence-in-depth, though thanks to American incompetence were seldom forced to do so. Militarily, the contest between the Americans and British around the Great Lakes was decided on Canadian soil.

What else accounted for the near total lack of success by the Americans in the northern theatre of operations, in Canadian and British favour? Command of the large lakes and the vital lines of communication that facilitated transportation and movement was essential. Naval power, or at least the provision of sufficient naval forces directed in a meaningful and decisive manner, accorded the ability to fight over, contest and dominate control of waterways to the advantage of either side. The Royal Navy expanded and up-gunned the existing Provincial Marine from a transport service under the army quartermaster general to a full-fledged fighting force, with a dockyard and base at Kingston on the eastern end of Lake Ontario and a lesser yard at Amherstburg on Lake Erie. The Americans constructed fleets of new warships on Lake Ontario based on Sackets Harbor due south of Kingston and Presque Isle on the south shore of Lake Erie. The natural physical barrier of Niagara Falls prevented transfer of ships between Lake Ontario and Lake Erie, though the upper Great Lakes were accessible from the latter. The American naval victory at the Battle of Put-in-Bay in September 1813 over a numerically and cannonade inferior British naval force achieved control over Lake Erie – used to good effect in transporting William Harrison's merry band of brothers to a date with destiny and then thrown away by redirecting almost all available warships to operations in the strategically marginal upper reaches of Lake Huron to subdue Fort Mackinac, a choke-point important to the fur trade. Opposing commodores on Lake Ontario meanwhile embarked on a frenzied naval arms race to out-construct the other side in terms of numbers and size, neither especially willing to risk any decisive naval engagement or even losses while supporting armies in the conduct of joint operations, despite the potential shown in 1813. They were content to stay in port spending vast sums of money and manpower on warships that would never be used, if indeed finished, before peace came. Jacob Brown's last military campaign on the Niagara frontier was clearly impeded by the US Navy's abandonment of any pretence to joint operations in conjunction with the army.

The sure way to win on Lake Ontario, and arguably the whole of Upper Canada, was to attack and seize the primary naval base, which required the cooperation of naval forces for lift and fire support. The British tried once at Sackets Harbor and failed; the Americans, for their part, felt Kingston too well-defended and only planned, never executed, a full-out assault. The war might have turned out differently if the Americans had captured Kingston straightaway, sat on the place over the winter with total command of Lake Ontario, and then used it as a base of operations for a big push on the main prizes Montreal and Quebec City in the next campaigning season. No doubt, the Canadians and British would have also done their utmost to evict the Americans at the earliest opportunity.

In fact, the British Empire soon struck back with vigorous, direct, offensive operations against the United States. Napoleon's abdication and forced exile to the island of Elba following the sixth coalition's invasion of France in the spring of 1814 released large numbers of seasoned British troops and warships for employment in North America. The United States stubbornly refused to make peace with Great Britain, so obviously further encouragement was needed. Halifax, erstwhile haven for privateers and home to part of the Royal Navy's fleet on the North America and West Indies station, became a hive of activity and preparation under a new aggressive naval commander, Vice Admiral Alexander Cochrane. Cochrane's warships provided escort and transport for a sizeable expedition of British troops led by Major General Robert Ross up Chesapeake Bay to strike at the very heart of American political power. The British landed, drove away the scratch Maryland militia at Bladensburg, and occupied

Washington DC. The White House and other government buildings were burned, ostensibly in retaliation for American actions at York in Upper Canada the year before. Cochrane, however, found the defenders at the port of Baltimore, the next target, stronger and more determined and decided to withdraw in order to husband strength for another planned major amphibious assault against New Orleans in the southern gulf. The British were now the ones to waste strategy and military effort on the margins.

Lieutenant General George Prevost, the senior commander in Canada, tried to move in force down the Champlain valley from Lower Canada in loose support of the planned British operations and without firm command of the lake, which was contested. At Plattsburg, the Americans soundly beat the British first in battle on the water and then compelled Prevost's troops to retreat. The French-Canadian militia mocked and jeered the sullen British regulars when they passed back across the Canadian border. The big plans to put the United States in its place, perhaps even undo the American revolution, came to naught. A peace treaty between Great Britain and the United States was duly negotiated and signed at Ghent, Belgium, in December 1814, but military operations continued afterwards until ratification by the US Congress in February 1815. With this turn of events, Canada remained solidly under British influence instead of American for the time being.

Canada, as a nation, remembers the War of 1812 in a highly idealised and self-serving way. It has become part of national mythology and the historical narrative, in a country that struggles with identity, sense of history, and uniqueness. We are told that Canadians defended territory and homes against invading Americans and consequently won a course to nationhood. Bicentennial arrangements celebrate the likes of Isaac Brock, Tecumseh and Laura Secord as heroes and heroines in the long-ago struggle. That the events took place long before Canada achieved Confederation in 1867, when the British basically grew tired of paying for the defence of North America and shifted the burden onto reluctant populaces in the guise of self-government, is only inconvenient. Since then, Canadians have grown very comfortable with the United States, for economic livelihood, shared culture, winter getaway vacations and perimeter continental security. The two countries have the longest undefended border in the world. Unlike 200 years ago, war is simply unthinkable. Naturally, the strongest connections and memories surrounding the War of 1812 are in Central Canada where the fighting actually took place. Numerous historic heritage sites have been preserved for posterity that interpret and relive the experience. Canada's four western provinces, on the other hand, were settled later in the century and have no direct attachment to the war with the Americans. What does a person in British Columbia, for example, really think about the War of 1812? Probably not much. The subject is casually taught in grade school and periodically seen in Heritage Minute infomercials presented on television and websites.[1] Still, the war was a time when Canadians of the day, whether English, French or first nation, came together in a common purpose. They may not have been motivated for all the same reasons, or even liked each other, but they stood united. As a symbol, participation in the War of 1812 has become part of broader Canadiana, alongside love of hockey, maple syrup, loon-faced coins, the time-honoured beaver, red-serged Mounties and Canadian Tire money. It contributes to a sentiment that makes Canada and those who live in such a fortunate, resource-rich country that much stronger.

Suggested Further Reading

Barbuto, Richard V, *Niagara 1814: America Invades Canada* (2000).
Hitsman, J Mackay, *The Incredible War of 1812* (1965).
Malcomson, Robert, *Lords of the Lake* (1998).
Turner, Wesley B, *British Generals in the War of 1812* (1999).

---

1 Heritage Minutes are short dramatisations funded by the Canadian government to promote history and heritage in the country. They are shown on Canadian television, especially during televised hockey games and special events such as the Olympics (the War of 1812 ones played almost constantly during the 2012 Winter Olympics in Vancouver). In North America, a television spot that has no overt commercial motive is called an infomercial; in the British context, you might call it a public service announcement.

PROVO WALLIS (1791–1892)

Provo Wallis was born in 1791 in Halifax, Nova Scotia. His father, a clerk at the Naval Yard had him registered as an able seaman on HMS *Oiseaux* at the age of four and subsequently on the crews of other warships. By the time he actually went to sea on the *Cleopatra* as a midshipman in 1804 he had amassed nearly a decade of seniority.

He joined the *Shannon* in January 1812. Since Broke was badly wounded in the battle and the first lieutenant killed, Wallis served in temporary command for six days escorting the *Chesapeake* (now flying the Blue Ensign above the Stars and Stripes) into his home town of Halifax. An eyewitness recorded: 'This circumstance naturally added to the enthusiasm of the citizens, for they felt that through him they had some share in the honour of the achievement.'

His later commands were again on the Halifax station and in the West Indies and Mediterranean. In 1857, he was appointed Commander-in-Chief on the southeast coast of South America. To prevent two admirals from dying as paupers, a special clause in the naval retirement scheme of 1870 provided that those officers who had commanded a ship during the French war should be retained on the active list. The few days Wallis was in charge of the *Shannon* meant he was on the active list until he died, having automatically reached the rank of Admiral of the Fleet, purely by seniority. The Admiralty suggested he retire when he reached his late nineties, as otherwise he could be required to take a seagoing command. Wallis replied that he was ready to accept one, and that, though from the age of sail and without experience of modern steamships built of iron, he was willing to learn.

After a final period sheltering 'in Blanket Bay, under Cape Rug' (his own words), Wallis died in 1892 at Funtington near Portsmouth just short of his 101st birthday with a combined service of 96 years from his name first appearing on the books of an RN ship.

Colin Reid

4

Prize Laws in the War of 1812

Gabriela A Frei

Maritime warfare is not only about battles; it also involves contention over the legal grounds for the stopping, searching and capturing of ships and the claiming of prizes. In the lead-up to the War of 1812, American ships were captured and prizes claimed, and battles were fought in the British Admiralty Courts over the lawfulness of this capture. In 1806, James Madison, then US Secretary of State, anonymously published a pamphlet, *An Examination of the British Doctrine which Subjects to Capture a Neutral Trade not Open in Time of Peace*, in which he argued for free trade by neutrals and condemned the British practice at sea which violated the neutral rights of the United States. He referred to cases of capture which were, in his opinion, unlawful and contrary to the law of nations. Although Britain's extensive blockade and anti-neutral policies in the Napoleonic Wars offered a reason for the United States to declare war on Britain, they were by no means the only causes for the outbreak of the War of 1812.

Prize laws were part of international law, which was then understood as a body of customs and rules established by states. Affirmed in court rulings, these customs and rules provided precedence establishing whether prizes were lawful capture of property. The right of search and capture enabled a belligerent to control trade and offered an instrument to suppress the enemy's economy. While enemy ships were generally subject to capture, this also allowed the stopping of neutral merchant ships in order to identify the ship, and the destination of the ship and cargo, as well as the nature of the cargo. International law acknowledged the right of search and capture and states regularly affirmed it in their treaties. A neutral ship was lawful capture if it resisted search and capture, fled, or destroyed the ship's papers. These acts constituted suspicious behaviour which justified detention. Before a prize could be claimed, a prize court had to verify the prize, for which the prize had to be brought into port, usually a port of the belligerent. Whether a prize could also be brought into a neutral port or destroyed was disputed practice. Although prize courts decided on matters of international law, their rulings reflected national policies and thus their impartiality was not beyond doubt. At the outbreak of a conflict, mariners received information from their own state or sovereign as to the conditions for a prize to be lawful. While a lawful prize could mean a fortune, the wrongful detention of a ship could lead to ruin, since the ships' commanders were liable for any costs and damages incurred. For good or for evil, the capture of prizes was lucrative, albeit a personally risky endeavour, as Broke would have been well aware.

A good illustration as to the prize laws and to the practices of different sea powers can be found in Henry Wheaton's book *A Digest of the Law of Maritime Captures and Prizes*, published in 1815. Wheaton was an aspiring young American lawyer, born in Providence, Rhode Island, where he had studied law at Rhode Island College (known today as Brown University). During the War of 1812, he was an editor of a New York newspaper and regularly commented on legal issues. He became a US Supreme Court Reporter in 1816, and later an American diplomat in Denmark and Prussia.

All British prize cases during the War of 1812 were in the first instance tried by the Vice Admiralty Courts established in the colonies; in this case, Halifax in Nova Scotia and Bermuda. The High Court of Admiralty in London acted as a court of appeal, and in the last instance a further appeal could be brought to the Lords Commissioners of Appeal in Prize Causes. The Vice Admiralty Courts were organised in the same way as the London court and followed the same rules, but they acted mostly independently because of the slow correspondence between the colonies and London.

Sir William Scott, Lord Stowell, who was appointed judge at the High Court of Admiralty in 1798, was the towering figure at the court until his retirement in 1828. Before his appointment to the Admiralty Court, he was Advocate-General and as such gained vast experience in prize cases. His decisions as admiralty judge shaped the British prize laws until the outbreak of the First World War in 1914. His judgements were praised far beyond the British realms as sharp, precise and fair, and Wheaton respected him for his rigour. However, Wheaton also pointed out that the principles upon which British practice was based reflected the interests of a major sea power and trading nation.

One of the principles of British practice was that enemy property could be seized on a neutral ship. On the other hand, neutral non-contraband goods were to be restored, if found on an enemy ship. The British practice was intended to hit the enemy economy by suppressing the export of goods. At the same time, neutral property and neutral waters were to be respected. Scott ruled in several cases for the restoration of a ship captured in neutral waters. He argued that these cases violated the integrity of neutral waters and thus compromised the sovereignty of a state. Whether neutral ships sailing under convoy were subject to the right of search and capture was disputed by the British. The High Court of Admiralty insisted on the exercise of the right of search and capture as a lawful instrument of a belligerent to identify a ship. Scott argued that resistance to the right of search and capture raised suspicion as to the intention of the ship.

A related question was whether the owner's residence or domicile determined enemy or neutral status of property. The nationality of subjects, and thus of the owner of goods, was of importance to merchants who often resided outside their native country. The question was also relevant in cases of impressment, where American sailors were suspected to be British subjects. The British practice followed the principle of residence, which meant that a neutral subject, who lived for a period of time before the outbreak of a conflict in an enemy state, was treated as an enemy subject. Scott defined the principle more precisely and ruled that a British subject who resided in the United States prior to the War of Independence was to be treated as a US subject, while a British subject, who only resided in the United States for a short period before the outbreak of the War of 1812, was to be treated as a British subject; the length of this period was not specified, so the prize court had to decide the 'real' intention in each case.

Britain's wide definition of contraband was another area of dispute. Belligerents were free to declare any good as contraband, and generally distinguished between absolute and conditional contraband. The former described goods for direct military use such as arms and ammunition, while the latter described goods which could be used for civilian as well as for military purposes, such as timber, food, pitch or tar. Since conditional contraband left room for interpretation, the destination decided the nature of the goods. So, if naval stores were destined for a port in which enemy ships were built, then the cargo was declared conditional contraband because the goods assisted the enemy war efforts. On the other hand, if the same goods were destined for a civilian port, then they were not declared contraband. Instead of condemning the cargo of a neutral ship, which had been declared conditional contraband, Scott ruled that the cargo could be sold in Britain. This transaction was called pre-emption, offering a compromise to the condemned neutral, but nevertheless favouring the interests of a belligerent.

Blockade was legally one of the most controversial issues because of its vague definition. Scott prohibited paper blockades by ruling that a lawful blockade had to exist in practice. A lawful blockade further needed to be notified and established by an authority. A ship could only be condemned if it actually violated a blockade, for example by attempting to ingress or egress a blockaded port. However, practice differed from theory. When, in November 1807, the British Government proclaimed by Order in Council a blockade on all French ports in reaction to Napoleon's land blockade, neutrals were only allowed to trade with France if they first paid a duty in British ports. Not only did these measures favour British trade, but the proclamation of blockade was also unlawful with respect to Scott's definition. Yet, Scott justified the Orders in Council as a retaliatory measure because the enemy did not respect the law of nations.

A final point of dispute was the British practice of the Rule of 1756. The rule was established during the Seven Years War when Britain imposed trade restrictions on neutrals which prohibited them from undertaking in wartime trade that was usually closed to them in peacetime. The policy aimed at cutting off colonies from their mother countries. The principle underscoring the Rule of 1756 was that enemy property was not safe in neutral ships. While trading with the enemy was legal, trading for the enemy was not. To circumvent the Rule of 1756, American ships en route from the West Indies to France stopped at a neutral port in the United States, and then argued that their voyage started from a neutral port. Scott, however, ruled in these cases that the cargo remained enemy property for the entire voyage, even though it was trans-shipped in a neutral port; this was called continuous voyage, another policy which aimed at the interruption of trade between a colony and its mother country.

The American prize cases were in the first instance tried before the district courts, and the US Supreme Court acted in cases of appeal. The decisions of the US Supreme Court underlined the principles for which the United States had fought during the Napoleonic Wars as a neutral power, such as the principle of free ship, free goods; that neutral goods were safe in enemy ships; or that the destination decided whether goods were declared conditional contraband or not. These principles reflected the values of American policy with regard to neutral rights and the freedom of the seas.

The American practice followed in many aspects that of the British. It acknowledged that neutral property on enemy ships, with the exception of contraband, was exempt from capture; that the destination decided the character of the goods; and that residence decided the nationality of an owner. Yet there were also differences of principle between American and British practice. The United States recognised the principle of free ship, free goods, which meant that enemy property, with the exception of contraband, transported in neutral ships was safe from capture. Several rulings of the US Supreme Court during the War of 1812 reaffirmed this principle, and the policy was subsequently included in various state treaties.

With regard to the question of contraband, the United States advocated the abolition of the concept of contraband altogether. As this effort proved unsuccessful, they pushed for a limited list of contraband. Yet, when the War of 1812 broke out, the American government did not issue a list of contraband. The United States also objected to the British practice of the Rule of 1756, against which the pamphlet from Madison was directed, and regarded neutral trade between two enemy ports as lawful. Finally, the United States urged for an agreed definition of the term blockade, since this had been one of the key issues which had led to the War of 1812, and demanded that a lawful blockade needed to be effective. The American government went so far as to propose the immunity of private property at sea, which meant that neutral and enemy property be exempt from capture with the exception of contraband and blockade. This proposal was never adopted by any sea power.

The prize laws of both belligerents and the decisions of the prize courts reflected national interests. British practice strengthened belligerent rights and only made minor concessions to neutrals. On the other hand, American practice strengthened neutral rights, and thus supported the protection of neutral property from capture. The most significant cases underscored the principles laid out in the two countries' policies. When the War of 1812 came to an end with the Treaty of Ghent in 1815, none of the diverging practices of war at sea had been resolved. In one of the last American prize cases of the War of 1812, considered by the US Supreme Court in 1818, Justice William Johnson demanded reforms to the diverging practices at sea. Ever since, these differences have continued to be unresolved and to represent challenges in international law.

Suggested Further Reading

Bourguignon, Henry J, *Sir William Scott, Lord Stowell, Judge of the High Court of Admiralty, 1798–1828* (1987).

Hill, J Richard, *The Prizes of War: The Naval Prize System in the Napoleonic Wars, 1793–1815* (1998).

Wheaton, Henry, *A Digest of the Law of Maritime Captures and Prizes* (1815).

WINTER OFF NOVA SCOTIA, 1812–13

This was the last winter Captain *Broke* was destined to pass on this trying station; and it may be well to give the young sailor an idea of its inclemency, as often experienced on board the *Shannon*. The cold was so intense that it was impossible to handle the ropes without the fingers suffering from frost-bite. The sails were so frozen as to become brittle as glass; when furled they would not fall from the yards; and when forced down they broke like chips as they opened their folds. The ropes were so encrusted with ice that they cracked when moved, and so thickened were they that they could neither start nor run through the sheaves. If the ship had to wear (and to tack was impossible) it was necessary to haul the foresail up first, as no dependence could be placed on the tacks or sheets working in their blocks. The top-gallant-masts could not be got up when struck. The spray came over the gangway and quarterdeck, and froze on the guns and deck as fast as it fell. The ship's hull from ahead to abaft was a mass of ice. The *Tenedos*, *Shannon*'s consort, had fifteen men frost-bitten on one occasion of wearing ship. The *Shannon*'s crew, during this cruise, wore in winter a very thick worsted under-dress, mittens, and Welsh wigs.

Revd J G Brighton, *Broke Memoir*, p 148

5

Victories or Distractions, Honour
or Glory?

Tim Voelcker

The timing of the declaration of war could hardly have been worse for both Britain and the United States. Napoleon's control of the European mainland was at its height, France's 'running sore' of Spain not yet at its worst. Six months of tortuous secret negotiations to persuade Russia and Sweden to break free from French domination and form a tripartite alliance with Britain to rescue Europe's other nations had yet to reach agreement. Britain had the ships but too few men to man them; she had the financial resources but too little hard cash. On the other side of the Atlantic, President Madison had made little preparation for actual conflict either on land or at sea, despite the growing anger of the United States against what they saw as the arrogance of Britain. The belief expressed by Jefferson that 'Providence has placed their richest and most defenceless possessions at our door'[1] and that American troops could just walk into Canada had encouraged over-confidence. Neither country was militarily prepared for what was to come. Had Madison delayed a month and so received in time the news that Britain had agreed to suspend the Orders-in-Council as far as American shipping was concerned, he would have achieved his chief domestic political objective of preventing a split in his Republican party, avoiding the loss of blood, property, finance and stability that, to this day, is too often the result of resorting to a war of aggression. But whether he would have had the wisdom to see this is open to doubt. For future Canada, fighting a war of defence, the situation was very different.

At least the US Navy had acquired valuable combat experience in its

---

1 Quoted in Rodger, *The Command of the Ocean*, p 565.

efforts to control the Quasi War against the Barbary pirates in 1798–80; as the War of 1812 was to show, its gunnery was excellent, especially the effectiveness of its sharpshooters. How far that is attributable to the presence of frontiersmen in the crews is not known; the presence of experienced former Royal Navy gun crew will certainly have brought advantages. Additionally, the ships were relatively newly built or refitted and three of the six frigates were of a size and weight of broadside that greatly exceeded the standard 18pdr frigates of the British. Yet half of them were not ready for sea at the declaration of war, so that they were not fully able to make use of the great advantage that aggressors had in those days of slow communications – of attacking opposing ships before they are aware that hostilities have broken out. Britain had made use of this eight years before, after the end of the Peace of Amiens when still at peace with Spain. A squadron of four frigates was sent to intercept four Spanish frigates returning to Cadiz with treasure from the Indies, capturing three and destroying the fourth of the unprepared Spaniards. The captured cargoes brought in over a million pounds.

Fig 5.1 Captain James Lawrence of the USS *Chesapeake*.

There was no clear plan of campaign given to the individual US captains or even to their commodores when they were put together in a squadron. Commodore Rodgers, on receiving notification of the declaration of war, had sailed with two of the super-frigates, *President* and *United States*, and two brigs. His instructions were to protect returning American merchant ships since the value of the customs dues and excise was essential to the war's finances. He ignored this, hunting for a West Indies convoy instead, insisting to his superior, Hamilton, that he was permitted to be 'governed by circumstances' and claiming that he 'hoped to fall in with some of the British cruisers before they were apprised of the war'.[2]

Paul Hamilton, appointed Secretary of the Navy by Madison in 1809, had little naval experience, having previously been governor of South Carolina. He also had no clear strategic policy and no real understanding of the demands on the Navy in the event of war with a maritime power as strong as Britain. In November 1811, he maintained that the existing navy 'would be ample to the protection of our coasting trade; would be competent to annoy extensively the commerce of an enemy;[3] and uniting occasionally in operations with the gunboats already built and brought into service, and our fortifications also, afford complete protection to our harbours'. This reflected Jefferson's strong but unjustified belief that a gunboat navy was 'the only <u>water</u> defense which can be useful to us, & protect us from the ruinous folly of a navy'. Yet the following month Hamilton asked for funding for twelve 74-gun ships of the line and a further ten frigates. This was hotly debated in the House of Representatives, being cut back in stages until finally reduced to a paltry figure for the repair of just three of the five existing frigates 'in ordinary' (reserve).

Hamilton was not to survive. Captain David Porter, later to achieve success as captain of the American frigate *Essex,* commented to a friend in October: 'There must be a change in our Department or we never can expect to do any thing except on our own responsibility – there is no energy nor will there be while a pint of whiskey can be purchased in the District of Columbia'. By the end of the year Hamilton had been persuaded to resign. He was succeeded by William Jones, who had quite a different background and was described in the press as 'a man

---

2 Quoted in McCranie, *Utmost Gallantry*, p 27.
3 Quoted in McCranie, *Utmost Gallantry*, pp 19–20.

of talents and a practical seaman'. He was a shipowner who had suffered bankruptcy while trading in Russia, as a result of the Embargo Act and the difficulties of trading within Napoleon's Continental System.

Within a few months he demanded a new strategy where American warships would: 'cruise the Ocean <u>singly</u> and if I mistake not will make such havock among their commercial fleet, and light cruizers of the enemy as will divert him from the Petty Larceny in our Bays and Rivers to the protection of his own commerce and colonies'.[4] On 6 May, he sent the following instructions to Captain Evans of the *Chesapeake* just before he was replaced by James Lawrence. They were quite specific and set out both the strategy and the reasons behind it. A copy was sent to Lawrence, accompanied by a letter telling him to accept them as his own instructions as *Chesapeake*'s new captain and to render a strict observance of them:[5]

It is impossible to conceive a Naval Service of a higher order in a National point of view than the capture and destruction of the enemy's stores, ships with Military & Naval Stores, destined for the supply of his armies in Canada, & Fleets on this station, & the capture of transports with troops destined to reinforce Canada or invade our own shores. With this in view no better position can be better chosen than the range of the coast of Nova Scotia & the entrance of the Gulph of St Lawrence & Straights of Belle Isle, along the coast of Labrador, or round the east coast of Newfoundland (as information & prospects may determine) to the coast of Greenland, where the entire whale fishery of the Enemy being without protection may be speedily and completely destroyed.

This should have made it quite clear to Lawrence that the role of the *Chesapeake* was to be that of commerce-raider – an unglamorous task where there was little glory to be won, or even much profit. After the initial successes of American privateers against undefended and unprepared merchant shipping, the establishment of a comprehensive blockade progressively along the eastern seaboard, especially at its southern end, had led to the frequent recapture of prizes by British

4 Jones to unnamed correspondent, 5 April 1813.
5 Pullen, *The Shannon and the Chesapeake*, pp 43–5.

cruisers. Their job was both to prevent the privateers putting to sea and to stop their prizes from reaching port to be sold and so finance continuing operations. Privateering ceased to be profitable and the 'private' arm of the American attack on Britain diminished; it was left to the regular navy to do what it could since it was not dependent on financial gain. This combination of close-to blockade and a regular convoy system by Britain had proved effective in the Baltic in defeating Napoleon's Continental System during the previous five years to the cost of his ally Denmark/Norway. It was to be employed again with success in the two Great Wars of the twentieth century.

William Jones shows also in this letter that he was conscious of the need for a commerce-raider to remain at sea as long as possible. Not only did this minimise the number of times that a ship had to breach Britain's naval blockade with the dangers that this involved; but wandering undiscovered for as long as possible on the high seas from Cape Ann to Bergen, and later into the Pacific and Indian Oceans, stretched British ships and manpower to the limit – for them, lack of action was almost as demoralising as a defeat. There is little doubt that Rodgers' three long cruises in the summers of 1812 and 1813, despite the small number of prizes he captured, had substantial impact. Jones was also aware that space on board and keeping conditions for water and food were limiting factors:

By the time this could be accomplished the same route may be retraced home, so as to enter some eastern port in all the month of September. In this route you will find great resource & refreshment in the fish with which those seas abound, as well as in that of the fishing vessels you may capture & destroy; moreover the moderate temperature & humidity of the climate will admit of a very moderate consumption of water.

It was probably unnecessary to make his next point about burning prizes rather than unsuccessfully trying to send them through the British blockade:

The force of the Enemy now on our coast & the expected increase, forbids a reasonable expectation of getting prizes safe into our ports during the summer months. The risk of recapture is so great that the public interest seems to demand rather the destruction of every prize, than to weaken your crew by attempting to send them in, particularly those with <u>military</u> or <u>naval stores</u>. A question never can arise between the honourable patriotism of our gallant officers & the pecuniary interest they may be supposed to have, in attempting to send them into port, when the doubtful chances of success, & the very great advantage the enemy would derive from recapture are considered.

The three early victories over Royal Navy frigates (*Guerrière, Macedonia* and *Java*) by other US captains (see Historical Note, p xxii), which had so excited America after the failure of the land forces, combined with his disappointment at not being allowed to wait until the *Constitution*, whose captaincy he had been promised, was ready for sea, had given Lawrence a burning desire for glory. This could only be achieved by his own victory over yet another frigate. It was a longing that had spread to other captains, particularly the younger ones. When Captain Henry Allen of the 16-gun *Argus* sailed from Sandy Hook on 18 June, his instructions were clear: having dropped the newly appointed minister to France at Lorient, he was to target trade in the Irish Sea; 'this would carry the war home to their direct feelings and interest, and produce an astonishing sensation'. He left Lorient on 20 July and in the next three weeks captured twenty-one prizes, to the confusion of the Admiralty and the fury and dismay of the British press and public. However, the Royal Navy's 18-gun *Pelican*, following information from a merchant ship, had tracked the *Argus* and, led closer by the sight of a burning ship, caught and attacked her.[6] Allen had evidently welcomed the battle as the *Argus* made no effort to escape, but he was mortally wounded in the first few minutes and his ship was captured. Madison's reaction to the news was to suggest that US cruisers should be instructed never to fight where they could avoid it and to employ themselves entirely in destroying the commerce of the enemy. However sensible that might have been strategically, it was too late. Emotionally, the standards had been set by those first victories and for Lawrence anything less than repeating *Hornet*'s triumph over the *Peacock* was unthinkable. Master Commandant John Creighton,

---

6 James, *Naval History*, vol 6, pp 220–22.

returning safely from a cruise and being offered command of the newly-built and larger *Argus*, expressed the feelings of other officers as well: 'The *Rattlesnake* is of that class of vessels only calculated for the destruction of the Enemy's commerce, and I freely give her up for the command of a ship on board of which I shall not always be obliged to flee before the foe'.

Jones' next instructions were again sensible – and again appear to have been disregarded:

The cruising ground herein designated, also embraces a vast & valuable mercantile trade for the supply of the British Provinces & of the Indians, & also a rich return in furs & pelteries. The enemy will not in all probability anticipate our taking this ground with our public ships of war, & as the enemy's convoys generally separate between Cape Race & Halifax, leaving the trade of the St Lawrence to proceed without convoy, the chance of captures upon an extensive scale is very flattering. It is of the greatest importance that an account of prisoners should be kept as full as possible, & the returns regularly made to this Department, in order that the exchange of our gallant seamen may be effected without delay, & that by the magnitude of the pledge in our hands the enemy may be induced from policy, if not from disposition, to treat our citizens with less vigour than he is accustomed to do. The fogs which prevail in the seas in which you are to cruise may be considered as forming an objection, upon the presumption that a superior enemy cannot be discovered until close on board, but admitting the fact, it is counterbalanced by the facility it affords to a fast sailing vessel to escape from a superior enemy, that it conceals your own ship until an inferior in force & sailing is under your guns – that the [*sic*] running close in with the land you are sure to have clear weather although the fog may be ever so thick two or three leagues off & that by taking a position off some known land fall usual for ships entering the St Lawrence, you may intercept them as they approach the land the moment they develop from the fog bank. After all vigilance & preparation are the only safeguards in any & every situation . . .

Unfortunately, Jones added a rider that Lawrence considered enabled him to ignore the instructions and do what he saw fit:

If in the course of your cruise you should derive such information of the force of the enemy, or other sufficient cause, as to render a strict observance of my instructions prejudicial to the public service, you are at liberty to exercise your own judgement & pursue such other course as may in your opinion be best calculated to accomplish the important objects of your cruise . . .

Captain A T Mahan's verdict in 1905, as an eminent American naval historian, was damning:

The bearing of these facts is not to excuse the defeat but to enforce the lesson that a grave military enterprise is not to be hazarded on a side issue, or on a point of pride, without adequate preparation. The Chesapeake was ordered to a service of very particular importance at the moment – May 1813 – when the Canada campaign was about to open. She was to act against the communication of the enemy; and while it is upon the whole more expedient, for the morale of a service, that battle with an equal should not be declined, quite as necessarily action should not be sought when it will materially interfere with the discharge of a duty intrinsically of greater consequence. The capture of a single enemy's frigate is not to be confounded with, or inflated to, that destruction of an enemy's organised force which is the prime object of all military effort.

As John Hattendorf has put it in Chapter 1, p 11: 'A turning point came at sea on 1 June 1813 with the British victory over Chesapeake and the blockade of Decatur's squadron at New London, removing nearly half of the US Navy's operational force in a single day. Certainly, this was a pair of British successes with cumulative strategic consequences, while, in contrast, the earlier single-ship actions were displays of American tactical prowess in battles that brought little strategic advantage to the American side.'

When Jones reviewed the state of his frigates at the end of the year, their state was depressingly inactive:[7]

---

7 McCranie, *Utmost Gallantry*, p 195.

Chesapeake.	Captured.
Congress.	Blockaded at Portsmouth. Needing repair and undermanned.
Constellation.	Blockaded at Norfolk
Constitution.	Blockaded at Boston. Under repair.
Essex.	Successfully commerce raiding in the Pacific.
Macedonian.	Blockaded at New London.
President.	Blockaded at Rhode Island. Needing refit.
United States.	Blockaded at New London.

That is not to say that British command and control, the relationship between the Admiralty and those in command where the action was taking place, was any better than the American. Admittedly, this was 3,000 miles away in a very fluid situation, in an era when communications took a month or more to be received and when the politicians were preoccupied with the need to maintain the naval blockade of the whole of mainland Europe at the same time as finding men and money to support Wellington's growing success in Spain – a sentence whose complexity illustrates the near impossibility of Admiral Warren's role as Commander-in-Chief. He had at least seven tasks:

1 Blockade. Capture or destroy American privateers that had speedily seized the economic opportunities of taking poorly defended British merchant ships as prizes.
2 Find sufficient escorts to establish an effective convoy system which would have to cover the whole clockwise North Atlantic sailing route predetermined by the prevailing winds.
3 Protect the Caribbean Islands and their vital wealth-producing sugar crops.
4 Catch and destroy the US Navy frigates which were more powerful than their British opposites and faster than ships-of-the-line.
5 Blockade the southern states to bottle up the would-be exports of food and raw materials to French-controlled ports.
6 Recover some of the 9,000 British seamen said to be serving in American ships, to help crew his under-manned ships.
7 Avoid upsetting American policy-makers in the vain hope that they would come to the peace table to negotiate, while at the same time

widening the divide between the Federalists of the north and the Republicans of the south and west.

Powerful lobbying groups – planters, shippers and merchants, newspapers, members of parliament for major ports or manufacturing areas – pressed the government from all directions, each believing that their own cause should have priority. It was easier for Lord Melville at the Admiralty to send letters criticising Warren for not using his resources properly than to find the extra ships for which he repeatedly asked.

Was Warren the right man for the job? His former diplomatic experience in Russia appeared to make him a suitable candidate, but that was on the assumption that there was a realistic hope of a speedy end to the war now that the Orders-in-Council had been suspended. If Broke was correct in his opinion, expressed in a letter to his wife Loo on 13 October 1812, that 'pacific overtures were no more likely to check the flames of war than a mild remonstrance would the raging of a tiger', that part of Warren's instructions was a distraction leading in a hopeless direction. As that 'loose cannon' (and brilliant orator) George Canning was to say in Parliament on 30 November: 'nothing has happened in consequence of the American declaration of war, except that America has captured our ships and attacked our provinces'. The British Government's response was 'mitigated and half afraid hostility'. Warren's earlier career had been that of a highly successful frigate captain and leader of small frigate squadrons off the French coast, not managing fleets and multi-tasking. To quote Broke again, writing to Loo on 22 September: 'He does not decide very quick.'

There were only three admirals of that era to whom the Admiralty might have turned with some hope of success – Collingwood, Saumarez and Samuel Hood Jnr – and two of them had recently died. There is no record that any approaches were made to the one still extant, Sir James Saumarez. He had returned to Portsmouth in the *Victory* on 4 December at the end of five years in command of the large, scattered Baltic Fleet, acting on his own initiative in a quasi-diplomatic/political role. By his humanity, restraint and confident delegation, he had used the threat of his naval firepower to bring about peace in a region outwardly totally dominated on land by France and her allies, thereby breaking the same Continental System that had led to war on the other side of the Atlantic. It was the return westward of his fleet, their task completed, for which Warren waited in hope of the extra forces he craved. But Saumarez had just been allowed to haul down his flag on the sudden death of his much-loved eldest daughter. Unless his sense of duty was called upon sufficiently persuasively, he would not have left his home in Guernsey again for a distant command of indeterminate length.

Warren was superseded in January 1814 and replaced by Melville's fellow-Scot, Sir Alexander Cochrane, whose nephew Thomas was later to further his established swashbuckling reputation in the freedom fights of South America. The new admiral arrived in March. By then the blockade had been extended to cover as much of the coast as possible and Sir George Cockburn was raiding towns and villages along Chesapeake Bay with mixed forces of marines, sailors, soldiers, French prisoners-of-war and former slaves (his 'Colonial Marines') making the most of amphibious warfare. The thinking of the new command team was now that this was 'the true way to shorten this Yankee war, whatever may be said in Parliament against it' – a policy that was no more likely to succeed than the earlier diplomatic approach since it hardened the resistance of those affected, stiffening the will of the US Government to resist even when they knew that economically they could not continue.

For the true passage to victory was being pursued monotonously and without ostentation by the horde of British blockading cruisers, crippling the American economy without much open violence, suffering more from the extremes of weather, accidents, disease, boredom and the dangers of little-known waters than from military action. Broke expressed his feelings clearly in his letters to Loo. But, as Brian Arthur summarises in his excellent book *How Britain Won the War of 1812*, 'Intelligent, targeted economic warfare enabled Britain to fight the United States to a standstill with a fraction of its armed forces, without compromising the total war effort against Napoleonic France'. This aspect has already been covered here by Andrew Lambert in Chapter 2, but to explore it in depth you need to read Arthur's book.

Broke should be remembered for his contribution to this continuous, wearing, yet ultimately successful battle – one year in the fast but old and leaky frigate *Druid* and then seven years almost without another break, as captain of the newly-launched *Shannon*: Cork, Spitsbergen, Madeira, the French Atlantic coast, till on 21 August 1811 he opened his sealed orders off Lisbon and found he was to sail to Halifax: 'I have discovered our destination my beloved Looloo but must not tell you as my orders are marked secret again ... I shall not tell my officers till they find out by the way we steer ... but you may enquire about a house in Suffolk as there is every possibility I shall be <u>a year away.</u>'

HOME THOUGHTS

'Another Sunday already! You can't think how busy we have been doing nothing. Gales of wind and rain – then moderate – repair damage and dry sails – <u>encore</u>, wind and rain – repair again . . . and so we murder our time – in doing and undoing . . . I am very weary . . . (3 November 1811)

that vile convoy wasted us three weeks (8 January 1813, off Azores)

And as to prizes, I would never leave my lovely L[ouise] for all our flag has ever taken. I have never been fortunate at all that way; but supposing I was to retire with eight or ten thousand pounds no (instead of one or two), it would be no more than I might have saved in the time I have been serving, by retiring to live in quiet domestic comfort with my L ... upon £400 or £500 a year, like some contented parson; and I am sure you will believe I should have passed the time *more happily*. My being poor is no disappointment to me. To return without any successes, to prove how we have been exerting ourselves in so long and tiresome a pursuit, and which we feel conscious of deserving is mortifying; but my L ... must comfort me when I come to her. Indeed, you can't imagine the pains I have bestowed on this *graceless wooden wife* of mine, particularly since she ran away with me here; and I perhaps, shall have to leave some other person to reap all the credit of her beautiful play, unless we have somebody to *open a concert with* very soon. But when tempted to think of home, I am constantly reminded that naval success will be my speediest liberation from exile.'

Broke to Loo (14 February 1813)

Honour or Glory[8]

There is a great difference between these two words although, so often, they are linked together as one. It shows clearly when we look at the respective captains in the Battle of the *Shannon* and the *Chesapeake*. Lawrence was an ambitious young man who had become a public hero through his stunningly swift capture of the *Peacock*. 'A brilliant, dashing, audacious, and lovable officer, at times he seems to have delighted in quarrelling with his superiors.'[9] He had been indignant that one of his fellow officers had been promoted to captain before him, threatening to resign from the service, and had been slapped down for lack of loyalty. His victory had restored him to favour, to promotion and to the promise of appointment to captaincy of the super-frigate in which he had already served as first lieutenant. The delays in her being repaired and got ready for sea had led to his appointment instead, despite his protests, to the *Chesapeake* with instructions to sail north to the St Lawrence to attack undefended transport ships. She was said by some – mostly afterwards – to be an unlucky ship. When he arrived to take command, he certainly found a discontented ship lacking a first lieutenant and undermanned, with a serious dispute over prize money. Earlier clashes with the Royal Navy, in his view impugning his dignity, had made him very hostile towards the British.

After a brief handover from the outgoing sick captain, the next ten days saw Lawrence whirling into action to restore order. The money problem was resolved; active recruitment saw boatloads of men coming out to be vetted, with strict selection of only those considered suitable; and gun drill, both with the great guns and with small arms and boarding, took place each day – the log records ten sessions. There were stories put about after the defeat that *Chesapeake* was not 'fit for purpose' when she put to sea on the morning of 1 June. Despite Admiral Chadwick's claim in 1913 that 'Not a gun's crew had been exercised, not a sail had been bent before the day of action',[10] the *Shannon*'s 'butcher's bill' of killed and wounded is ample evidence of the gunnery skills of the *Chesapeake*'s crew. No more true was the report of the court martial on her loss stating that, but for the accident

---

8 See also Chapter 16.
9 Pullen, *The Shannon and the Chesapeake*, p 117.
10 Quoted in Pullen, *The Shannon and the Chesapeake*, pp 47 and 62.

of her hooking on to the *Shannon*'s anchor, the *Chesapeake* was so badly damaged that she 'must have very soon surrendered or sunk'.[11]

Lawrence was a skilled leader, determined to succeed, who would not have sailed, in breach of his orders, if he had not been confident that he had sufficiently transformed his ship and her crew to be ready for action. The fault was his own misjudgement in loading his cannon with star shell to cripple the rigging from a distance and then changing his mind to come to close quarters and repeat tactics that had been so successful against the *Peacock*. His battle had to be swift, his hurts quenched, not a drawn-out duel of stroke and counterstroke. He wanted glory; the public recognition that he was an outstanding officer, a hero, who would go down in history as the man who had defeated the arrogant Briton who had sailed up to Boston light and fired a challenging gun. Even when mortally wounded, he produced the words that would live on to make his name immortal and like so many heroes he died in the attempt. The *Boston Repertory* wrote on 22 June: 'The glory of our departed hero cannot be tarnished by mischance and the remembrance of his services and worth is only rendered dearer by misfortune.'

Broke's name too would have lived on louder and longer if the cutlass that cleaved a 3in wound in his skull had gone that little bit further. Like Lawrence, he had seized a moment of opportunity. Seeing his opponent's quarterdeck empty, he had leapt over the bulwarks by her aftermost carronade with the cry of 'follow me who can' and led the rush of men that in just four minutes overwhelmed the officerless Chesapeakes. Had he died those words too might have echoed down the years, confirming his heroic stature. Captains do not usually lead boarding parties unless they are Nelsons. But his motivation was not the search for glory.

It was for honour. His letters to Loo speak repeatedly of his need to do some act of honour that would enable him to give up the ship, his 'wooden wife', and return to her and family life in England. It was a matter of his own personal repute, of how he saw himself:

Honor and peace with my Loo will content <u>me</u> (30 July 1812)

---

11 James, *Naval History*, vol 6, p 210.

We are all very angry at hearing that the American frigate *Constitution*, whom our squadron <u>hunted</u> so lately has taken one of our frigates and burned her. However this will all forward the chance of *Shannon*'s making an <u>honorable</u> game of it as the enemy will be saucy now (20 September 1812)

I would not stay here for all the <u>salaries</u> and honors of all their governors and chiefs put together . . . now the unlucky events of *Guerriere* and *Frolic*'s actions bind us all to the service until we have restored the splendour of our flag (26 November 1812)

Honor is a jewel of more value than whole fleets & armies (14 December 1812)

I will come as soon as honour will let me, my Loo, and not go to sea again,

In the circle in which he lived, honour was of supreme importance, not to be confused with outward honours. As Admiral Lord St Vincent said, 'The honour of an officer may be compared to the chastity of a woman, and once wounded may never be recovered'.

It was for this, combined with his sense of duty, that Broke had endured the days and weeks of dreary blockade and convoy duties, that he had spent his own money on motivating his gun crews in competition, innovating ways of improving accuracy and control, that he had foregone the comfortable life of a country squire and the company of a loving wife, that he had burnt his prizes to avoid diminishing his crew by sending them to Halifax, that he had lived the lonely, pressurised life of a ship's captain for seven years. He had made good use of his time, his brains and his skills of leadership to create the most effective fighting machine for its size of his time. In the battle itself, he covered the approach of the *Chesapeake* as an America's Cup yacht covers its opponent, watching each move and trimming his sails or adjusting his course, until he could let loose his specially placed 9pdr that destroyed her helm and helmsmen, leaving her nearly bereft of officers and helpless. His objective was achieved and he could now return home, with honour.

Suggested Further Reading

Latimer, Jon, *1812: War with America* (2007).

Pullen, H F, *The Shannon and the Chesapeake* (1970).

FROM AN OFFICER'S JOURNAL ON BOARD HMS *NYMPHE*

9 June   A flag of truce came out to ransom the schooner *Welcome Return*. We share with *Junon*. Received vegetables of all kinds from Boston, green peas for the first time. Newspapers, and in short anything we choose to send for is brought by these rascals. No occasion to use force, a hint quite sufficient and frequently even that is not wanting. Federalists pretend to be friendly to the English. They hate the war on their own account, hate the war because it prevents their making money, and like the English as a spendthrift loves an old rich wife; the sooner we are gone the better. [p 23]

On 11 June the boats returned after having been amazingly successful in capturing and destroying about 800 tons of shipping. Brought the *Rosebud* schooner, a wood sloop, and a beautiful packet schooner, called the *Orient*. Destroyed all the vessels in Scituate Harbour but one, the skipper of which was a Democrat and a traitor but for his good services to the boats was restored; it is right to keep one's word but I question whether the destruction of such a rascal would not almost justify its being broken. Run a vessel, called the *Concord*, loaded with iron, on shore and detained the skipper as a hostage for a ransom of $1000. Also captured the *Experiment* sloop, bound to Truro with notions. This expedition of the boats alarmed the whole coast as far as Boston, particularly the unfortunate women and children, who had least reason to be alarmed. Making prize money resembles killing a sheep; one likes to eat it but cannot bear the distress of the animal's death. [p 24]

13 June   I returned with the boats after having been in shore all night without success. Went into the harbour of Annisquam, burned two vessels, let one go clear because she belonged to an old man who had a wife and eight children and had lost $20,000 within two years. Destroying this, his last, would have ruined him. Spared another, as I told them, because her name was the *Federalist* but the truth is she was aground alongside of the town and I could neither get her off, or set fire to her there, without burning a number of poor people's houses. These little things, when constantly done, may cause distrust, or heighten that which has already broken out with great violence between parties. Saw a beautiful girl, sister to the two people we took in the *Welcome Return*; assured her and her old mother of the safety of her brothers. [p 25]

27 July Made the unfortunate master of a fishing boat, who formerly had permission to fish and came out, trusting to that protection, pay $200 for a ransom. The poor creature has a wife and seven children, no money, and was in debt for his salt and fishing lines even. He with great difficulty scraped up by sixpences and shillings the amount of the money at Provincetown and came on board with tears in his eyes. This is an ungenerous war against the poor and unworthy of Englishmen. I am ashamed of Captain Epworth's conduct. [p 38]

Henry Napier, *New England Blockaded 1814*

COURT OF INQUIRY INTO LOSS OF USS *CHESAPEAKE*

The court are unanimously of opinion, that the *Chesapeake* was gallantly carried into action by her late brave commander; and no doubt rests with the court, from comparison of the injury respectively sustained by the frigates, that the fire of the *Chesapeake* was much superior to that of the *Shannon*. The *Shannon*, being much cut in her spars and rigging, and receiving many shot in and below the waterline, was reduced almost to a sinking condition, after only a few minutes cannonading from the *Chesapeake;* whilst the *Chesapeake* was comparatively uninjured. And the court have no doubt, if the *Chesapeake* had not accidentally fallen on board the *Shannon*, and the *Shannon*'s anchor got foul in the after quarter-port of the *Chesapeake*, the *Shannon* must have very soon surrendered or sunk.

William James, *Naval History*, vol 6, p 210.

6

Broke – His Youth and Education

John Blatchly

Philip Bowes Vere Broke was very much a Suffolk man. Born at Broke Hall in the small village of Nacton near Ipswich, on 9 September 1776, he was the eldest son of Philip Bowes Broke and his wife Elizabeth, daughter of the Revd Charles Beaumont, Rector of Witnesham. It may be significant that Charles and his brother Robert were educated at Ipswich Grammar School, and that Charles was a member of the six-man committee that made new regulations for the school in 1746.

Broke Hall is on the north bank of the Orwell and from his earliest years Philip could enjoy long walks on the sandy shore of a river busy with the arrivals and departures of merchant and naval ships, many of them built in the Ipswich shipyards a few miles upstream. It is no wonder that he was fired with an enthusiasm for the adventurous life which the sea promised, and like many other sons of Suffolk gentlemen he would obtain an officer's commission in the Royal Navy.

Admiral Vernon, former neighbour on the Nacton shore

Philip will have known about Edward Vernon, who after his victory at Portobello in the Spanish Main in 1739, had become a national hero overnight. Streets and pubs then renamed Vernon and Portobello still commemorate that triumph today. Others may be more aware that the following year he instituted the practice aboard ship of adding three parts of water to the daily rum issue, hence its name 'grog' from the old grogram cloak he wore.

In retirement Vernon lived in a modest farmhouse on the Broke Hall estate and sat as a Whig member of Parliament for Ipswich from 1747 until his death ten years later. In the House of Commons his passionate oratory (usually on naval and military subjects) bordered on the uncontrolled. 'He quite lost his temper and made himself hoarse again,' wrote the Earl of Egmont in his diary.

Whilst Vernon was struck from the flag list for publishing his critical correspondence with the Admiralty and thereafter lived and died a plain esquire, his nephew and heir Francis, a mere colonel in the Suffolk Militia, became Baron Orwell and then Earl of Shipbrooke. Just a mile upstream from Broke Hall he built the dignified colonnaded Orwell House which the enormously wealthy Colonel Tomline transformed into the vast mansion which is Orwell Park School today.

Philip Broke at school, 1784–1788

All accounts of Philip Broke's youth agree that his schooling began at the age of eight, and that he managed to persuade his somewhat reluctant father to allow him to join the Royal (Naval) Academy at Portsmouth when he was twelve, the regulation minimum age for entry. Thomas Harral of Ipswich wrote an eight-page biographical memoir of the newly famous Broke in the first (January 1814) number of *The East Anglian*, a monthly journal which limped through only five issues.

Harral's brief treatment of Broke's schooling is confused and erroneous, beginning with Cheam School in Surrey under Dr William Gilpin, known as the original for Combe and Rowlandson's cartoon clergyman/schoolmaster Dr Syntax.[1] As Gilpin handed the school over to his son and namesake (except he was *not* a Dr) in 1778, this cannot be true. We know for certain that Broke was at Ipswich Grammar School under the Revd John King, master there from 1768 to 1798. We can only suppose that Philip or his father was unhappy with Cheam and that the school in nearby Ipswich, where teaching took place in Foundation Street and boys boarded with the head's family in the Master's House at 19–21 Lower Brook Street, suited them better. From the school it was a matter of a mere hundred yards to the quayside on the Orwell which had inspired Thomas Cavendish and Thomas Eldred to embark on the second English circumnavigation of the globe two hundred years earlier.

Proof positive that the young Philip was at Ipswich under King, followed three years later by his brother Charles Broke Vere – how the Brokes juggled with their names – came when, more than seventy years after his heroic victory off Boston, Philip's son, Admiral Sir George Nathaniel Broke-Middleton, Bart, presented an indoor swimming pool

---

1 See especially vol 3, *Dr Syntax in Search of the Picturesque* (1812).

to the school in memory of his father. Lady Broke-Middleton laid the foundation stone in late February 1884, and the Latin inscription it bore on the outer wall ran:

HOC MONVMENTVM
VICTORIAE NAVALIS CELEBERRIMAE
AVSPICIIS
PHILIPPI B V BROKE
SCHOLAE REGIAE GIPPOVICENSIS QVONDAM ALVMNI

It would be marvellous to be able to produce from the school archives some documents or artefacts to illustrate Philip Broke's time under King, but on his retirement that long-serving headmaster regrettably had a great bonfire and priceless records of the school since its earliest days went up in smoke in the yard of the Master's House.[2] The best one can do in this vacuum is to cite the names we know of men who may have shared their schooldays with Broke (between 1784 and 1788 at most), as listed by William King MD, fourth son of the headmaster and twenty years younger than Broke, writing his own autobiography in 1864–65. King was the pioneer of the Co-operative movement, which flourishes nationwide today and particularly in East Anglia. His seventh child, Richard Henry born 1790, was on the muster roll of Broke's *Shannon* but, as a midshipman, was away in command of a prize and missed the battle, rejoining the ship at Halifax. He stayed in touch with Broke in later years; there are letters in the Broke archive and King made four drawings of the battle which were later engraved and published. Like Broke, Richard King eventually reached admiral's rank.

Humphry Repton comes to Broke Hall

Philip Broke had a deep affection for his childhood home and during his long years at sea frequently looked forward to returning to spend the rest of his life there. During his youth his father was planning extensive changes to the house and its surroundings and one wonders

---

2 For more about Ipswich School in Broke's time, see *A Famous Antient Seed-Plot of Learning*, published by the school in 2003 and available for purchase from the archivist there.

how much the son, who had already left home, was involved in the discussions.

Like Admiral Vernon, Philip Bowes Broke (senior) sat to Thomas Gainsborough, and had the good taste to send for the great landscape improver Humphry Repton. In due course he, like all Repton's clients, received a volume bound in red morocco, a Repton Red Book, which would show and explain what ought to be done and how. After several pages of elegant prose and a plan or two, the chief delights were the before-and-after watercolours cut and pasted with hinged flaps to reveal transformed vistas. The effect was quite magical, akin to the cardboard cut-out toy theatres becoming popular at the time. Repton claimed to have made over four hundred Red Books in all, including three others in Suffolk for Henham, Shrubland and Livermere.

Repton undertook landscape gardening mainly as a profession but it also gave him enjoyable opportunities to mix with landed society. He was pleased and flattered to find that Philip Bowes Broke at Nacton remembered that they had been boys together at Norwich School in the early 1760s. Repton wrote that that had 'awakened in my bosom the most grateful emotions' and so he declared 'my advice will be delivered *con amore*' but not, of course, gratis. The survey for the Broke Hall Red Book was carried out in November 1791, when Philip would still have been at the Naval College, and delivered early the following February.

The ingratiating tone continued when Repton deplored the extent to which Francis Vernon's newer Orwell House tended to degrade the character of the home the Broke family had occupied since Tudor times. 'The more lofty situation of Orwell House, its park being fed with deer, and even the name it has assumed, all contribute to lessen the consequence of the property by which it is in fact surrounded.' Across the Orwell, the Woolverstone Park of the newly arrived Berners family was by contrast a 'beautiful view', but then distance always lends enchantment.

Repton called in James Wyatt to improve Broke Hall, 'crippled proof of another architect's want of judgement', for it was 'hardly possible to give much dignity of appearance to a modern square red house'. Giving Nacton a new white frontage in the gothic style would counterbalance with its more conspicuous colour the loftier situation of the intrusive and alien Orwell House. Repton referred to the avenue leading to the house from Nacton as 'incorrigible', but as there was no other possible means of access, he felt that when the house had 'resumed its Gothic dignity' it would be 'perfectly consistent with its Character'. The receipt of a Repton Red Book after breakfast will never have been all joy.

Broke at the Royal Naval Academy at Portsmouth, 1789–1791

This establishment was set up in 1733 to provide potential naval officers with a better education than their predecessors, most of whom had gone straight to sea and depended on the naval schoolmaster on board. Entrants aged twelve were either the sons of noblemen and gentlemen or of serving commissioned officers in the fleet, and the syllabus was broad. The subjects taught were writing, arithmetic, drawing, navigation, gunnery and fortification. French language, dancing, fencing and the exercise of the firelock added variety to the young men's studies.

The Academy has at last received a balanced assessment, from H W Dickinson. In *Educating the Royal Navy* (2007), he confidently refutes the 'sink of abomination' reputation which earlier writers had given it. Dickinson describes an academy which was well staffed and ruled by only five headmasters over its seventy years, three of sufficient distinction to be elected Fellows of the Royal Society. The last of them, William Bayly, never FRS, arrived from a life of considerable adventure three years before Broke joined.

Bayly's father was a small farmer in Wiltshire, but William had a talent for mathematics, which he took every opportunity to develop. He taught at fairly humble schools until Nevil Maskelyne, the astronomer-royal, heard of his talents, and engaged him as an assistant at the Royal Observatory. On Maskelyne's recommendation, Bayly was sent out by the Royal Society to North Cape, Norway, in 1769, to observe the transit of Venus just as James Cook was observing the same phenomenon from Tahiti on his first voyage of discovery. In 1772, Bayly accompanied William Wales as an astronomer on Cook's second voyage to the southern hemisphere. He also sailed on the third and final voyage in the course of which Cook was killed in a skirmish with some Hawaiians. It would be good to know to what extent the boys under Bayly profited from the excitements of his seagoing career. Surely he was more of an inspiration to his young charges than the typical dreary pedagogue found in many schools of the time. The fees charged by the Academy were comparable to those of Eton and Harrow, but the facilities were in many ways superior. In a report written on Broke in 1791, as he neared the time to depart for the fleet, Bayly found him 'industrious and well-behaved'.

Broke will have known two of Jane Austen's brothers at the Academy. Francis and Charles Austen were his contemporaries; like him they went on to become admirals. Graduates of the Academy could earn two years of sea-time as part of their studies, and would be able to take the lieutenant's examination after four years at sea instead of six. The Academy did not, however, achieve the objective of becoming the preferred path to becoming a naval officer and after 1837 shore-based training was abandoned. Thereafter the traditional means of a sea-going 'apprenticeship' remained paramount. William IV summed up this view when he remarked that 'there was no place superior to the quarterdeck of a British man of war for the education of a gentleman'.

Suggested Further Reading
Blatchly, John, *A Famous Antient Seed-Plot of Learning* (2003).

WRITING HOME

'. . . As I am not under my gentle wife's spells, I shall tell you more of my plans and prospects which you will consider as less influenced by her smiles and soft looks than when I was at Stonehouse [Plymouth]. They are the result of many years' reflection and consideration and I am now an old philosopher. Had the admiral given me into a 74[-gun ship-of-the-line] at home or in the Mediterranean it was my intention to have resigned her in less than a year unless some hopes of brilliant service had arisen. Under my present circumstances and with the prospects of war here I shall continue to serve tho' I cannot tell how long. Now it is not civil to put ladies in mind of such circumstances but I am now, my dear mama, thirty five years old and considering the age which my family have previously reached I can hardly look forward (indifferent of war) to twenty years to come in this world. Not two years of my life have I yet enjoyed as a domestic man or in a fixed home. The most of my time has been spent in service or seeking employment. I shall soon have completed a course of seven years' banishment for this war only – time which can never pass again, or its loss be atoned for. . . Having been, by favour of providence bound to the inheritance of an English gentleman it is my duty to fill that situation in a useful manner, both by example and influence amongst those I was born to preside over.

  . . . I have hitherto served on a [seat] of duty, considering myself as attached for the war, but times are changing and war is life. The conditions of service are of course altered. I am not a mere professional man attached to the service by necessity and having no other pursuits or duties to consider. Having been, by favour of providence bound to the inheritance of an English gentleman, it is my duty to fill that situation in a useful manner, both by example and influence amongst those I was born to preside over – it is true that such men should set an example of privation by serving in war and it is a desirable thing in a political view that our officers, some of them, should be independent men and such as have an immediate interest in their country as well as in professional advancement – but let all take their time. I have served my time fully . . . I am now becoming anxious to share in the education of my little ones.'

Broke to his mother
(Undated, but marked before the American War of 1812)

7

In Arctic Waters

Michael Barritt

Most accounts of the involvement of the Royal Navy in exploration of the Arctic leave a gap. The probe towards the pole led by Captain Constantine Phipps (later Lord Mulgrave) in 1773 is well covered, though too often with the focus on the mythical encounter of Midshipman Nelson with a polar bear. Attention then turns to the long campaign in polar waters which John Barrow, Secretary of the Admiralty, launched in 1818 with the despatch of Captain John Ross to resume the search for the Northwest Passage, and of Captain David Buchan to attempt another penetration of the ice in the Greenland Sea. However, when Lieutenants Franklin and Beechey of the *Trent* surveyed an inlet on the west coast of Spitsbergen they were in fact following in more recent naval footsteps, those of Philip Broke.

In the years of war between 1793 and 1815 the British whaling fleet operating in the Greenland Sea and Davis Strait had been a target for warships deployed by France and her Northern European allies, and latterly by the United States. The Admiralty had responded by sending units on patrol, at the very least to escort the homebound whalers with their valuable cargo. This task took the Royal Navy into unfamiliar waters for which the published navigational information was scant. Admiralty regulations directed captains and their navigational specialists, the ship's masters, to gather and report back data to remedy this deficiency. Such publications as there were could be purchased from the London commercial outlets. David Steel had recently issued *The Greenland Pilot, being Three Charts for the Fisheries of Greenland and Davis Strait*. Thomas Henderson, master of the *Sybille* (44 guns) (Captain Clotworthy Upton), who was sent out in 1809 to cruise between Greenland and Labrador, supervised Midshipman Shannon in laying down the ship's track between astronomical fixes on a blown-up outline of a chart published by Steel. Henderson was an alert observer who had rendered valuable data to the Hydrographer to the Admiralty Board during service in the Danish Belts. His remarks, scribed on the plot, are based on observations of lunar distances, compass variation and ocean currents. He was particularly critical of the information available for the important Greenland landfall at Cape Farewell.

Enemy depredations had reached a peak in 1806 when a French frigate squadron took or destroyed twenty-nine whalers and merchantmen. The *Blanche* (38 guns) and *Thames* (32 guns) were deployed into the region in response, and a similar frigate presence was sustained as long as there was intelligence of further substantial French incursions. In 1808, the *Thalia* (36 guns) and *Medusa* (32 guns) patrolled the approaches to the Davis Strait, now becoming the favoured ground for the whaling fleet. The two masters, encouraged by enlightened captains, brought back surveys to the Admiralty. As had been the case much earlier with James Cook and other naval explorers, this region provided a demanding but fruitful school for hydrography. George Thomas, a midshipman in the *Medusa*, took part in this work on the remote coasts of Newfoundland and Labrador. He later became Admiralty Surveyor on the Coasts of Great Britain, serving with distinction for over thirty years in the burgeoning RN Surveying Service.

Broke's *Shannon* (38 guns) had deployed in April 1807, with the *Meleager* (32 guns) in company. The whalers were believed to be operating in the Greenland Sea, and soon the ships were getting a taste of arctic conditions. Broke kept a highly descriptive Remark Book of their experiences, which you can find in Revd Brighton's *Memoir of Admiral Sir P B V Broke*, published in 1866. Since the frigates would need all their speed to intercept and deal with an enemy cruiser, they could not be strengthened for navigation in ice as the whalers were. Broke felt his way carefully, exploiting open passages, checking likely haunts of enemy ships around Jan Mayen Island and aiming to pick up the trail of the whalers at their bases in Spitsbergen, the southern part of which was reached in mid June. At the beginning of July he reached as far north as 80° 6' N before the pack ice forced him to turn west. Eventually he located and spoke to several whalers before making landfall on the coast of Greenland on 23 July. The two ships then moved south to cruise off the Shetland Isles during the autumn to cover the return of the whaling fleet. Broke took great care with his remarks on the deployment, recording lessons learned for the benefit of those who might follow in his wake, especially on fitting out for ice work, on conditions to be expected, and general navigation in the polar region.

His Remark Book reveals the limitations of the guidance held onboard. It included Laurie and Whittle's small-scale sheet: *A New Chart for the Whale Fishery and the Archangel Traders or the Navigation in the Northern Seas*. This proclaimed that it was 'Drawn from the most Accurate Surveys *Regulated by the latest Astronomical Observations*'. The most recent information was from Phipps' voyage of 1773, thirty-four years previously, his track and observations of the ice fields being depicted. However, there was a lack of firm data of help to the navigator. Broke recorded that, whilst 'the positions of the most remarkable headlands in Spitsbergen, as laid down in the charts, agreed with our own observations; the form and inlets of the coast – as far as we could judge by that part of it which we had leisure to examine – are by no means accurately drawn in any of those charts which I have been able to procure'. Broke also noticed the scant information on compass variation, none of which tallied with his own observations. At worst they differed by fifteen degrees. He was prepared to accept that his compasses might have been faulty, though careful observations of azimuth and amplitude had given consistent results. He concluded that information on Spitsbergen 'was very scanty indeed . . . The charts now extant of the island must have been drawn in the earlier time of this fishery'.

The Laurie and Whittle chart bore small plans of the two anchorages in Spitsbergen where Phipps had encountered whalers. That of Fairhaven (Smeerenburg) had been made by the Phipps expedition during a five-day stay. It has been derided by later authorities. In 1906, Sir Martin Conway, a distinguished mountaineer, wrote: 'There was some surveying attempted and a wonderful chart was produced, which is still the marvel of those who take an interest in Spitsbergen surveying, for its extraordinary badness.' It was, however, considerably more detailed than the accompanying plan of Magdalena Bay which Broke would describe as 'altogether a very indifferent place of shelter'. His squadron remained there from 27 June to 4 July. They estimated that ice had only cleared from the outer part of the bay two or three days before their arrival, and they saw 'some huge islands wandering in the offing'. The anchorage in English Cove shown on their unsatisfactory

83

chart was still frozen up. Nor had they derived much benefit from any of the whaling veterans. Broke commented tartly: 'I have to remark that there appears to me no positive necessity for a Pilot to take a ship in to Magdalena, nor is it easy to procure one acquainted with the place; few have been there above two or three times in their lives and perhaps at such remote periods, that they have forgotten what knowledge they had acquired. Their ideas of the Bay are not more accurate in general than the common Charts.'

Broke and his officers set about conducting a thorough survey, plotting it at 3in to the mile. The *Shannon* survey is in itself an excellent piece of work, worthy of emulation. It is perhaps a tribute to the subsequent fame of Broke and the *Shannon* that the rough collector sheet for their observations has survived later culls of ancillary documents in the archive of the Hydrographic Office. It bears an annotation 'surveyed by Captain Broke of the Shannon'. Not only did Broke himself compose the comprehensive remarks to accompany the survey, but he also drew some fine views.

The topography on the sheets conveys the impact of the dramatic landscape on Broke and his officers and men. The depiction of 'Roach hill, a lofty Pyramidical Mountain, remarkably regular in its form and proportions' with the nearby 'Devil's Waggonway, a black track like a Road upon the snowy surface of the Waggonway Ice Berg' is particularly effective. 'Ice berg' is the term used throughout the memoir when referring to the glaciers that descend to the bay.

As soon as the ships had anchored, Broke had set off with Captain Broughton of the *Meleager* to sound and seek for water. Over the following three days the survey was progressed, the boats were sent away to sound and sample the seabed in the bay, including the location of the drying 'Shannon's Rock' on the edge of the deep water channel. Broke compiled clear directions for entry, either for an ice berth in English Cove, or for two recommended anchorages on the banks below the glaciers in the outer bay. He acknowledged that they had not tried the anchorage near Shannon's Rock, and described their berth on Adam's Bank as a 'tolerable summer anchorage [where a ship] . . . would probably hold on a long time with the wind on shore, but if near the edge would be in danger of driving off with the squalls that come off the iceberg in strong SW gales'.

In his remarks Broke is honest about the difficulties of observing for position and compass variation with the plain instruments available in a vessel not employed on official exploration. They did not have a theodolite or any watches onboard that could be trusted to. The horizon to westwards was limited and often bad. Better results in Spitsbergen would have to await the arrival of the two ships of the 1818 expedition with their fully equipped observatories and allocation of chronometers.

The only significant shortcoming of the survey was the failure to identify an isolated 6-metre shoal in the western approaches to the bay. Broke had noted the irregular depths 'near the land off Magdalena' and the tell-tale green colour that warned of shoals, but even the most rigorous deployment of their 120-fathom lead line would not guarantee the location of a hazard of such limited extent. He and his team had produced most creditable results, which were fully acknowledged in the subsequent survey by Franklyn and Beechey. Broke's report of a reconnaissance may also have prompted their examination of the South Gat leading into Smeerenburg. When the Hydrographic Office issued its first coastal chart of the archipelago in 1860, Broke was cited amongst the sources. In 1866, Brighton had written that his extensive quotation of Broke's journal and remarks was prompted by his judgement that they would 'not prove uninteresting at a moment when earnest endeavours are being made by some of our most gallant and enterprising naval officers to induce the government and the country to send out another expedition to the north pole'. The preservation of two copies in the Hydrographic Office is testament to their worth. However, it would not be until the last two decades of the century that the relevant volumes of the *Arctic Pilot* would be published.

Meanwhile, at least one of Broke's young officers was inspired by the experience, and put the lessons learned into practice. Douglas Clavering would command a polar exploring voyage in the *Griper* in 1823, naming Shannon Island off the coast of Greenland after the ship in which he had distinguished himself in the great fight with the *Chesapeake*.

8

Letters to his Wife 'Loo'

Ellen Gill

'I will come my Loo, as soon as duty will let me; for not all the fame of Nelson, or Lord Wellington would reconcile me to destroying the happiness of an affectionate wife, and whom duty has already compelled me to desert so long and so cruelly. Whenever I can retire without reproach conscious of having done my duty to my country, no view of honors however splendid shall tempt me to surrender my own happiness, and to sacrifice that of my beloved Loo to my ambition.'
Philip Bowes Vere Broke to his wife Louisa (11 December 1812)

Philip Broke was a talented officer, dedicated to the service and driven by a sense of duty to his country. He was also a loving husband and affectionate father. His correspondence with his wife Sarah Louisa, 'Loo', provides a fascinating insight into the man who rekindled hope and restored British naval pride during the war of 1812. His sense of duty to the service and his country was complicated by his sense of duty to his family and his love for his wife, and this is reflected in his correspondence. Correspondence played an important role in the lives of naval officers such as Broke. It allowed them to maintain and develop their relationship with their families throughout prolonged absence. It is through correspondence that we get a glimpse of how Broke saw his family and his duty, both afloat and ashore. Broke's sense of family continued onto his ship, with *Shannon* playing the role of his 'wooden wife' and the young midshipmen and lieutenants his 'sea children'. This familial approach to ship and crew shows through his letters, reflecting the importance of family and paternalism in the life of Broke and his contemporaries.

Broke was born, in 1776, at Broke Hall in the small village of Nacton, near Ipswich in Suffolk, into a family of three sons and five daughters. Unusually for an eldest son, who was normally groomed to take over the estate, Broke pursued a life at sea. He trained at the Naval

Academy at Portsmouth before entering the Navy in 1792, joining the sloop *Bulldog* as a midshipman under Captain George Hope. Broke then received a commission as third lieutenant aboard the frigate *Southampton* on 18 July 1795. Less than four years after this first posting, Broke was appointed to the brig *Falcon* as Commander on 2 January 1799. He went on to make post-rank in 1801. His rapid progress through the commissioned officer ranks is testament to the strength of his social position.

During the brief Peace of Amiens, Broke took the opportunity to wed. On 25 November 1802 he married Sarah Louisa Middleton, his 'Loo', in her home parish of Crowfield, Suffolk. On the recommencement of hostilities with France, Broke immediately reapplied for active command of a ship, but among the flood of applications his request was unsuccessful. To aid his campaign for active command, he needed to assert and demonstrate his qualities as a deserving officer and as a patriot, loyal and committed to the country. He therefore took the step of raising and commanding a local militia in order to be seen to be serving his country even when the Navy did not need him. Broke applied again to the First Lord of the Admiralty, Lord Melville, for promotion, and his continued public service, along with a recommendation, encouraged Melville to respond favourably on 1 June 1804:

I have received your letter soliciting active employment, which I hope to be enabled to give you before any considerable lapse of time, as the public spirited and candour manner, in which you have been acting since the war commenced, has, together with a particular recommendation I have received in your favour, given you a claim to an early appointment as circumstances will admit of.

Patriotism was an important component of an officer's identity, even when not on active service. Militia reforms and debates from the 1750s publicly asserted the patriotism, masculinity and courage of the militia. The militiaman was also praised for his defence of family by taking up arms and in turn considered truly English and truly manly. By raising his own battalion of militiamen, Broke tapped into this patriotic, public-spirited sentiment that surrounded the militia. Over six months after his letter to Melville, and after a stream of ships received new captains, Broke again wrote to the First Lord, on 27 January 1805, to plead his case:

> Having observed that a great many Frigates & smaller ships have been lately commissioned, I take the liberty of reminding your Lordship of the promise you favor'd me with in the <u>summer of last year</u> that I should be <u>employ'd</u> <u>soon</u>. As your Lordship was pleased w' your letter upon that occasion, express[ing] your approbation of the manner which I was exerting myself here, I have continued to support my Battalion of Peasantry, in <u>hopes</u> always that such service would recommend me for an early appointment, than if I remained idle, where I could be of use . . . . I again request your Lordship will place me in an active situation & flatter myself that my not having made more frequent application by letter will be attributed to a reliance upon your Lordships promises & not to indifference to the service. A worthy friend high in an office having assured me your Lordship would not forget me I thought it would be importunity to write oftener.

In April 1805, he was appointed to an elderly fifth-rate, the 32-gun frigate *Druid*, which was tasked to patrol the Channel and the Irish coast. Broke's father had died shortly after he received his promotion to Captain in 1801 and, as the eldest son, Broke inherited his father's estate, taking his place amongst the elite landed gentry. Like the ideal eighteenth-century gentleman, Broke took his responsibilities seriously and believed that his duty was to serve his country during war. He wanted to return to the Navy because he felt that he would be of greater use to the nation at the helm of a frigate than at the head of a 'Battalion of Peasantry'. Broke was not alone amongst his contemporaries in answering the call to duty. When he first received his commission in 1792, there were 2,000 commissioned naval officers. By 1806, when Broke took command of *Shannon*, that figure had increased to 10,000, 40 per cent of whom came from landed backgrounds. Not all members of the gentry were rich, and for many the financial rewards of the service would have had equal, if not, greater, allure than any patriotic considerations. Yet once Broke was on active service, with a young family waiting for him at home, the competing forces of family and national duty came into play.

Broke's desire to perform his national duty was not only relevant on the public stage. He also felt the need to set a good example to his children. At sea off Brest in September 1810, Broke wrote to Loo expressing not only his own sense of duty, but also his expectation of her duty: 'I must set an example to my children of that sacrifice to public good, which all men must make to their duty to their country: of a good patriot to my boys, as my gentle Loo does of a kind and patient and affectionate wife to her girls.' After eighteen months' continuous absence in the western Atlantic, Broke's letter to Loo of December 1812, quoted at the head of this chapter, neatly captures his sentiments towards his wife, his family and his country: 'Whenever I can retire without reproach conscious of having done my duty to my country, no view of honors however splendid shall tempt me to surrender my own happiness, and to sacrifice that of my beloved Loo to my ambition.'

From all of Broke's letters and indeed the three surviving letters from Loo, it is evident that she, like many contemporary naval wives, remained anxious and eager for Broke to return to her and the children. It was Broke's sense of duty that kept him away from his wife and his domestic responsibilities. Although he was committed to the patriotic cause, there is no evidence that he subscribed to the cult of heroism that many of his fellow officers, most notably Nelson, embraced. Broke therefore tried to strike a balance between the competing demands. Once he could honourably discharge his duty to his country, Broke would then be free to devote himself to his family.

Broke was appointed to the newly commissioned frigate *Shannon* (38 guns) in August 1806. That Broke received a brand-new ship reflects recognition of his reputation as a skilled officer, noted for his dedication to gunnery training, putting his crew through gun drills six days a week. His emphasis on target practice resulted in unprecedented proficiency. His primary duties initially consisted of blockading Brest and Bordeaux as part of the Brest Squadron in the Channel Fleet. Blockading was an essential part of Georgian naval policy. The close blockading of important enemy ports such as Brest allowed the Navy to observe and limit both enemy warship movements and trade, to contain the French and to prevent a feared invasion of Britain. As a frigate, *Shannon* undertook reconnaissance and intelligence work; with her size and speed she was able to go close into harbours to observe enemy preparations. Blockading was important, but it was boring, uncomfortable and often unrewarding with little opportunity for action or prizes. It was psychologically draining for the officers and the men, with some ships remaining at sea for over twenty weeks at a time. Despite his dedication to the Navy, Broke became frustrated with the tedium of blockading duty, writing on 8 July 1810:

> I am certainly (without vanity) becoming a better man, as every day I think more and more of my wife; though I doubt I am not the better officer for that circumstance however, what can't be cured &.c, and so they must put up with me; as I do with blockades and dull cruizes, and other grievances; by flattering myself that some time or other I shall enjoy my Loo's society at home in peace and comfort . . . another tiresome, useless week! The only variety a little foul weather to tear our sails and make us swear at the wind.

Broke and the *Shannon* remained on blockading duty on the eastern Atlantic coasts until 1811, with only brief 'hunting' expeditions breaking the monotony.

The increasing tensions building between America and Britain saw Broke ordered to Halifax, Nova Scotia, in August 1811. As the pressure mounted, Broke and his fellow officers eagerly anticipated war with America. Whilst Loo dreaded a war, presumably for the danger and continued separation it entailed, Broke believed that it might prove to be the 'happiest event' for them. He felt that a war would be to his advantage, providing him with 'some honorable opportunity of retiring home, at least till Boney's Navy [is] intitled to [my] attention'. Shortly after war was declared by the United States on 18 June 1812 he wrote:

> I grieve at this war, as a patriot, my Loo, but as [a] Naval Officer must rejoice in it: England has borne much insult from these graceless people, and latterly has tried every device to soothe them, but they are determined to throw themselves into the arms of France, and one way or another shall be punished as they deserve: . . . Shannon is getting old and this campaign I think will justify her return home to rest herself . . . My tender Loo prays for no American war, but it is perhaps the happiest event for us, for suspense would have kept me in Shannon perhaps a year longer; she will now probably be in England in a shorter time. [2 July 1812]

Before the outbreak of war, Broke had wondered how far he needed an honourable action to fulfil his obligations to the nation. Writing to Loo on 14 April 1811, he debated whether he ought to retire or not before peace was obtained:

Oh what a dismal stupid week we have passed! fogs, calms and gales, to pester us, but not a creature to chase or to give us the news . . . we have seen nothing, the winds have been rude and capricious, constantly whanging and appear to be quarrelling amongst themselves, but always scolding us. I suppose you will say this is a judgement on us for accepting this cruise: I shall be very penitent indeed, if we do not thrive better next week: and then the bad weather and solitude make me read and think, much more than is good for sailors; and I consider how long I have been serving this war, and whether I ought in conscience retire, or not, before peace is obtained; and I think I have settled that point in my favour, but when? And whether I am bound in duty, or only by vanity to wait for some opportunity of retiring with *éclat*? It would relieve me from so much in public business at home, particularly in a military way.

However, as the war with America unfolded, his sense of national duty and his desire to uphold the reputation of the service came to the fore and he decided that only success in battle would discharge his responsibility. As he wrote to Loo on 21 July 1812, 'I have no chance now of enjoying domestic tranquillity but by some glorious victory: war, I trust, will be peace to me, martial honour will be my passport to love'.

Broke patiently and diligently blockaded ports and chased any ships they saw, of whatever nationality, stopping, capturing, ransoming, recapturing and destroying many of their vessels. The US seagoing Navy was small in number but the might of the Royal Navy did not prevail as anticipated, and the British suffered a series of humiliating defeats. The American 24pdr frigates posed a serious threat to the smaller British frigates, which the Admiralty had not anticipated. There had been little serious opposition from the French except in the Eastern seas; captains had grown slack and apparently more interested in spit and polish than preparing ships and crew for action. Few officers were interested in gunnery. Broke was an exception. His dedicated and innovative approach to gunnery made him one of a small group of officers who experimented and developed new techniques. This he did at his own expense since the parsimonious Admiralty would not allow money for sights on the guns or for practice, considering them unnecessary. That the Royal Navy was losing single-ship battles shocked not only the Navy, but the British public. Broke, through his relentless blockading and his willingness to adapt to the demands of a new enemy, was searching for a way to restore the tarnished reputation of the Navy: 'I trust in God and my brave crew, in brightening up the honor of our flag, and soothing the feelings of our country men for the late mortifications,' he wrote on 28 May 1813.

Just four days later, on 1 June, Broke's 'glorious victory' took place, nineteen years to the day after Admiral Howe's victory of the 'Glorious 1st of June' 1794, the first great naval battle of the French Revolutionary and Napoleonic Wars. Broke and his men aboard the *Shannon* took the *Chesapeake* in fifteen minutes off the coast of New England, in what was described in *The Times* of 16 August as 'one of the fairest, shortest, severest, and most decisive actions that ever was fought between two ships'. For Britain, this was a decisive, important and much celebrated victory in the War of 1812; as the first major naval success, it rekindled national hope and faith in the Navy. It brought Broke honour and fame; and most importantly, it allowed him to discharge his national duty and 'retire with honor' to his beloved Loo and his family. He wrote to Loo in September 1813 whilst waiting to return to England:

one happy quarter of an hour has repaid all my ten years toil and enabled me to retire to the enjoyment of that fond society in which only I think life desirable – & that with a reputation which secures me from that restless anxiety which so often disturbs a military man, who, tho' satisfied he has done his duty, has no opportunity of proving it to the world.

Broke, therefore, not only performed his duty but secured public recognition. He did not seek glory for its own sake, but the massive public recognition success brought ensured that he could truly believe that he had discharged his duty with honour.

Broke remained at Halifax recovering from his head wound until 4 October when he embarked with *Shannon*, for England. Of his injuries

Broke initially wrote to Loo 'I was wounded in the head which also deprives me the use of my right hand, but I mend fast'. He spent his time convalescing at the home of the Dockyard Commissioner, Philip Wodehouse, whence he reported to Loo on 11 June 1813:

> I sit and read idle books, or creep about Woodhouse's [sic] lawn for air, and the Ladies have very kindly sent me flowers to decorate my room, so I dress them and plant them on the tables round me, to gaze at them, and think of my Loo . . . Woodhouse [sic], Capel and Byron . . . come and chat quietly to me, and some other friends, and to-day some of my fair acquaintance came to congratulate me and to prattle and smile on me, to comfort me in my confinement. Oh my poor Loo, what a delight it would have been to have been at home in all this painful nursing, with my gentle and tender wife to watch and soothe me!

As Broke's victory and success became widely known, congratulations, praise and admiration flowed in from every quarter. Loo, waiting anxiously in England for the return of her wounded husband, charged her own brother to enquire at the Admiralty when she might be able to expect his return. On 26 June, she wrote movingly to Broke:

> As my Brother is now in town I told him the greatest kindness he could do me, would be to enquire and find out of his friends at the Admiralty when I was likely to see you, and I yesterday got his answer . . . he says 'No one can stand higher in the opinion of the Admiralty than Captain Broke, they consider him one of the first officers in the service, and as such think they will not order him home, as long as it is possible for him to remain there,' he spoke of your having given up the certainty of immense Prize money to Convoy the Jamaica Fleet safe, and my Brother adds, 'Nothing could be more gratifying than the manner in which he spoke of you, and which he trusts will repay me fully for the disappointment of not seeing you so soon as I had expected' but my Husband cannot stand higher in my opinion than he does, therefore nothing in this world can compensate me for the loss of his dear and valuable society, time never to be recalled, which now passes in constant anxiety, excluding the possibility of our happiness while separated, which otherwise might glide on as

tranquilly as it is possible to expect in this mortal life; or at any rate when afflictions did arise, how much softened would they be by mutual affection and tenderness towards each other! When will the time arrive my love when I shall be made happy by your unwearied, & unceasing affectionate attentions towards me (which distance now so cruelly denies us), or allow the power of returning which I so much delight in, to the best of my abilities but feel sensible how incapable I am of performing the extent of my wishes.

Broke wrote often to Loo during the months of his convalescence, planning his homecoming and his reunion with his wife and children, as well as reflecting on his naval career and the careers and prospects of his crew. He arrived in England on 2 November 1813 and, in his final letter on 3 November, writes 'my interview here (with the Admiralty) changes my plans; come to me in Portsmouth'; Loo rushed to his side and they were at last reunited on 5 November 1813.

The importance of letters to naval officers and their families
Personal letters were of the most profound importance to individuals in the eighteenth century. For naval officers, such as Philip Broke and his contemporaries, letters were their main means of communicating with their family and friends and home, and were essential to maintaining and developing relationships during periods of prolonged absence. To get a better understanding of their importance, it may be necessary to remind ourselves, in our age of electronic communication, of the physical characteristics of the handwritten letter. The paper, the ink, the seal, the address, the postmark – all its outside appearance – would tell the recipient a great deal about not only who the letter was from but also the nature of its content. The postmark included the date and the location the letter entered the postal system. An additional stamp was also added if the letter passed through one of the docks or if it was a 'Ships Letter' (carried by a ship returning to England, rather than entering the postal system). These markings would give some indication of the whereabouts of the sender. In times of war especially, this was a key consideration as it could signal homecoming or further separation. Eighteenth-century letters were not contained within envelopes, but instead the paper was folded in on itself. A space was reserved for the name and the address of the recipient and the letter

was secured with a wax seal. This was also important. Letters written by all classes were generally sealed with red wax. A black seal, however, was a sign of death and mourning. For men serving in the navy or the army, receiving a letter with an unexpected black seal would have caused distress. When, in July 1812, Loo chose not to seal her letter with black wax after the death of an uncle, Broke wrote in reply: 'I suppose you did not black-seal, to save me from any alarms'. By closing the letter with a regular (red) seal, Loo saved Broke unnecessary anxiety that one of the children or a close relation had died. Broke's comment on the seal reflects it was common practice to use colour-coded seals. For elite families, family crests were often used as seals, particularly for official correspondence. Broke and his wife had seals made with their Christian names, 'Philip' and 'Louisa', which they used only for letters between themselves. This illustration of intimacy between husband and wife emphasises the importance of correspondence for married relationships. In 1801, George Bass, naval surgeon, explorer and circumnavigator of Tasmania, who was parted from his wife Elizabeth just weeks after their wedding, wrote of how crucial correspondence would have to be for strengthening their marriage and maintaining their relationship: 'Since we could not add to the cement [of our love] by living together let us at least do it by frequent correspondence'. After three years' absence, George Bass set sail from Australia on an expedition to South America in 1803, but was never seen or heard from again. His letters were the symbol of their married life, and would have taken on extra poignant value for Elizabeth, who took three years to resign herself to the fact that she was a widow. These little details on the letter, which can only be obtained from the original document, afford us a glimpse of the letter-writing process. An intact seal, bearing the name of the writer, takes us back to when the letter was written, sealed and later carefully prised open by its recipient.

Letters mattered immensely to individuals and their families and were anxiously and desperately longed for. This was especially the case in wartime when prolonged absence, poor communication channels and the inherent danger associated with active service meant that families left at home were forced to wait with uncertainty, sometimes for months at a time, for news of their loved ones. Similarly for men at war, the wait for letters from home was no less anxious. Illness and misfortune just as readily found those on shore as those at sea and at war. Broke regularly sat down on a Sunday to begin his letter to his wife, keeping it open until an opportunity to send it presented itself. He constantly wrote of the means of conveying letters home as well as the anxious wait for letters from home. During wartime there was always a danger that letters would be captured and destroyed, which created added anxiety. Broke wrote of his correspondence half in jest, but with an underlying acknowledgement of its importance and the dangers of sending letters during wartime:

> We met on Monday a Bristol ship from Oporto, and trusted her with my letters, of which the quantity was important at least; of the quality I will say nothing, but I sent, to my wife 3, to both Mama's, to Mr Beck, and various other worthy people, so I hope the privateers won't take her, as I shall lose credit with all my correspondents, and though she may be insured to her owners, I am under no legal obligation to write all my letters over again; but I will write a little to my Loo, in readiness for chance postmen. [30 December 1809]

Broke, like many of his fellow officers, was always on the lookout for a means to convey letters back to England. Ships or officers returning to home ports were often called upon to act as postmen, with the officers either delivering the letters by hand or putting them into the Post Office once ashore. Prize ships were potential postmen and Broke frequently wrote, in jest, of using them as such: 'I will try and find some little prize or recapture, that ought to be sent to England, next cruize, so that she may be a prize to my Loo too' [4 December 1812].

Correspondence was seen as a form of conversation. Broke described one of his letters as an 'enormous long chattering letter' and wrote of 'looking over my Looloo's last chats to me'. The conversational tone of these letters suggests their effectiveness for couples in maintaining and developing their relationship and combating the loneliness endured by officers at sea, although the flow of correspondence was not reliable, and was often disjointed. Correspondence enabled them to discuss their hopes, fears and anxieties, and to keep a running dialogue open about day-to-day activities. Indeed, contemporary letter manuals suggested letters should 'replicate the ease of polite, familiar conversation' and writers were encouraged to write as they would speak. The ease with which Broke and Loo converse through the intimacy of their letters shows how successfully they maintained their relationship through long and trying separations.

For naval officers, their removal from the domestic hearth was often painful and distressing. Although surrounded by fellow officers and their crew, life at sea could be lonely, especially if a man had left behind a loving wife and children in England. Many men retreated into their imaginations to conjure up the sounds, sights and sentiments of home. For Broke, imagining home became both an escape from, and a hindrance to, his naval service. Broke used his correspondence with Loo to allow himself to retreat from the pressures and traumas of his naval life. He imagined himself in 'domestic tranquillity' at Nacton with all his dear family around him. Broke frequently imagined Loo as his rose, his 'gentle, quiet, soft, mild-looking, rosy Loo!' For a time, he kept a rose bush in his cabin to transport him in his mind back to his wife and children. In a particularly poignant letter, Broke tells Loo of his reaction to receiving a packet of letters from her:

I have just got my dear Loo's letters, of 23rd and 29th, and am charmed to hear so favourable account of the dear children, and so I put my rose by my side, and sat down and kissed the letters, and the rose, and the Loo, in imagination, and felt very happy for a few minutes, till I began to reflect that the real real, true Loo was not there! But I hope yet to enjoy soon a more rational interview! [29 July 1810]

Broke was clearly not afraid to express his emotions and feelings in his correspondence. For many officers, personal correspondence provided a welcome emotional outlet from the demands and discipline of naval life. For Broke, faced with both a letter and a physical metaphor for his family, his reaction was both powerful and emotional, such that he feared it might distract him from his duty. Broke wrote to Loo of his struggle in the face of such an emotional challenge:

No! These roses must not stay! They haunt my imagination with wifish ideas, and won't leave me a moment for myself, or King George; if it was even a picture of the Loo's soft countenance, I could shut it up; but these things flaunt their beauties in my face, and yet look so mild, and so innocent in their bloom, that I can't help thinking of her. [24 June 1810]

Such a strong symbol of home threatened to upset the balance that Broke had worked so hard to achieve between his duty to the nation and that to his family.

Throughout his letters Broke created a distinctive persona for his ship. He cast *Shannon* as his wooden wife or mistress who had dragged him away from home and his family. Imagining a ship as a woman was common throughout the period. Satirical prints such as Newton's *Launching a Frigate* (1809) provide a crude, highly sexualised image of a woman as a 'frigate'. Such prints were common, demonstrating the connection between maritime culture and prostitution – an association that is far removed from Broke's imaginings of his 'wooden wife'. Rather than a sign of infidelity, Broke used his 'wooden wife' to express his love for Loo. It also can be read as an analogy for his national duty, keeping him away from home against his will and desire. When he wrote to Loo, it was an opportunity for him to forget 'Mrs Wooden Wife', and return to his family. Broke's constant attempts to gain his passage home were often prevented by the wicked ways of his wooden wife:

> You can't imagine the pains I have bestowed on this graceless wooden wife of mine, particularly since she ran away with me here; and I perhaps shall have to leave some other person to reap all the credit of her beautiful play, unless we have somebody to open a concert with very soon: But, when tempted to think of home, I am constantly reminded that naval success will be my speediest liberation from exile so then I turn to *Shannon* to see if she is perfection. I think she will do me credit if she finds an opportunity, and I am sure the other wife will make me happy if I quit this game of honour; so I must make the best of it, and pray God to let us soon meet in joy and security.

In this letter of 14 February 1812, Broke uses his accustomed metaphor to resolve the constant conflict in which he found himself: by imagining his ship as a wife and his crew as his sea family, he carries the importance of family duty into his life at sea.

Whilst he was away on active duty Broke asked Loo to create a family-like network around her on shore. At the same time, he too depended on a familial community within the Navy. The idea of a naval family was partly forged through fraternity amongst officers, which

Nelson too promoted with his 'band of brothers'. Similarly, Jane Austen, whose own brothers were in the Navy, and were in fact friends with Broke, writes in *Persuasion* of 'brother-officers'. Officers formed networks of support and friendship in their years of training and during their time at sea, and maintaining such friendships constituted part of their duty to the navy. Those brother officers provided an essential support network for both Loo and Broke. In turn, Broke maintained a strong sense of duty towards his fellow officers. He felt guilty that, whilst other men suffered silently, performing their duty to their country, he was seeking a way out. Couples might not hear from each other for several months at a time, and during these long intervals they relied on verbal communication through fellow officers relaying family news. After the birth of his son Charles, Broke heard the news of Loo's safe delivery from Captain Brenton of *Spartan* who had heard that she was doing well but could not tell Broke 'who was arrived to share [her] maternal attentions'. The naval network went further than that, however, as Brenton had heard the news from Captain Henry Hotham, a 'particular friend' of Broke's. Broke then arranged a meeting with Hotham in order to learn that the new baby was in fact a 'loo-boy'. This network was not limited to news of births, and the common practice of getting fellow officers to deliver letters in person allowed them to reassure Loo of his health. Officers also wrote to each other to convey news of home, with Hotham writing to Broke on a separate occasion to inform him that Loo and the children were well. On a visit to Plymouth, Hotham went for a walk with Loo and then wrote to Broke that 'she said she and her children were all well; we spoke of the probability of your return to England, which I hope may arrive as soon as you wish it may, but I shall regret it very much on my own account'. The system worked both ways, with Loo reporting the health of a fellow officer's wife to Broke, which greatly delighted the concerned officer. Broke also commissioned Loo, when holidaying in Bath, to tell Lady Faulkner, the mother of one of his lieutenants, 'that her boy is well and is a fine brisk entertaining fellow'.

The strength and interconnectedness of the naval community, and the naval family, is particularly evident in Broke's relationship with Samwell, a young officer aboard *Shannon*. Broke saw the young midshipmen and lieutenants on board his ship as his 'sea children', and his correspondence reflects the paternal care and attention that he gave them. Samwell's father was also a captain in the navy and his mother, 'an excellent worthy kind woman', lived near Loo and was a major source of support for her, helping to care for her and the children. Broke expressed his gratitude to Mrs Samwell in his letters and used the networks of naval communication to send her news of her son. He communicated with Mrs Samwell through his letters to Loo, writing that he 'gave her son a little pocket money whenever we come into harbour, and have no complaints of him now from his little messmate Mr Mayne'. This was common practice as captains often kept midshipmen's funds, giving them spending money when they came into port. When Samwell's box arrived on the ship from Portsmouth it contained within it a letter for Broke from Loo. Broke's paternal attitude towards the young men in his care was here matched by 'Mrs S' in her care for his children. He showed a genuine interest in Samwell and longed for his promotion, which he hoped would come as soon as he was of age. During Loo's pregnancy with their son George, Mrs Samwell attended Loo and corresponded with Broke, for which Broke was very grateful.

Samwell was wounded in the thigh during the battle with *Chesapeake* and, despite being severely wounded himself, Broke made sure to write of the boy's condition, knowing that the news would be passed on to his mother. In his first, brief letter to Loo after the battle he added a line after his signature: 'Samwell slightly hurt but almost well'. Unfortunately, despite initially doing well, Samwell died suddenly from a ruptured blood vessel. Broke wrote to Loo of Samwell's death and promised to write separately to Mrs Samwell. He knew that she would turn to Loo for comfort and to 'vent her grief'.

Broke also suggested that Loo prepare Mrs Samwell for the blow by telling her that her son had weakened, but feared such action would prove futile, as Mrs Samwell would read about his death in the papers. Broke expressed his grief for Mrs Samwell in his letter, and also for Loo, who, he believed, would 'feel for a person who has been so kind to her and to the dear children'. Broke's affection and sense of responsibility for Samwell continued after his death. He wrote to Loo that he would settle the boy's affairs as he would 'his own private accounts' to make things as easy as possible for Mrs Samwell.

The naval family that Broke created with his fellow officers extended to his relationship with his crew, as witnessed by his frequent references to the midshipmen as his 'sea children'. Broke fulfilled the paternal role on his ship, providing education and moral guidance to his 'boys'. He sought to help them advance in their careers, writing to Loo that he hoped 'to see [his] sea children settled' before he left them. The role he played at sea in many respects mirrored the role he so longed to play ashore with his own children. Such a naval family was essential to creating a sense of shared experience and community which helped families such as Broke's cope with the demands of warfare and naval life. After the battle with the *Chesapeake* Broke wrote to Loo of leaving his naval family:

It is a great happiness for me to be able now to leave them all in so prosperous a way, to see my sea children settled before I leave them (except poor Samwell), but we were altogether very fortunate in that rank, our enemy lost 8 or 9! All my old *élèves* [students] will make good officers and do Shannon credit: indeed I regard bringing up such a family, as an essential part of my 8 years' services, and it is one that has cost me much care and anxiety: I have a right now to bring up my own children surely, and please God will, with my gentle Loo's aid. [20 July 1813]

Broke looked on his ship and his crew as his family. His duty to the Navy was, in part, forged through a sense of familial, paternal duty to his officers and men. As well as the captain of the ship, Broke was also the father and school master, and fulfilled the role of affectionate, instructive and moral fatherhood for his sea children. Broke was able to leave *Shannon* with honour and without regret. His sea children were now ready to go out into the world, naval and otherwise, on their own. Having completed his duty to his naval family, Broke felt that he had earned the right to return his attention to his own children and at last lay down his sword, and his pen, and take up his role of father ashore.

Broke was everything that one would hope for in a good post captain. A tall stalwart figure, a calm, kindly, and devoted man, a firm disciplinarian with the ability to inspire trust, confidence and loyalty in his officers and men, a superb leader and a first-class fighting seaman with a keen and inquiring mind. Such was Philip Bowes Vere Broke, the creator of that splendid fighting ship, the *Shannon*, and the exponent of the art of naval gunnery.

Rear Admiral H F Pullen RCN, *The Shannon and the Chesapeake*, p 119.

A RADICAL VIEW OF BROKE'S VICTORY

This is of far greater importance than the victories of Lord Wellington and as such the public appear to feel it; for everyone runs cackling about it to his neighbour with as much glee as a long-married husband carries the news of the birth of his first child. Why there is more boasting about the defeat of one American frigate than there used to be about the defeat of whole fleets. This is no small compliment to the Americans.

William Cobbett, *Political Register*, 17 July 1813

11. HMS *Shannon* under sail, a sketch by Admiral King.

12. Broke as a young captain.

13. Broke in old age, drawing by Sir William Ross in 1833.

14. A section through the breech of a Blomefield cannon showing the cartridge, roundshot and wad *in situ* in the bore. The vent is represented by the black line. The gunlock above creates the spark which ignites the quill primer, sending a stab of flame into the cartridge causing the gunpowder within to explode instantaneously.

15. A replica of one of Philip Broke's designs for a tangent sight fitted to the breech of the cannon behind the gunlock.

16. The quarterdeck of HMS *Trincomalee*. Restored and preserved afloat in Hartlepool the *Trincomalee* is a *Leda*-class frigate and sister ship of HMS *Shannon*, albeit built some years later in India of teak not oak. Although HMS *Trincomalee* features a combination of 32pdr carronades and 9pdr guns as in the original upper deck armament configuration of *Leda*-class frigates, significantly changed on the HMS *Shannon*, in every other respect this is identical to the quarterdeck from which Philip Broke commanded the *Shannon* in action against the *Chesapeake*.

17. Gun drill; here, in a dumb-show exercise, the gun has been hauled inboard by two members of t[he] crew using the train tackle to bring the muzzle inboard of the port to facilitate reloading.

18. A romantic vision of the death of Lawrence.

19. Celebration of the victory that Americans believed was confirmed by the Treaty of Ghent.

20. *Preparing John Bull for General Congress*, a satire on the failed Congress of Prague, 1813 (see p 162–3).

21. *The Fall of Washington or Maddy in Full Flight*, venting the tale that Madison had had to abandon a celebratory dinner, an echo of the Shannon story (see pp 165–6).

22. *Bruin become Mediator or Negotiation for Peace*, between John Bull and Columbia, over the Orders-in-Council (see p 167).

23. The frigate *Trincomalee*, sister-ship of *Shannon*, restored in 2000 and now lying afloat in Hartlepool.

9

A Gunnery Zealot: Broke's Scientific Contribution to Naval Warfare

Martin Bibbings

'The captains of the guns, the lanyards in their hands, bring the dark artillery to bear, . . . and the iron tempest, with which it is loaded, bursts in fire and thunder upon her decks.'
Reminiscences of a Naval Officer by Captain A Crawford RN

Had it not been for the events which occurred off the Massachusetts coast in the late afternoon of 1 June two hundred years ago, few people would remember the name of Philip Bowes Vere Broke or his ship *Shannon*. Because of those brutal eleven minutes off Cape Ann, however, his name was immortalised following one of the most famous frigate actions ever to take place. Without it, Broke's career might have been largely forgotten and his gunnery improvements and methods overlooked long since. In the wake of that stellar victory, and in particular the speed and manner of the defeat of the *Chesapeake*, experts began to look in detail at the techniques and innovations Broke used on board his ship to bring her and her crew to such a perfect state of combat readiness. As a result his reputation was established as one of the leading gunnery experts of the age.

Even up until the end of the eighteenth century gunnery was still considered by many to be more of an art than a science. Apart from improved methods of ignition, the cannon itself and techniques of muzzle-loading artillery were unchanged from Elizabethan times. The army had already begun to adopt a far more scientific approach to aiming and sighting but of course they did enjoy the big advantage of firing off a stable platform – the land. Gunnery at sea took place on a platform that usually was continuously moving, up and down and side to side; this, coupled with the limitations imposed by the poor engineering tolerances of the era, had encouraged the belief that long-range accuracy was unachievable. It led to the view that the only tactic employable at sea was to hit the enemy hard and fast at short range with heavily concentrated broadside fire. Broadside fire was the tactic of choice in major fleet actions, as a result of rigid Admiralty instructions. Manoeuvres in single-ship engagements were more fluid and required a variety of different gunnery skills and sailing tactics.

Broke's frustration at the unimaginative use of gunnery by his colleagues during the Napoleonic Wars is clear from his letters. A few of the more enlightened frigate captains like him saw how gunnery could be improved from the 'old ways' using a modern scientific approach and mass simultaneous broadside fire began to fall from favour. A letter to the *Naval Chronicle* on 22 March 1813 argued that 'The firing of each gun should solely depend on the man that lays her . . . it is he alone that can discover the exact moment for discharging the gun'.

There were of course huge practical difficulties with accurate naval gunnery, not least the moving platform from which it was delivered (ie the ship) and condition of the medium on which it sat (ie the sea). William Spavens, an experienced gunner, wrote in his *Narrative* of 1796:

It is always necessary that he who points the gun should have judgment of the ship's motion, to do execution; for if the side be rising, he must take his aim below the water's edge, or he'll fire over the object; if it be lowering, he must level above the gun-whale, or else he will fire into the water: Some attention must also be had to the motion of the object; it is not like fighting ashore.[1]

Shannon's armament

Philip Broke had been captain of *Shannon*, a 38-gun frigate, since September 1806 and over the years had gradually developed and implemented his gunnery theories through a rigorous daily training programme for his crew. *Shannon* was one of the large frigates of the *Leda* class of 1794 designed on the lines of the captured French frigate *Hebe*. Displacing 951 tons and with an overall length of 150 feet these

---

1 Spavens, *Narrative*, pp 55–6.

vessels were rated for 38 guns and were originally configured for a broadside weight of 425 pounds with armament comprising:

Main deck	28 × 18pdr, 40cwt, 9ft short Blomefield guns[2]
Forecastle	2 × 9pdr, 24.5cwt, 7ft 6in, long Blomefield guns
	2 × 32pdr, 4ft 17cwt carronades
Quarterdeck	8 × 9pdr long Blomefield guns
	6 × 32pdr carronades

Carronades were classified as secondary armament and were not included in a ship's official rating.

By the time *Shannon* met the *Chesapeake* seven years later, Broke had removed all but two of the quarterdeck 9pdr carriage guns and replaced them with 32pdr carronades and had added two further carronades to the forecastle's armament. He had two 12pdr boat carronades pointing through the stern ports on the quarterdeck, and an old brass 6pdr mounted in the larboard entry port (a further 12pdr carronade was in the starboard entry port). The *Shannon* also had a small swivel gun mounted in each of the fore and main tops for anti-personnel use to sweep the exposed enemy weather deck with canister shot or langrage (small pieces of iron and other metal scraps). American ships, including the *Chesapeake*, used 3in howitzers in their tops. She also had at least two 1pdr swivel guns per side mounted on the quarterdeck bulwarks, loaded likewise with canister or small shot.

The 9pdr long guns on *Shannon*'s forecastle and quarterdeck were mounted on specially adapted carriages to enable the guns to fire over the top of the bulwark rather than through a gun port. These 'barbette' guns had a vital role to play in Broke's strategy:

a ship should always have at least one long gun of a side on the quarterdeck and forecastle ready to fire *en barbette* over her barricade or gangway rails. We had two long nines thus placed in the Shannon – being the foremost quarterdeck and aftermost forecastle guns. These were mounted on higher brackets than usual and would elevate to about 33 degrees – so that by crossing their fire

---

2 Guns designed by Major General Sir Thomas Blomefield, inspector of artillery for the Ordnance Board in Woolwich from 1780 to 1822.

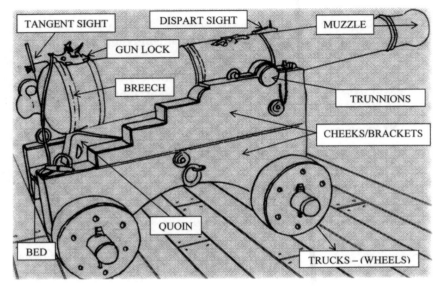

Fig 9.1 The parts of a cannon.

as required – or if <u>foul of an enemy perhaps</u>, turning the gun on the unengaged side we could have <u>commanded a top</u> with a powerful fire . . . such guns, firing overall, would bear anywhere athwart or fore and aft . . .

. . . It is certainly desirable when fighting under sail and particularly with an enemy who is likely either to try to escape, or to manoeuvre for position – to always keep some guns appointed to dismantling services . . . It is only however from the long guns that much service might be expected in this way, they will throw the grape or case close and sharp enough at fifty yards distance to cut shrouds or slings away, will make great havock in the running rigging, and <u>if under press of sail</u> will materially damage a top mast . . .[3]

Broke's relationship with one of *Shannon*'s other armaments, the carronade, was rather a troubled one. Of all the weapons at his disposal, it gave him the most cause for concern and he described the carronade as 'a very awkward engine'. Whilst he was fully appreciative of the huge value of these powerful weapons, as can be seen from his addition of a further eight to *Shannon*'s original armament, his genius

---

3 Suffolk Record Office [hereafter SRO] HA 93/9/311, Broke's Critique and Observations on Sir H Douglas's *Treatise of Naval Gunnery* published in 1820.

for solving the practical problems of gunnery was sorely tested in finding ways to maximise their efficiency and minimise their problems.

The advantages of the carronade were considerable – they delivered a very heavy 'punch' for their small size and were murderous at short range. They took up less room on deck, they were light and easy to manoeuvre, and they needed only a small crew, freeing up others for secondary duties, particularly as boarders when required at short notice as in the engagement with the *Chesapeake*. However, their effectiveness declined rapidly with range and they were a problem to secure. If mounted outboard, the crew were very exposed when reloading and the gun was difficult to prime as the vent lodged right under the gun-port sill when run out. Mounted inboard, their ability to traverse was severely limited by the narrowness of the gun port. Because of their short barrel length, the flame from their discharge sometimes had the unfortunate consequence of setting fire to the ship's own heavily tarred lower rigging! Worst of all, their lightness in relation to the heavy weight of shot they fired made their recoil extremely violent; in consequence, they were continually pulling ring bolts out of the ships side, breaking their breechings and destroying their slides (carriage mounting).

Significance of gunlocks and quill primers

In line with all other Royal Navy ships of size, *Shannon*'s guns were equipped with gunlocks, bolted to the breech of each gun to the side of the vent. They were a larger version of the same flintlock mechanism used in muskets and pistols of the period except that they were triggered by a long lanyard. The gunlock produced the spark which lit the priming powder at the vent and started the chain reaction which resulted in the ignition of the main charge in the chamber of the gun. This replaced the former method of manually igniting the priming using a linstock – a short stick with jaws at one end holding a length of smouldering slow match. The gunlock was used with quill or tube primers in the vent and it was the combination of the two which enabled very significant advances in naval gunnery.

The Royal Navy had been experimenting with gunlocks since the middle of the eighteenth century but it was Sir Charles Douglas who really pioneered their use in HMS *Duke* from 1778. Douglas bought gunlocks for the ship and had them fitted at his own expense. These were used in combination with quill primers (which some credit

Douglas with actually inventing). These innovations led to the outstanding performance of the ship at the Battle of the Saintes in April 1782.

In effect the quill was a little rocket. It was inserted into the top of the vent and was ignited when the priming flashed across from the pan of the gunlock. The quill then sent an instantaneous stab of flame down the vent into the cartridge and the gun discharged almost immediately. By the old linstock method there could be a delay of a second and a half between the priming being lit and the gun going off, with obvious consequences for precision firing.

Claims that the new method increased rate of fire significantly are an exaggeration. The speed of ignition was made faster by a fraction as described above but overall this had little effect on the overall time it took to load and fire a gun. What the gun lock and primer did do, and this *was* a significant advance, was to give the gun captain absolute control over the exact moment the gun fired; this was crucial to the cause of greater accuracy when firing from an unstable platform and in 'catching the roll' (see p 121). Furthermore, the long lanyard allowed the gun captain to aim the gun from directly behind and to sight down the line of metal, safe in the knowledge that the breeching rope would stop the gun short (even though he was instructed to 'hop' to one side!). Again, this was a very important move forward in gun aiming and accuracy; previously the gun captain had to approach the gun from the side in order to avoid his feet being crushed by the recoil. Broke sums it up perfectly:

> Instantaneous discharge is of high value in naval practice & our locks & tubes (quills) give us vast advantage in that respect over the old gunner who was obliged to wait the slow ignition of a deep touch-hole filled with coarse powder & to be fired with a smoldering match – how they could hit anything in a rolling sea (unless very close) is astonishing.[4]

Organisation

There were two distinct phases in the organisation of a ship and its crew for battle. First, there was the preparation of the ship ('clear for

---

4 SRO HA 93/9/311.

action') which included the distribution of a huge quantity of equipment and munitions from the gunner's store, and then the dispersal of the crew ('beat to quarters'). Sometimes these two activities were separated by several hours; if an encounter with the enemy was thought probable but the convergence of the two protagonists was slow, the ship would be cleared for action and the men then dispersed for other duties, to relax or eat, or even exercise at the great guns (as the *Shannon*'s crew did during their wait for the *Chesapeake*), before being sent to quarters (action stations) as the engagement became imminent. At other times, when the prospect of action was sudden and immediate, the two activities would be virtually simultaneous.

Able Seaman Samuel Leech described in his memoirs (*A Voice from the Main Deck,* p 72), the scene when he was a powder boy aboard *Macedonian* going into action against *United States*: 'The drum and fife beat to quarters; bulk-heads were knocked away; the guns were released from their confinement; the whole dread paraphernalia of battle was produced; and after a lapse of a few minutes every man and boy was at his post, ready to do service for his country.'

The partitions which formed Broke's great cabin, dining and sleeping quarters at the aft end of the gun deck and all his furniture and personal effects would be removed and struck down into the hold or placed in the ship's boats being towed astern, creating a clear unbroken sweep of deck from bow to stern inhabited on either side only by the twenty-eight great guns and all their attendant equipment. Brian Lavery has recorded the Captain's Standing Orders for *Amazon* written in 1799 by Edward Riou, another outstanding frigate captain.[5] Riou, who was sadly killed at the first Battle of Copenhagen in 1801, set out everybody's duties in great detail:

> By this all possible preparation is meant that the shot, wads, matches, match tubs, powder horns, lanterns etc. should be placed in amidships, . . . breechings middle seized, guns hanging by the train tackles, hand-spikes, sponges and worms down by their guns, small arms, pikes and ammunition disposed of upon deck . . .
>
> . . . gun locks (and flints) in order; handspikes, rammers and sponges by the right side of each gun and powder horns, and priming

---

5 Lavery, *Shipboard Life and Organisation,* pp 165–82.

wires amidships; and shot of different qualities, . . . tubes, vents, spare flints and a piece of blanket or woollen rag to wipe the lock and flint in possession of the captain of the gun; cinders or sand in tubs between every two guns to be strewed upon deck in case the deck should become wet or slippery; . . . train tackles bighted alongside the guns; relieving tackles hooked.

Principal responsibility for the distribution of small arms and all gunnery equipment lay with the Gunner himself – this important position as one of the ship's warrant officers was filled on board the *Shannon* by Richard Meehan. Weapons and equipment were issued from the gunner's store, which was the ship's armoury located forward on the orlop deck. Here most of the ship's arms were kept securely, under Royal Marine guard when not in use. The marines' weapons were racked in their own berthing area, aft of the crew's.

Muskets were hauled up into the fighting tops, together with arms chests containing ammunition for the muskets and swivel cannons. In preparation for rigging repairs spare coils of line and tackles were also hoisted up to the tops, along with buckets of water for firefighting. Chain slings were fitted to the larger spars to support them in the event that their lifts and halyards were cut by dismantling shot. Here, Riou again:

topsail sheets stoppered, preventer bracers rove,; and in short everything in its place ready for battle . . . Slings on the topsail yards if the weather is very settled and the breeze not likely to increase so as to render it necessary to reef the topsails; quarter slings (or chains) for the lower yards; puddings, dolphins, preventer braces rove; stoppers on sheets; spare tiller shipped and with it a spare tiller rope; fire buckets to every gun; engine and hose in good condition; fire booms unlashed; wings clear; passages clear to the store rooms and magazines; all the store room (and arms chest) keys etc. given into the charge of the purser or some other officer . . . and such sails (placed in the after hold) as will least likely be wanted (to be bent) and some cots and frames ready slung for the wounded.

For night action, twenty-eight lanterns hung amidships opposite to each gun on the main deck, the signal lanterns likewise ready. Lanterns for the lower deck and after cockpit; screens placed round the hatchways near to the magazines. Good sweet water for drinking on different parts of the decks; spare arms and ammunition, cutlasses, pikes, tomahawks etc, disposed of carefully in different parts of the ship for the seamen quartered on the main deck, forecastle and quarterdeck, for boarding or repelling boarders ...

So 'clearing for action' was no small task, but a complex and highly organised evolution involving the entire crew of 300 men or more, requiring very careful planning. These actions had to be performed quickly and efficiently with every man knowing his own responsibilities. Only when these preparations were complete was the ship ready for action.

The document which determined where each man was stationed was the quarter bill. When 'Beat to Quarters' was sounded by marine drummer William Jones playing the *Grenadiers March* every regular crewman knew exactly where to go: Second Lieutenant Provo Wallis had command of the aftermost main deck guns whilst Third Lieutenant Charles Falkiner had the forward guns, each with their own midshipman and quarter gunners. One hundred and eighty-two men manned the fourteen 18pdr guns on this deck, thirteen per gun when manning one side, or, if the ship was likely to be engaged on both sides simultaneously, dividing themselves between two guns opposite each other, sharing one powder boy.

Each man within that thirteen-man crew had specific responsibilities in the aiming, firing, cleaning and reloading sequence of the gun drill (see Figure 9.2). The gun captain led the team and aimed and fired the gun, his second captain primed the vent and managed the gun lock, other men used the handspikes to elevate and traverse the gun under the captain's direction, hauled the gun back up to the port with the side tackles, passed and loaded the powder, ball and wad, one man wielded the unwieldy rammer, swab and worm on their ten-foot ash staves in the close confines of the gun deck, the powder boy ensured the gun's salt box (ready magazine) was continuously supplied with cartridges, one man clinched the train tackle to hold the gun in its run-in position to give the loaders room to access the muzzle for cleaning and reloading.

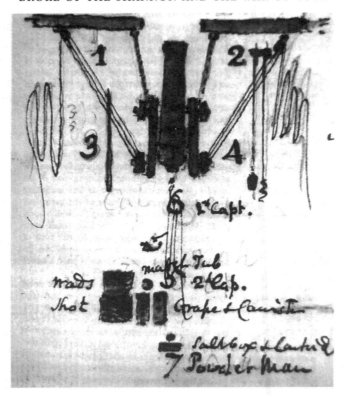

Fig 9.2. Contemporary drawing showing the manning and layout of equipment for firing an **18-pounder with 7 man crew**. (From the Captain's orders for HMS *Amazon* (1799), in Lavery, *Shipboard Life and Organisation*, p 179.) The numbers 1 to 7 in the drawing represent the gun crew and their positions:

1. Loader: places the cartridge, shot & wad into the muzzle of the gun and mans the side tackles.
2. Sponger: rams the cartridge, ball and wad during loading, worms and sponges the gun after firing and mans the side tackles.
3. Handspikesman I: mans the side tackles and uses the handspike (wooden lever) to traverse and elevate the gun under the gun captains (6) instructions.
4. Handspikesman II: mans the side tackles and uses the handspike to traverse and elevate the gun under the guns captains (6) instructions, and attends the train tackle.
5. 2nd Captain: adjusts the quoin (wedge) for elevation during handspike deployment, works the gun lock, primes the vent, stops the vent, manages the slow match, fires gun with match if gunlock fails.
6. 1st Captain: directs the gun crew, aims the gun and fires with gunlock.
7. Powder Man: supplies powder to the gun and its opposite number (one starboard and one larboard) and ensures each guns salt box is continually supplied with cartridges. Transfers cartridges from the salt box to the loader.

The guns on *Shannon*'s main deck were spaced at roughly ten-foot centres, and as the carriage axles and wheels were about five feet wide, there was only five feet of space between adjacent guns. Allowing a few inches' margin, each man had a channel no more than two feet wide in which to work; heaving on tackles, passing side arms, cartridge shot and wad, using handspikes, standing clear of the recoil – step six inches too far and he could lose his toes under a truck or his eye on the end of a wad hook. Gun drill had to be as exact as a choreographed ballet with every hand, foot and bodily movement synchronised precisely with every other member of the crew – and all this in the thick of the smoke, deafening noise and horrendous carnage of battle whilst stupid with fatigue from the physical effort involved. Mercifully, the actions were so familiar and required such intense concentration that a man would rapidly become robotic in his actions and completely oblivious to the maelstrom of smoke, noise, injury and perhaps death going on around him.

All the primary guns had marines in their gun crews, one each in the quarterdeck and forecastle crews, and two for the main deck guns – thirty-eight in all out of the total number of fifty-six marines on board. Others manned the quarterdeck swivels, and guns at the entry ports and provided musket fire from the weather deck and tops.

Each man in a gun crew had at least one secondary job and half the combined crews of each pair of guns, larboard and starboard, were designated as boarders. Three of these were called *First Boarders* and were usually issued with a cutlass and a pistol; three more were designated *Second Boarders*. Of these, two were assigned pikes, and the third assigned the tomahawk or boarding axe. The First Boarders were the ship's assault party; the Second Boarders could be mustered for a second-wave assault or as a defensive force. Additional responsibilities as firemen and sail trimmers were also allocated as required. This explains how the *Shannon*'s boarders followed Broke so quickly and with their weapons (see Chapter 10). The quarter bill goes on to allocate another 100 gunners to the carronades and 9pdrs on the quarterdeck and forecastle.

Ammunition supply

The popular image of the 'powder monkey' running back and forth from the magazine to his gun to keep it supplied with ammunition has been questioned in recent years with regard to the practicality of being able to do so fast enough given the distances and obstacles involved. Nonetheless, this was the system employed on at least some ships. Samuel Leech wrote:

> My station was the fifth gun on the main deck. It was my duty to supply my gun with powder, a boy being appointed to each gun in the ship on the side we engaged, for this purpose. A woollen screen was placed before the entrance to the magazine, with a hole in it, through which the cartridges were passed to the boys; we received them there, and covering them with our jackets, hurried to our respective guns.[6]

On *Shannon*, for safety's sake only a small amount of powder was kept by the guns, and the cartridges, being vulnerable to damp, were not filled long in advance. Her well-organised ship's company would have only the minimum amount of powder in transit from the magazine, on the disengaged side if possible. In the magazine, cartridges as they were filled were immediately inserted into cylindrical wooden cartridge cases and passed through the dampened 'fearnought' screens to a 'bucket line' of nine men – along the magazine passage, up the ladder, then to the fore hatchway and up its ladder to the fore scuttle and the gun deck. Only once there did the powder boys transfer them directly to their own gun, where they were placed in the safety of the salt box (saltpetre), ready for use as required. Another six men were given the physically exhausting job of handing shot up from the main hold and onward to the gun decks.

Broke's gunnery innovations

Speed
Statistics relating to the speed of fire achieved on ships during the muzzle-loading, smooth-bore era are very scarce but the achievements of one man stand out. Cuthbert Collingwood, Nelson's second in command at Trafalgar, was renowned as a gunnery enthusiast and it is recorded that during his command of *Excellent* during 1797–99, his gun crews were achieving a rate of fire equivalent to three broadsides

---

6 Leech, *A Voice from the Main Deck*, p 326.

in three and a half minutes. This outstanding achievement reflected his belief that in order to defeat the enemy 'the fleet must bring overwhelming firepower to bear, faster, more accurate, more determined and more prolonged'.[7]

Such rates of fire could only be achieved by rigorous and continual practice with minute attention to detail. Contemporaries of Collingwood felt uncomfortable with his severity and reserve, and even considered his attention to detail demeaned and compromised his dignity. However, it was almost certainly Collingwood's 'attention to detail' and 'meddling' which enabled a succession of his commands to achieve the most outstanding gunnery performances.

On board *Shannon* Philip Broke had created a strict, but benevolent regime dedicated to achieving the highest professional standards of seamanship and gunnery. In exactly the same way as Collingwood before him, the standards Broke maintained were a direct product of his outstanding attention to detail and the creative innovations his enquiring mind brought to the practical problems of gunnery at sea. His archive at the Ipswich Record Office is full of instructions, detailed computations, drawings, sketches, correspondence and theories relating to all aspects of gunnery, including tables with recommended loads of projectiles and powder for hulling, disabling masts and rigging at differing ranges (cable's length, half-cable, close or foul) and accuracy in rolling seas or still water. Among this wealth of documentation are tables with recommended loads for achieving specific results against differing targets with aims to dismast, disable, rake, or silence (the latter meant causing death or injury to so many of the enemy's crew that the guns could no longer be worked); crib cards for himself and his officers with optimum ranges and shot variations; designs for salt boxes, elevating screws for carriage guns, carronade restraint and innovative breeching mechanisms, pivoted traversing guns, and ships with *redan* bulwarks designed to permit increased arcs of fire, deck plans showing the exact distribution of arms and munitions at quarters, boat guns, various designs for tangent sights and quadrants, notes on canister shot composition and effect, mounting of carronades on the inboard or out-board principle, and so on. In short, the output of a lively and creative mind

---

7 Adams, *Collingwood*, p 49.

Amongst the most revealing documents in the archive are Broke's correspondence with Sir Howard Douglas, then writing his *Treatise on Naval Gunnery*, published in 1820. Here, he generously shares the benefit of his experience on a very wide range of subjects relating to naval gunnery (see p 149).

Shannon's *training regime*

Admiralty Regulations demanded that crews be trained and practised at the great guns but how regularly this was done depended entirely on the commanding officer. In some ships there was little or no commitment: 'It is customary in many ships in a general exercise to go through the motions without loading or firing once in a year, and in others to exercise a few guns every day, and seldom to have a general exercise or to fire the guns.'[8] Not so on board *Shannon* where the weekly training took place on five days out of every seven. Brighton sets out the weekly timetable in his *Memoir*:[9]

On Monday, forenoon, the watch on deck exercised at great guns; and, in the afternoon, the first division of the watch exercised at small arms.

Tuesday, forenoon; watch on deck at great guns: afternoon; first division of watch on deck at small arms.

Wednesday, forenoon; the watch on deck at second deck guns: afternoon; second part of watch at small arms.

Thursday, forenoon; watch on deck at second deck guns: afternoon; second part of watch at small arms,

Friday, forenoon; midshipmen at great guns: afternoon; at small arms,

Saturday, wash clothes before breakfast, and wash lower deck in the forenoon,

Sunday, church, and not any work,

It was Broke's philosophy to give the men detailed explanations of what they were doing and why: 'to give a man <u>confidence</u> [in] his <u>gun</u> &

---

8 Lavery, *Nelson's Navy*, pp 172–8.
9 Brighton, *Broke Memoir*, pp 148–9.

shew him what service he alone might effect against an enemy by <u>cool courage</u> and <u>patient skill</u>'.

As well as practice at the great guns, time was given to the swivel gunners and sharp-shooters in the tops: 'In regard to the enemy's topmen – the only . . . way of being on even terms with them is to have our own tops <u>well</u> but not <u>numerously</u> manned with brave active men who are good marksmen and who have been accustomed to practice from the tops at targets floating alongside.'[10]

Although *Shannon*'s gunner Richard Mehan had primary responsibility for gunnery training, Broke himself was the inspiration behind the drive for perfection with his exacting standards and the training scenarios he devised to prepare his men for every eventuality:

Few days passed at sea without some warlike practice of great guns or small arms, frequently <u>field days</u> when [in] full force we practiced our powers & resources in every position we could suppose the ship placed – engaged with one or more adversaries – either ships or gun boats, & in every situation le fortune de guerre could throw at us, every man in the ship being used to his small arms & all but the Marines (& most of them) & the very dullest of our waisters being qualified to serve a great gun . . .

. . . This gave great room for varied practice, in the supposition of boarding or repulsing boarders, & of making the most of our force against an enemy [who] entangled with us in a position where few guns would bear . . . The kinds of shot were varied according to [the]object . . . which the guns were to be directed (against), & the guns being frequently worked in different divisions for affecting particular sorts of service as for hulling, or dismasting, at various distances, the men were prepared for any practice wanted, & also for making the utmost use of their arms in every situation, whether <u>complete</u> or more or less disabled by loss of men or material damage.

Although not a rich man, Broke nonetheless could afford to supplement the allowance of powder and shot allocated by the parsimonious Board of Ordnance with his own purchases for live firing practice; the fact that he was prepared to do so further demonstrates his absolute

---

10 SRO HA 93/9/311.

commitment to achieving the highest standards on board his ship. He even motivated his gun crews to greater achievement by rewarding good performance from his own pocket. In addition to the rewards Broke gave out as a result of good practice at the mark, he also had his gun captains rated as petty officers when it came to the distribution of prize money.

Accuracy
> 'the balls left the barrel all right but the Lord alone knew what happened to them after that'
> C H J Snider, *Under the Red Jack*

The two components of aiming the gun were the 'point' to give lateral direction and the 'elevate' to achieve range and trajectory – the two elements of gunnery on which Broke invested a great deal of his time.

> The idea of aiming the guns at the enemy seemed almost superfluous. No sights were fitted to the guns, and the captain of the guns looked along the top of the barrel and roughly pointed the gun at anything he could see through the smoke. The guns however, were short and considerably tapered toward the mouth, so that the line along which the aimer looked was at a definite angle to the actual direction in which the bore of the barrel was pointing and along which the shot was actually fired. As a consequence it was generally assumed in the fleet that the shot always rose as it left the gun.[11]

The tapering shape of a cannon barrel described above was known as the dispart. The cannon barrel was designed to be considerably fatter at the breech end than at the muzzle (the breech needed to be the strongest part to contain the exploding gunpowder charge). It was this taper or dispart which created the biggest problems for gunners in the days before proper sights were fitted.

The gun captain who simply sighted his piece down the length of the barrel and made no allowance for the dispart would inevitably send his shot flying harmlessly over the target. Blomefield guns had degrees of elevation crudely incised around the perimeter of the breech and a

---

11 Baynham, *From the Lower Deck*, p 219.

simple notch cut halfway down the flare of the muzzle. By lining these up, the gun captain could in theory lay his gun horizontally (o degrees) or incline his gun up to 3 degrees of elevation. According to William Hutchinson in 1781:

> The Captain of the gun is to look by the side sights first, and apply one hand to the bed or coin, and make motions with the other hand, upwards or downwards, for the men on each side looking at him with handspikes to rise or fall the breech of the gun, 'till it points level to the object, then looking along the top sights, tap with his hand more or less on the side of the gun, as it requires to be breeched fore or aft by the men with their crows or handspikes, 'till it points directly to the object, then he is to make the motion to fire by slapping the gun, with both hands at a time, jumping briskly on one side abaft the gun.[12]

This however, made no allowance for the 'sheer' (the curve fore and aft) and 'camber' (side to side) of the gun deck. Even more importantly, the heel and motion of the ship depending on the strength of the wind, set of the sails, sea conditions, and whether the ship was engaging to windward (uphill) or to leeward (downhill). So, to compensate for the sheer, Broke had his carpenter cut the 'high' side of each gun carriage until the bed was horizontal by spirit level.

In the confident belief that the way to defeat an enemy was always to hit the ship rather than the masts and rigging, to cause maximum material damage and casualties, the 'holy grail' that Broke was seeking was a method to achieve horizontal fire for 'hulling' the enemy at point-blank range consistently, whatever the sea conditions, inclination of the ship or wind strength. Point-blank range was considered to be the distance to a target at which the shot would travel parallel to the surface of the sea without appreciably dipping from the force of gravity; this varied from 300 to 400 yards, according to the nature of the gun. Broke called it 'blindfold firing':

> My dear Sir, I must begin by returning my best thanks for your invaluable remarks, especially that part in which you supply me with

12 Quoted in Padfield, *Guns at Sea.*

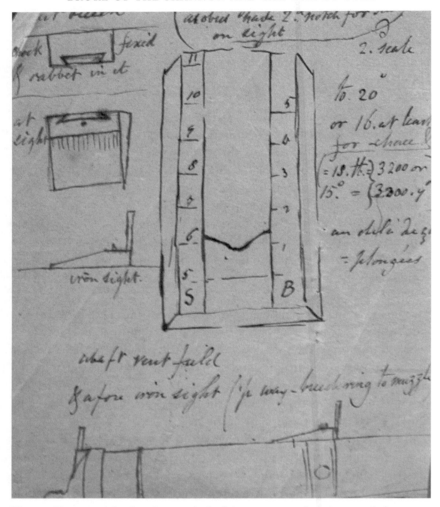

Fig 9.3. Tangent sight drawing, typical of the numerous drawings made by Broke.

such cogent and additional reasons for using in my battles, not with an enemy, but with many officers who are nearly as bad, and who will not, or cannot, be made to understand the use of horizontal and, as you properly call it, blindfold firing.[13]

---

13 Broke to HRH The Lord High Admiral, 11 January 1828: SRO HA93/9/311.

To achieve the standards he sought from his gunners Broke introduced several initiatives: he gave his gunners the opportunity of live practice firing at targets, he taught them to anticipate the movement of the sea and 'catch the roll' to ensure precision, he introduced sights and other methods whereby the guns could be laid with precision and finally, perhaps the most groundbreaking of all, he gave himself control of the entire battery with his revolutionary director fire system.

'Firing at the mark' (target exercising).   Each gun was allowed three shots. The mark was a beef-cask, with a square piece of canvas of about four feet. It was always cut to pieces; the distance about three to four hundred yards.

'Catching the roll'.   This exercise for gun captains improved their ability to fire their guns at precisely the right moment in the cycle of the ship's up-and-down movement as she rolled, in order to send their shot horizontally at the target. On calm days two sailors would heave the barrel of one of the lighter quarterdeck 9pdrs up and down with a handspike inserted in the bore, imitating the rise and fall of a rolling ship. Gun captains took it in turns to stop the movement by inserting the quoin, a wedge-shaped block of wood that supports the breech of the gun at the required angle of elevation, at the moment the sights lined up with a target fixed in the fore part of the ship. During live practice and in action, Broke favoured his experienced gunners firing on the up-roll, novice gunners on the down-roll.

This exercise, which was a test of the gun captain's reactions, eyesight and anticipation, underlines just what an important innovation the gunlock and quill primer combination was, as previously discussed, giving for the first time, the ability to time the discharge of their piece with complete precision. As Broke observed, in the vertical plane 'the ship will aim her'. It is no exaggeration to conclude that all later attempts to improve naval gunnery would have been as nothing without the immediate and instant form of ignition the gunlock and primer provided. From this technological advance championed so enthusiastically by Sir Charles Douglas, all subsequent improvements became possible.

'Horizontal fire'.   Early in the *Shannon*'s first commission whilst the ship lay at anchor in the calm waters of Dungeness Bay, Broke had a

plumb line suspended from aloft down the main hatchway and weights moved from one side of the ship to the other until the deck was absolutely horizontal. Next, each of the main deck cannon had a crude gunner's quadrant inserted into the bore. This was a wooden T-square with a small plumb line suspended from the top of the T and a graduated scale of degrees below (see Figure 9.4). The gun was elevated or depressed using the quoin until the plumb line crossed the quadrant at zero degrees showing the bore of the gun was exactly horizontal. A deep score was then incised into the side of the quoin and a corresponding one in the bed of the carriage. Thereafter, whenever the two marks were lined up (and the ship on an even keel) the gun captain knew the gun would fire horizontally.

Later, two more marks were added to indicate the gun was horizontal; firstly, when the ship was inclined to leeward, 'That level on which the gun would be point blank for the horizon when it was on the lee side and the ship under the heaviest press of sail on a wind'. Then, secondly, a corresponding mark was added for the same inclination to windward.

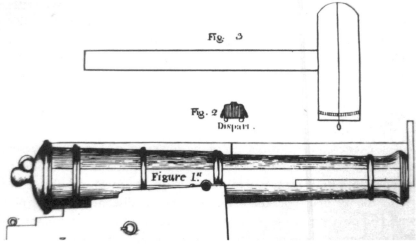

Fig 9.4. Line drawing by Sir John Pechell of Broke's 'T' piece pendulum for obtaining a horizontal or zero mark for guns. This simple wooden gunner's quadrant was inserted into the bore of the gun. With the barrel levelled and the plum bob hanging vertically, a zero mark was incised on the quoin and bed of the carriage, so that the gunner would know when his gun was horizontal. A string attached to the widest diameter of the gun at the breech was then stretched to a corresponding point on the upright of the quadrant to determine the required height for the dispart sight to compensate for the taper of the gun (Padfield, *Guns at Sea*, p 141).

Contrary to the commonly accepted theory that the windward position was always the most advantageous tactically, from a gunnery perspective Broke considered the leeward position had its own benefits:

> I must . . . advert to the peculiar advantage of the lee-gauge in regard to use of grape or case, – an enemy's decks are laid very open & considering the quick fall of those charges from double shotted guns . . . the men on a ship's lee quarter-deck have but little shelter unless close to the side.

This, of course, was exactly the position of the *Shannon* and the *Chesapeake* when they met on 1 June 1813, although in the light prevailing winds the advantage was probably slight.

Despite the above, Broke went on balance with the accepted wisdom which favoured the windward position, especially if the ship to leeward 'may completely expose her copper' – 'a few shot striking them underwater or just *fleur d'eau* [between wind and water] will soon drive them to their pumps'.

Sights. Next, Broke had dispart sights added to the guns. A string was stretched from a square inserted into the muzzle of the gun to the base ring (where the cannon barrel is at its maximum diameter at the breech) exactly parallel to the bore. Then a small saddle of wood with a vertical metal spike was attached directly above the trunnions corresponding to the exact height of the string at that point. With the string removed, a gunner squatting behind the gun could squint down its length; with the top of the breech ring aligned with the top of the sight spike he knew that his line of sight was precisely parallel to the bore.

Finally (and in a process which was developed over a period of years), Broke had tangent sights added to his guns. These might be best described as 'back sights' and were attached to a block of wood at the breech above the cascabel loop. They consisted of a small copper plate with a 'V' notch which could be slid up and down within a small wooden 'ladder'-like frame marked with degrees of elevation (previously calibrated using the gunner's quadrant). Lining up a mark on the plate against a degree of elevation and then aligning the top of the dispart sight half way down the barrel within the 'V' by making fine adjustments with the quoin, the gunner could now precisely lay the cannon to an exact degree of elevation. Broke had these sights made up and fitted at his own expense, almost certainly by *Shannon*'s own armourer and carpenter, and clearly their form was one of continual refinement. The Ipswich archive contains sketches of numerous different designs (see p 120).

Director fire. Broke now had the means to control the entire battery from a central command position:

> to secure this power of horizontal fire in all situations is of vast import, by frequent observation of a pendulum we knew in the Shannon what depressions or elevations . . . would place our guns horizontally under different presses of sail & the quoins were marked for several adjustments each way so strongly that the marks could be felt in the dark – & this enabled us to order the guns at any moment to be all put into such a position that whatever list the ship had, our shot would <u>skim</u> the <u>surface</u> horizontally to full point blank & through smoke or night provided that he was abreast of us, the men would be sure to hull him though they saw nothing of him but only fired on a <u>prescribed</u> <u>horizon</u>.

This concept was finally realised in its entirety with the addition of angles of training cut into the deck inboard of each gun and filled with putty or white lead, and a central compass at Broke's command centre on the quarterdeck inscribed with marks corresponding to those at the guns. Now, with a single order, Broke could train all his guns on one target simultaneously (see Figure 9.5):

> To suppose a case: you are coming up with your enemy on a dark night; the Captain judges what her distance *will be* and how many degrees of the wooden quadrant (tangent scale) will give that distance. Then he orders the guns to be elevated and trained to so many points before the beam. All being ready the Captain watches the bearing of the enemy by the compass on the tank (before the main mast) and when that bearing corresponds with the point to which the guns are trained, he gives the order to fire.[14]

14 SRO HA 93/9/311.

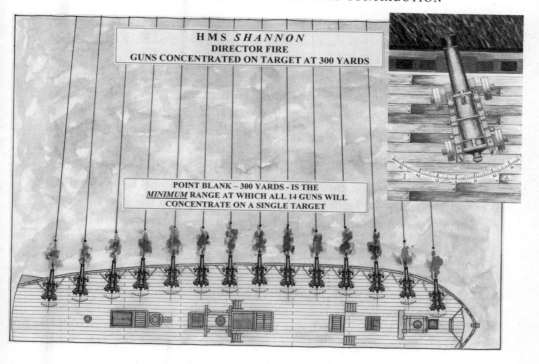

Fig 9.5. Two drawings depicting Broke's director fire arrangements. An arc of degrees was incised into the deck behind each gun, angled according to the gun's position relative along the ship's side and its situation fore and aft. At a single command from Broke on the quarterdeck all guns could be focused on a single target at a given distance. The traverse of the guns at the extremes of the gun deck were limited by the curve of the hull and width of the gun port. The author has calculated that 300 yards was the minimum range at which all fourteen guns on *Shannon*'s main deck could be brought to bear on a single target. (Drawings by the author.)

This system that Broke had developed, however crude and inexact it may be by modern standards was one of unprecedented refinement for its time, with the equipment at his disposal and in the face of blunt rejection by the Admiralty for any such scientific advancement. Their only reply to any application was: 'it was not according to the regulation of the service, and could not be complied with'. To an officer of no private fortune, this was equivalent to a prohibition. Luckily, for the future of both the service and the British flag, Philip Broke was both able and willing to ignore this.

It is ironic that, after all the time and attention spent perfecting such a novel system, Broke was so disheartened by events in the first year of the War of 1812 that he felt obliged to return to old ways after the Americans had so successfully bloodied the Royal Navy's nose on three occasions: 'Our only remedy for the disadvantages [of being out-gunned by the heavier American frigates] is to get alongside them as soon as possible, and stop all distant, scientific practice and hammer them "more majorum" [in the manner of our predecessors].' All his practice and rehearsal was not to be wasted, however; the pro-fessionalism he had engendered in *Shannon*'s crew and his immaculate organisation and technical efficiency had prepared the ship for every eventuality. The rapidity of fire his gunners could achieve and the pin-point accuracy that his dismantling guns were capable of, added to his crew's proficiency in small arms, made the *Shannon* an irresistible fighting force.

As Captain A T Mahan wrote of the British sailors of the earlier sailing Navy:[15]

The artist is greater than his materials, the warrior than his arms; it was in the man rather than his weapons that the British Navy . . . wrought its final triumph.

Suggested Further Reading
Douglas, Sir Howard, *A Treatise on Naval Gunnery, 1855* (1982).
Gilkerson, William, *Boarders Away II* (1993).
Padfield, Peter, *Guns at Sea* (1973).

---

15 Quoted by Bennett, *The Battle of Jutland*, p 172.

10

The Battle

Martin Bibbings

'An action rarely equalled and never surpassed'
    Secretary of the Admiralty William Croker

His Britannic Majesty's frigate *Shannon*, P B V Broke commanding, Tuesday 1 June 1813, Bay of Massachusetts, off Boston.

The tall red-haired Englishman paced up and down the scrubbed planks of the quarterdeck. The day was calm and the sea moved with just a gentle swell below a warm breeze from the southwest. Cape Cod was out of sight to the south; before him lay the low-lying coast of America, Boston itself, with its outlying islands and harbour approaches whilst to starboard he could make out the Massachusetts shoreline trending gradually northeast toward Marblehead and Cape Ann beyond.

Nothing about his unremarkable appearance gave any clue as to the true martial character of the man. In his plain blue frock coat and trousers, riding boots and top hat he looked every inch the country gentleman that he was in his native Suffolk. His confident bearing marked him out as a man of significant qualities – apart from the sword hanging at his side, his casual dress belied the fact that he was a military man of any sort. He was in fact a consummate professional seaman and an exacting and single-minded perfectionist 37-year-old captain of this ship. On that day two hundred years ago this man of action was about to meet his destiny – eleven minutes[1] that would change his life for ever.

---

1 The exact timing is uncertain except for the eleven minutes recorded by the Gunner on Provo Wallis's watch. Broke himself spoke of 'a quarter of an hour' in his letter to Loo of September 1813. See p 92 [Editor].

A few weeks earlier, on 14 April, he had written to his wife Loo:

> I wish much, for my people's sake, to make some good capture, for they have had hard cruising. I shall at any time feel contented with the attainment of my only object when I first embarked – an opportunity of retiring honourably, and with the consciousness of having done my duty as an Englishman. Eight years of my youth, and all my plans of rural quiet and domestic happiness, have faded away or been cruelly interrupted by this imperious call of honour. But surely no man deserves to enjoy an estate in England who will not sacrifice some of his prospects to his country's welfare.[2]

Philip Broke had been in command of *Shannon* since 1806 and the ship had been on almost continuous active service ever since. During that time Broke had never had the opportunity to test his ship against anything like an equally powerful opponent. After weeks of tedious blockade during which he suffered the bitter disappointment of allowing Commodore Rodgers to escape in *President* in company with *Congress* when adverse winds forced Broke and his consort *Tenedos* into the offing, his desire to confront the remaining frigate in Boston became more and more intense, as he expresses to Loo just four days before it was to end:

> We still haunt this tiresome place without any success to reward us, indeed I have been so particularly anxious to watch the <u>great</u> ships that it has thrown us much out of the way of the smaller tho' <u>richer prizes</u> – since Rogers [*sic*] escaped we have rarely hunted our game far from his Den which still contains another large <u>wild beast</u> [*Chesapeake*], if all the noble prey elude us we <u>must</u> chase the vermin, but have great hopes yet of an honorable encounter.

Not only was Broke frustrated, but he was concerned that the material condition of his ship would require him to him leave station for a refit before *Chesapeake* could be lured out of harbour. Her arduous service career had left *Shannon* in poor condition. She had been built by a

---

2 Broke Archive, Suffolk Record Office, Ipswich, SA 2/2, the source for all the letters to his wife.

commercial shipyard on the Medway with an experimental lightweight fastening system – in Broke's words: 'her topsides are slight and leak like a basket in heavy weather'. He had been in command of her since she was first commissioned and had driven her hard ever since. As he wrote to Loo, 'to wear out a new frigate is quite enough for one term of service for any man'. He was short of water and, to add to his problems, on 5 May *Shannon* had been struck by lightning which had severely damaged her mainmast, sprung her mainyard and set the fighting top on fire: 'providence saved us from destruction; thanks be to God, not a man was lost.'

Despite *Shannon*'s condition and outward appearance – she was described as 'a little black dirty ship' – efficiency was more important to Broke than smartness, and he had turned the his crew into a frighteningly effective fighting unit, superbly drilled in his scientific gunnery methods and highly trained in all aspects of hand-to-hand and small-arms combat. He had huge confidence in his ship and men and a burning ambition to test both against a worthy opponent, whilst at the same time crowning his career and avenging the recent humiliations of his beloved Royal Navy. He wrote to Loo on 28 May 1813: 'my wishes will be satisfied in regard to all prizes when some honorable action leaves me at leisure to homeward plod my weary way in poor old shattered Shannon'.

Almost in desperation he did everything in his power to try and tempt the *Chesapeake* out. On 31 May, he carefully drafted the following formal challenge to her captain, James Lawrence:

As the Chesapeake appears now ready for sea, I request that you will do me the favour to meet the Shannon with her, ship to ship, to try the fortune of our respective flags. To an officer of your character, it requires some apology to proceed to further particulars. Be assured, sir, that it is not from any doubt I can entertain of you wishing to close with my proposal, but merely to provide and answer to any objection which might be made and very reasonably, upon the chance of our receiving unfair support . . .

The Shannon mounts twenty-four guns upon her broadside, and one light boat-gun – eighteen-pounders upon her main-deck, and thirty-two-pound carronades on her quarterdeck and forecastle, and is manned with a complement of 300 men and boys (a large proportion of the latter), besides thirty seamen, boys and passengers, who were taken out of recaptured vessels lately . . .

If you will favour me with any plan of signals or telegraph, I will warn you (if sailing under this promise) should any of my friends be too nigh, or anywhere in sight, until I can detach them out of my way; or I would sail with you under a flag of truce, to any place you think safest from our cruisers, hauling it down when fair to begin hostilities . . .

I entreat you, sir, not to imagine that I am urged by mere personal vanity to the wish of meeting the Chesapeake, or that I depend only upon your personal ambition for your acceding to this invitation: we both have nobler motives . . .

You will feel it as a compliment if I say that the result of our meeting may be the most grateful service I can render to my country . . .

He even added a final note to say that, if Lawrence was prevented by special orders from responding to this challenge, he should keep it a secret but appoint a rendezvous within 300 miles of Boston where they could meet a given number of days after he sailed. 'Choose your terms but let us meet.'

Lawrence himself had sent just such a challenge in December 1812 from his sloop *Hornet* to the master and commander of Royal Navy sloop *Bonne Citoyenne*, at Sao Salvador (Bahia), in a failed attempt to get him to come out and meet him. Broke's challenge was described by the historian Capt A T Mahan as that 'of a French duellist'. The next morning he sent the letter in by a fishing boat he had captured. He followed into Boston harbour just off the lighthouse and fired a single challenging gun.

Her log records:

June 1st (Tuesday).

4.0.	Fresh breezes and cloudy. Land and several sail in sight.
9.40.	Tacked. Exercised great guns.
12.0.	Noon. Light winds; fine. Cape Ann NNE half E, ten or twelve miles.
1.0. pm.	Light breezes and fine. Observed the enemy's frigate Chesapeake under weigh. Kept away to gain an offing. At

	one the enemy rounded the light-house. Up foresail and down jib (steering off the land).
3.20.	Cape Ann north, six or seven leagues, the enemy still coming down under all sail, with several small craft around him, and a large schooner.
3.40.	In top-gallant sails and down staysails. The Chesapeake closing fast, with three ensigns up and a white flag, having on it 'Free trade and seaman's rights.'
5.10.	Beat to quarters. Hoisted the jib and filled the foretopsail.
5.30.	Filled the maintopsail and kept a close luff, the enemy coming down under his topsails and jib.
5.40.	The enemy luffed up on our weather quarter, within pistol-shot, and gave three cheers.
5.50.	commenced action within hail.

Shannon had cleared for action many hours previously. Her gun deck was a clean sweep from bow to stern with all the partitions forming Broke's stern cabin removed. Captain Marryat, writing in 1828, described a similar occasion:

> I cannot imagine a more solemn, grand, or impressive sight than a ship prepared as ours was on that occasion. Her noble tier of guns in a line gently curving out towards the centre: the tackle laid across the deck; the shots and wads prepared in ample store (round shot and canister); the powder boys each with his box full, seated on it, with perfect apparent indifference as to the approaching conflict. The captains of guns, with their priming boxes buckled round their waists; the locks fixed upon the guns; the lanyards laid around them; the officers, with their swords drawn, standing by their respective divisions.

At gun 14, on the starboard side of Broke's cabin, one of those gun captains, 27-year-old Able Seaman William ('Billy') Mindham from Surrey, waited as *Chesapeake* slowly approached. With him was his gun crew of six. They were soon joined by their opposite numbers from the larboard side, swelling the crew to a full complement of thirteen men as soon as it became obvious she was not going to cross *Shannon*'s stern.

With permission to fire as soon as his gun bore on *Chesapeake*'s second gunport from her bows, Mindham, squatting behind his perfectly levelled 18pdr, and sighting down the length of the barrel, watched her bow with its cut water and fiddlebeak above slowly fill the square of his open gun port. Resisting the urge to open his account too soon he gradually increased the tension on his trigger lanyard as the enemy's hawseholes and bridleport slipped past and then finally, as his target filled his vision just fifty yards distant, he yanked hard and the great gun fired.

Action

In the event Lawrence did not receive Broke's challenge and we can only guess what his motivations were for bringing out his ship to meet an opponent whose reputation for gunnery and fighting efficiency were well known on the coast.

Lawrence had only taken command of the *Chesapeake* on 20 May, just twelve days before. He was a disappointed man. After his impressive defeat of *Peacock* in his previous command, the *Hornet*, he had expected the command of the prestigious *Constitution* of which he had once been first lieutenant and in temporary command. Instead, when the captain of the *Chesapeake* fell sick before the *Constitution*'s repairs were complete he was given the lesser ship, which he considered beneath his merit and seniority.

Navy Secretary Robert Smith had told Lawrence to put to sea as soon as he was ready to proceed and to disrupt the important British supply route to the St Lawrence river. He could have waited for a favourable opportunity to evade the *Shannon* in poor weather or at night, as the *President* and *Congress* had managed, so one must question what other motives persuaded him to take out his new command in broad daylight, to an inescapable contest with such a powerful opponent, particularly when earlier he had expressed the intention to sail 'providing I have a chance of getting out clear of the *Shannon* and *Tenedos*'; this was before the *Tenedos*, had been sent by Broke back towards Halifax to persuade Lawrence it would be a fair duel.

Perhaps Lawrence arrogantly felt he could demonstrate his true worth to his supposedly unappreciative masters in the US Navy with yet another impressive American victory over a British frigate, or maybe he was just carried away with the public expectation of another success.[3] Indeed, the excited supporters of the war who thronged the Boston waterfront, and the host of pleasure craft which followed in the *Chesapeake*'s wake were all hopeful of yet another spectacular win and had prepared a victory dinner. To have delayed sailing, or to have crept out furtively in the dark, would have been odious to Lawrence's nature, particularly as he felt he had an audience to please. In his book *The Naval War of 1812*, C S Forester (creator of Horatio Hornblower) suggested that maybe the adulation Lawrence had received on account of the *Peacock* defeat had disturbed his judgement.

He had in the *Chesapeake* a ship that was at least a match for the *Shannon* in size, firepower and manning. She was marginally bigger and had a larger crew (see the table overleaf) but her armament was comparable, making the subsequent duel the closest matched frigate engagement of the 1812 War. Four 32pdr carronades and one long 18pdr had been removed from the ship before sailing. Some believe Lawrence ordered this in order to even up the *Chesapeake*'s firepower with the *Shannon*, but it is far more likely it was ordered by the Navy Department to ease the ship which was showing signs of hogging (sagging at the bow and stern).

Whatever his motivations, Lawrence confidently decided to accept the challenge *Shannon* posed, flaunting herself before Boston. He was confident and bullish, writing to Secretary Smith on the day he departed that he hoped 'to give a good account of her [*Shannon*] before night'.

Unfortunately for Lawrence, as Peter Padfield has written, his opponent on this occasion 'was not simply another lamb to the slaughter . . . she marked instead the final flowering and high point of the ancient art of broadside fire from carriage-mounted cannon and [that] a more destructive vessel of her force had probably never existed in the history of Naval warfare'.[4]

Battle

> 'Throw no shot away. Aim every one. Keep cool. Work steadily. Fire into her quarters. Don't try to dismast her. Kill the men, and the ship is yours.'
>
> Broke to the *Shannon*'s crew before the action with the *Chesapeake*

---

3 This is considered in Chapter 5 [Editor].
4 Padfield, *Broke and the Shannon*, p 151.

SHANNON & CHESAPEAKE COMPARISON			HMS SHANNON	USS CHESAPEAKE
LAUNCHED			1806	1799
DISPLACEMENT			951 tons	1,244 tons
LENGTH			150 feet 1½ inches	152 feet 6 inches
BEAM			39 feet 11 inches	41 feet
COMPLEMENT	See p 146		330 men	388 men
ARMAMENT				
WEATHER DECK	FORECASTLE	Carronade	4 × 32pdr	2 × 32pdr
		Long	2 × 9pdr	1 × 18pdr
	QUARTER	Carronade	12 × 32 pdr	18 × 32pdr
	DECK	Long	2 × 9pdr	
	EXTRAS	Carronade	3 × 12 pdr	1 × 12pdr mzn top
		Long	1 × 6pdr	
MAIN DECK		Long	28 × 18pdr	28 × 18 pdr
TOTAL GUNS			52	50
BROADSIDE WEIGHT Shannon's Chesapeake's	(Single shotted) Starboard Larboard		538 lbs	590 lbs

Shannon had long since cleared for action and her officers and crew were at their quarters. Broke himself was at his command centre on the quarterdeck with his First Lieutenant George Watt. The main gun-deck below was under the command of Lieutenants Provo Wallis and Charles Falkiner.

As *Chesapeake* ranged down *Shannon*'s starboard side the gun crews on both ships prepared to exchange broadside fire at pistol-shot range (40–50 yards). A tense but disciplined silence pervaded *Shannon*'s gun deck. No orders were given and none were required. Each man already knew exactly what was expected of him.

At 5.50pm, fractions of a second after Billy Mindham's main-deck gun number 14 was discharged, its 18pdr solid iron shot just over five

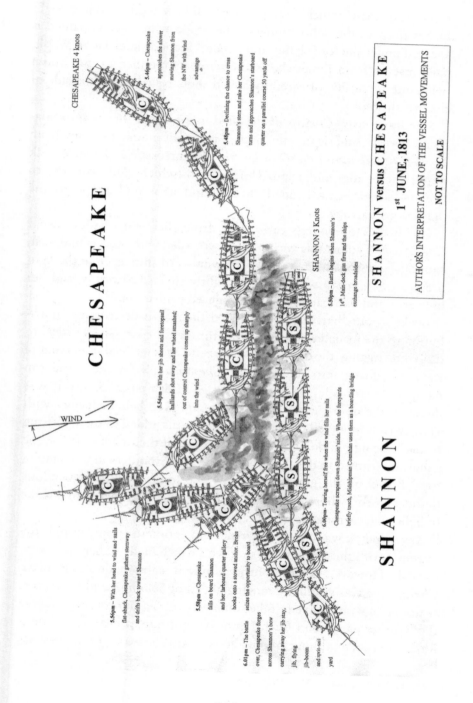

WIND

CHESAPEAKE

SHANNON

CHESAPEAKE 4 knots

5.46pm – Chesapeake approaches the slower moving Shannon from the NW with wind advantage

5.48pm – Declining the chance to cross Shannon's stern and rake her Chesapeake turns and approaches Shannon's starboard quarter on a parallel course 50 yards off

SHANNON 3 Knots

5.50pm – Battle begins when Shannon's 14". Main-deck gun fires and the ships exchange broadsides

5.54pm – With her jib sheets and foretopsail halliards shot away and her wheel smashed; out of control Chesapeake comes up sharply into the wind

6.00pm – Tearing herself free when the wind fills her sails Chesapeake scrapes down Shannon'sside. When the foreyards briefly touch, Midshipman Cosnahan uses them as a boarding bridge

5.56pm – With her head to wind and sails flat-aback, Chesapeake gathers sternway and drifts back toward Shannon

5.58pm – Chesapeake falls on board Shannon and her larboard quarter gallery hooks onto a stowed anchor. Broke seizes the opportunity to board

6.01pm – The battle forges over, Chesapeake forges across Shannon's bow carrying away her jib stay, jib, flying jib-boom and sprit-sail yard

SHANNON versus CHESAPEAKE
1st JUNE, 1813
AUTHOR'S INTERPRETATION OF THE VESSEL MOVEMENTS
NOT TO SCALE

inches in diameter struck *Chesapeake*'s bluff bow and buried itself eight inches deep in the solid timbers. The grape which accompanied it sprayed under the fore chains and whales. Seconds later Jacob Welsh, aged just 21 from Limerick, fired *Shannon*'s number 13 gun and a deliberate broadside of carefully aimed shots rolled down the side of the British ship.

Simultaneously, *Chesapeake* replied in kind with her main armament. Every American gun had a resonant name ranging from *Brother Jonathan* to *Liberty or Death*. Her forecastle and quarterdeck 32pdr carronades and 18pdr shifting gun (which could traverse to fire on either beam) added their round shot and grape to the murderous barrage.

On board *Shannon*, case shot from her carronades swept *Chesapeake*'s vulnerable weather deck crowded with officers and men, causing significant casualties. As the windward ship, even in the light breeze, *Chesapeake* was inclined slightly toward *Shannon* and her bulwarks and barricades provided reduced protection.

Broke's 9pdr 'barbette' guns added their own destructive contribution to the tornado of metal flying through the air. Given orders to dismantle rigging, the quarterdeck 'barbette' was inclined to maximum elevation, firing into the mass of *Chesapeake*'s foremast and top hamper. Meanwhile, on the forecastle, Midshipman Samwell was directing the 9pdr there, targeting *Chesapeake*'s helm. Marines with 1pdr swivels mounted on the quarterdeck rails added to the withering fusillade being put down by the musket fire of their colleagues on the gangway, seamen in the ship's boats and sharpshooters in the fighting tops. Below on the gun deck 'it was like some awfully tremendous thunder-storm, whose deafening roar is attended by incessant streaks of lightning, carrying death in every flash'.[5]

At 5.53pm, it was clearly Lawrence's intention to try and cripple the *Shannon* with the dismantling shot with which many of her guns were loaded. However, as this furious initial cannonade took place *Chesapeake* was gradually ranging ahead of *Shannon* and Lawrence, realising he would have to take some way off her in order to preserve the weather gauge and for his guns to continue to bear, luffed up a little. Even so, at a range of only 40–50 yards he was far too close for

---

5 Leech, *A Voice from the Main Deck*, p 73.

his guns to elevate sufficiently, nor had his gunners allowed sufficiently for the heel of the ship to leeward, with the result that many of his shot were striking *Shannon* too low to be effective.

To compound Lawrence's problems, a conspicuous target in his white vest, he now was hit by a musket ball behind the knee, fired by one of the men in the *Shannon*'s tops. Injured as he was, he remained on deck directing the *Chesapeake*'s faltering attack.

By 5.54pm *Chesapeake* was being systematically dismantled by the *Shannon*'s precision gun fire. With her jib-sheet and fore topsail-tie shot away, and with the yard fallen in its lifts, her wheel smashed and unattended since the death of her quartermasters, *Chesapeake* came up sharply into the wind, in irons, dead in the water. Now her stern and larboard quarter were horribly exposed to her opponent's broadside and she came under heavy fire which she was unable to return. *Shannon*'s aftermost guns began raking *Chesapeake* – their shot scything through the entire length of her gun deck, driving the Americans from the aftermost guns and causing terrible execution amongst their crews. Simultaneously, the shot from *Shannon*'s foremost guns, were entering *Chesapeake*'s ports from the mainmast aft, adding to the carnage. As Leech described *Macedonia*'s action:

> shot were pouring through our portholes like leaden rain, carrying death in their trail. The large shot came against the ship's side like iron hail, shaking her to the very keel, or passing through her timbers, and scattering terrific splinters, which did a more appalling work than even their own death-giving blows.[6]

At 5.56pm an open cask of musket-cartridges, standing upon *Chesapeake*'s cabin-skylight for the use of the marines, caught fire and blew up, but there is no evidence that this caused any injury. Even the spanker-boom, directly in the way of the explosion, was barely singed.

As *Shannon* had by this time fallen off the wind a little, and the manoeuvres of *Chesapeake* seemed to indicate an intention to haul away, Broke ordered his helm put a-lee; but scarcely had Shannon luffed up than *Chesapeake* was observed to be paying off. With her head to wind, and her yards flat aback with canvas flapping uselessly

---

6 Leech, *A Voice from the Main Deck*, pp 76–7.

against the masts, *Chesapeake* now began drifting back toward *Shannon*. Broke immediately ordered the helm up and the mizzen-topsail shivered in an attempt to turn *Shannon* away from the approaching enemy, trying to give his gunners more time to continue their destructive work. When *Shannon*'s jib stay was shot away, and with her head sails becalmed, she slowly fell off again and a coming together of the two ships became inevitable.

On board *Chesapeake*, Lawrence realising his ship was going to fall foul of his opponent immediately ordered his boarders up from below. The call for boarders should have been sounded by the ship's negro bugler William Brown, but terrified by the carnage going on around him he had deserted his post, being found later hiding under a boat. Brown had been selected for the role only days previously and it is not certain whether he could even play the bugle. He was made one of the scapegoats for the debacle and subsequently court-martialled for cowardice. Found guilty, he was sentenced to a flogging and loss of pay.

In Brown's absence, desperately, First Lieutenant Augustus Ludlow yelled down below and one of Lawrence's aides, Midshipman James Curtis, ran down the main hatchway to call for boarders by word of mouth. Only Fourth Lieutenant William Cox responded with a few men from the second division guns in the waist, who had been left relatively unscathed. When Cox reached the wreck-strewn quarterdeck he found that his captain had just been injured again. Lawrence had been hit by a second musket ball, this time in the groin – a wound which was to prove mortal. Having asked to be taken below, Lawrence left the deck exhorting his men with 'Don't give up the ship; fight her 'til she sinks'. Some accounts of the battle claim Lawrence made his rallying call only when he reached the wardroom which the surgeon had commandeered as a surgery: 'Tell the men to fire faster! Don't give up the ship!'

Still making sternway *Chesapeake* finally fell on board her opponent just before 6pm when her larboard quarter gallery ground into *Shannon*'s side between her fifth and sixth main-deck gun ports just forward of the main chains and temporarily hooked herself onto the fluke of an anchor. *Shannon*'s carronades had by now driven *Chesapeake*'s gunners from the after part of her weather deck, whilst the American marines, their ranks now decimated and without any officer, were falling back toward the forecastle. Running forward, Broke ordered the two ships lashed together and, recognising that *Chesapeake*'s quarterdeck was by now almost deserted, called for boarders. The sudden chance to board needed to be seized immediately if the opportunity was not to be lost; *Chesapeake*'s head was now being blown round before the wind and there was every chance her sails would fill and she would tear herself free.

At 5.58pm, without hesitation, Broke shouted 'Follow me who can!' and climbed over the hammock barricade just abaft the forecastle bulwarks and down onto the muzzle of *Chesapeake*'s aftermost carronade. Sergeant Molyneux of the marines was close behind with about twenty others. They dropped down onto the deserted quarterdeck. Broke and his men immediately ran forward across the corpse-strewn deck. Forward, they began to meet a desperate and disorganised resistance. Almost the first man to confront them was the ship's acting chaplain, Samuel Livermore, who took deliberate aim at Broke with his pistol only for it to misfire. Broke struck him down with his sword severely injuring him, and the boarders continued their determined charge.

Led by Lieutenants Watt and Falkiner and Midshipman Henry Leake, a second wave of thirty boarders soon followed with men mostly called up from the *Shannon*'s main deck. In all, seventy men boarded *Chesapeake* during this fleeting opportunity, comprising three officers, two midshipmen, fifty-one seamen, eleven marines and three supernumeraries. Watt, just as he stepped on *Chesapeake*'s taffrail, was shot through the foot by a musket ball fired from the mizzen top. In the meantime Lieutenant Falkiner and the marines rushed forward and, while one party kept down the men who were ascending the main hatchway, the others answered the destructive fire continuing from the main and mizzen tops.

Forward, Broke and his men began to meet stiffer resistance on *Chesapeake*'s gangways, where twenty-five to thirty Americans tried to make a stand, but they were soon driven back toward the forecastle. Here Lieutenant George Budd had rallied a small party of Americans from the gun deck which he had led up the fore-hatchway. Lieutenant Ludlow had also managed to gather a number of his men and led them up through the main hatchway where they emerged behind Broke's boarders on the forecastle. They were met by the second wave of

Shannon's boarders and forced back toward the bows. Here briefly the fighting was hotly contested – Budd received a cutlass wound across his arm and fell back down the hatchway from which he had just emerged, whilst Ludlow fell to the deck from a severe cutlass blow to the head.

Now without any officers to rally them, or any further support from below, the American resistance crumbled – some tried to force their way down the fore-hatchway while others fled over the bows plunging into the sea or making their way back onto the main deck through the bridle ports. Some of the remaining Americans began to lay down their arms. Broke restrained his men from slaughtering the few Chesapeakes still fighting, while directing other men aft where there were still pockets of resistance.

Up above, the battle was simultaneously raging in the fighting tops. As *Chesapeake*'s sails began to fill the ship lurched forward. As her side scraped down the *Shannon*'s forward end her foreyard fouled *Shannon*'s briefly. Seeing a momentary opportunity, Midshipman John Smith stationed in the foremast fighting top, ran out over the yard followed by five of his topmen and onto *Chesapeake*'s foreyard. Fighting their way up into the enemy foretop they forced the Americans there to flee down the weather-side shrouds

Seven men in *Chesapeake*'s mizzen top armed with muskets and a small howitzer were still causing great execution amongst *Shannon*'s boarders. Seeing this, Midshipman Philip Cosnahan across in *Shannon*'s main top began to pick them off one by one using a succession of loaded muskets passed down to him through the lubber's hole. He managed to dispatch three of them, and forced all but one of the others to flee below. The last, continuing to fire down on the English boarders, was only finally silenced when one of them scrambled up the shrouds into the top and physically threw him off.

Now free of any restraint *Chesapeake* forged forwards across *Shannon*'s bow, carrying away the British ship's jib stay, jib, flying jib-boom and spritsail yard. As the ships gradually lost contact with each other, the widening gap now prevented any further boarders. As it was, those seventy that had made it across had been enough, and the weather deck of *Chesapeake* was already virtually a British possession.

With victory apparently theirs, Lieutenant Watt made his way to the mizzen-halyards to haul down the American colours, but he found that some of the British crew had already raised a small ensign above the

Stars and Stripes. Determined to raise instead the larger ensign he had brought across especially for the purpose, he ordered the other flags to be hauled down in order to bend on the bigger flag.[7] At that moment he and his party were hit by a charge of grape fired from *Shannon* – probably the British gunners had seen the blue ensign coming down and assumed in the confusion that the battle was not yet over. Watt was instantly killed and five others with him wounded. Over on *Shannon* Provo Wallis immediately ordered the ceasefire.

Back on *Chesapeake*'s forecastle, perhaps emboldened by the confusion aft, three men rushed at Broke from behind with weapons they had picked up off the deck. Warned just in time Broke managed to parry the pike thrust at him by the first man and slashed him across the face with his sword. Even as he did so the second man dealt him a ferocious cutlass blow to the head whilst the third clubbed him with a reversed musket. Broke, with a three-inch cut in his skull, sank to the deck with blood streaming down his face and neck. There it mixed with the contents of a burst barrel of quicklime which lay scattered on the deck: William James claims that this was there to be thrown in the eyes of enemy boarders and there was another bag in the foretop. The presence of the lime was never fully explained by the American prisoners. Quicklime had been used up to the Middle Ages to blind opponents.

One of the Americans was about to finish Broke off when he was saved by marine John Hill who ran the attacker through with his bayonet. Midshipman Smith and Bill Mindham rushed to Broke's aid and helped him into a sitting position. Mindham was binding Broke's head with his scarf just as the British ensign was being raised: 'Look there, Sir. There goes the old ensign up over the Yankee colours!'[8] Broke was carried aft and sat on a carronade slide with his back resting against the bulwarks, faint with loss of blood.

The Shannons had driven the remaining Americans below and after some continued skirmishing on the gun deck, began securing the gratings to imprison *Chesapeake*'s crew. Suddenly there was an unexpected fire of musketry from the berth deck and marine William Young, standing guard at the main hatchway, fell mortally wounded.

---

7 Brighton's statement that it was a white ensign (*Broke Memoir*, p 172) is difficult to accept since Broke was under an admiral of the blue [Editor].
8 Brighton, *Broke Memoir*, p 173.

Angry Shannons had to be restrained by Lieutenant Falkiner from firing their muskets back down into the Americans below. Broke ordered the prisoners to be driven into the hold. It was his last order before he finally passed out. At 6.01pm the battle was over. By Lieutenant Wallis's watch just eleven minutes had elapsed since the action began.

The final analysis

The engagement between *Shannon* and *Chesapeake* was one of the more extraordinary contests in naval history. Most naval battles come about because of chance meeting between two ships, ambush or through tactical manoeuvring, but this was a deliberately contrived engagement between two men who knew little of each other and had no personal grudge. It was a duel in which Broke surrendered all advantages of manoeuvre to his opponent,[9] and in which Lawrence chivalrously declined to accept the tempting invitation to rake *Shannon*'s stern, for the alternative of an evenly matched contest, broadside to broadside. It was clear Lawrence wanted to repeat his success against the *Peacock* using the same tactics.

The consequences of these men's actions in their desperate search for 'honour' were truly shocking in terms of the casualties incurred during the short sharp engagement, which not least included themselves. Lawrence was mortally wounded, and died some days later en route to Halifax. Broke survived his severe injury but it was the end of his active service career. Of the 388 men on board the American ship 69 died and a further 77 were wounded. British losses were 34 killed or mortally wounded and 49 injured from a complement of 330. Such was the ferocity of *Shannon*'s gunnery and boarding, *Chesapeake* suffered more casualties in eleven minutes than *Victory* did at Trafalgar in several hours of fighting, and more men were killed per minute than in both Nelson's and Villeneuve's fleets combined.

The *Shannon–Chesapeake* action has been closely studied and a wealth of documentary evidence has survived. In particular, the reports which *Shannon*'s surgeon and carpenter made after the action give us invaluable information on the casualties sustained and material damage to both of the ships.

---

9 See Chapter 5 for an alternative view [Editor].

Many analysts have found it ironic that Broke's approach to scientific gunnery with his emphasis on long-range accuracy, horizontal trajectory and director fire played little or no part in the victory. But this is to misunderstand the comprehensive nature of Broke's approach to gunnery and to the overall preparation of his ship. First, as part of his meticulous training regime he had spent almost as much time exercising the crew in small-arms practice and hand-to-hand combat as on gun drill itself – and it was *Shannon*'s boarders who eventually carried the day. Second, it was the withering fire of *Shannon*'s guns which virtually cleared *Chesapeake*'s weather deck including most of her senior officers, and her devastating initial broadsides, in particular the work of Broke's dismantling 9pdr 'barbettes' on the forecastle and quarterdeck, which caused the loss of control and luff into the wind which created the opportunity for Broke to board. With so much of the enemy crew's fighting spirit already knocked out of them, Broke and his boarders were simply 'presenting the cheque for payment'. In Broke's own words:

> we practised our powers & resources in every position we could suppose the ship placed – engaged with one or more adversaries – either ships or gun boats, & in every situation *le fortune de guerre* could throw at us, every man in the ship being used to his small arms & all but the Marines (& most of them) & the very dullest of our waisters being qualified to serve a great gun. This gave great room for varied practice, in the supposition of boarding or repulsing boarders, & of making the most of our force against an enemy . . ., & also for making the utmost use of their arms in every situation, whether <u>complete</u> or more or less disabled by loss of men or material damage.[10]

Lawrence had been careless in not noticing that the boatswain had failed to sling the topsail yards on clearing for action – a basic precaution. One of the first broadsides cut *Chesapeake*'s foretopsail tie, the yard came down with a run, and the ship began to lose control. A sailing warship was a complex machine, and the failure of any component in the rig could have a significant effect on her ability to

10 SRO HA 93/9/311.

manoeuvre, especially at close quarters. The contribution of *Shannon*'s forecastle 9pdr was even more devastating in its pin-point despatch of *Chesapeake*'s quartermasters and resultant disablement of the ship's helm. This systematic assault directly resulted in the loss of control that signalled the beginning of the American's demise. It is a grim testimony to the accuracy of this gun that three of *Chesapeake*'s rated quarter-masters died during the battle or after and a further three were severely wounded.

The total number of shot recorded as hits from the great guns between the respective ships was in favour of *Shannon*: 362 as against 158 for *Chesapeake* in just over six minutes of the cannonade. These figures are distorted considerably by the quantity of grape, case and various other types of shot being used by both sides in addition to the traditional round shot. An 18pdr grape shot, for instance, consisted of nine 8oz balls (imagine iron golf balls 2.2 inches in diameter) quilted together with canvas and twine onto a steel plate and post.

> not having our choice at all of distance with Chesapeake, we never gave her more than two round-shot, or round and grape, but she fired three shot from her main deck & from many of her carronades & from none less than two, & the round shot from the latter even thus loaded came through the thickest part of the Shannon's bends [the thickest and strongest planks of a ship's side] into the gun-room. Perhaps the first broadside was exchanged at fifty yards & the second at 20/30 yards.

The *Shannon*, had her main armament of 18pdrs on her gun deck loaded alternately with two round shot in one gun and then one round and one grape shot in the next. In one discharge of her fourteen guns then, a total of 84 separate balls (plus iron plates and posts from the grape) were blasted at *Chesapeake* at 1,200ft per second with unimaginable destructive effect. From her weather deck 32pdr carron-ades, most likely loaded with case shot (a tin canister containing seventy 8oz balls: a total discharge of a staggering 630 projectiles) were directed at the enemy. Is it any wonder the casualties on *Chesapeake*'s weather deck were so numerous?

More important than the number of hits recorded on each ship was where the shots struck and in this respect *Shannon*'s were far more damaging. It was the smashing effect of the round shot which had the most destructive effect on the fabric of the ships. Peter Padfield sets this out very clearly and his conclusion is:

> The Americans had therefore been exposed to at least 44 round shot in about 6 or at most 11 minutes . . . while the British had only suffered from 10 or 11 round shot, most of which had arrived forward in the first 2 or 3 minutes of the action while the ships were still parallel or nearly so. All the rest of the Chesapeake's well-trained guns had been pointed too low; thus of 14 bar shot from the American main-deck pieces, nearly all struck the Shannon on her coppers just above the waterline and bounced back into the sea. American bar shot expanded into arms as it flew through the air and was designed primarily to dismantle rigging and sweep through men. The fact that nearly all of it, besides a great number of 18pdr round shot, struck so low is clear evidence that the American guns' crews had little conception of elevating their pieces for horizontal fire. They were firing on the lee side, and, under the press of a light breeze on topsails alone, they allowed their shot to follow the tilt and camber of the deck down almost to the Shannon's waterline at a separation of only 40 to 50 yards. Altogether they hit the Shannon with 39 round and bar shot, but only 11 were effective as killing or demoralising blows – as against the 44 at least from the Shannon.[11]

Generally speaking, American gunnery had been good during the War of 1812, not least that demonstrated by Lawrence himself when his *Hornet* sank *Peacock* earlier in 1813. (In the era of the wooden warship it was highly unusual for a ship to be sunk by gunfire alone.) *Chesapeake's* gunners by no means gave a bad account of themselves. It must also be taken into account that a significant number of casualties on both sides were not inflicted by gunnery at all but occurred during the brutal hand-to-hand combat on the deck of the beleaguered *Chesapeake*, and that at least six Shannons were killed, and possibly as many as twelve injured, by 'friendly' fire from their ship's own guns, including of course Lieutenant Watt and five others in his flag party.

---

11 Padfield, *Broke and the Shannon*, p 242.

Various factors have been put forward over the years to explain why the *Chesapeake* was overwhelmed so quickly by *Shannon*. There have been recurring suggestions of drunkenness amongst *Chesapeake*'s crew, of near mutiny over unpaid prize money from their previous cruise, that the ship was not ready for sea, that she had an untrained raw crew and inexperienced officers, and lastly that she was subjected to 'infernal machines' used by the British.

To deal with last first, Broke took great umbrage at the suggestion. On 19 June he told Loo:

> the <u>foolish</u> Americans have been [???? page torn] telling a thousand absurd lies – not liking to believe that their ship was bigger than Shannon and got such a <u>terrible beating </u>by fair play as she did – the simpletons say we used <u>infernal machines</u>. They are sadly disappointed they had <u>fetters</u> for <u>us all</u> upon deck <u>ready</u> which came to <u>their use</u>.

The *Chesapeake*'s men were not raw: of the 388 officers, men and marines on her pay list on 1 June, 279, or nearly three-quarters, had served in the previous cruise under Captain Evans, and for the most part those who accepted their discharge were, or rather had been, British men-of-war's men. Even so, of the 325 prisoners landed at Halifax subsequently, about 32, including the Gunner, Matthew Rogers, were recognised as British seamen. The actual number of men aboard *Chesapeake* is disputed. Some have suggested there may have been as many as 440. Recruiting criteria for American seamen were very strict. Candidates were examined by a board of officers including the master and surgeon. 'So fastidious was the committee of inspection, that frequently, out of five boat-loads of men that would go off to the ship in the course of the day, three would come back not eligible.'[12]

The *Chesapeake*'s crew showed they were well trained at the great guns during Lawrence's drills in harbour and although many were dissatisfied about not having had the money due for six prizes captured during the recent cruise, Lawrence had settled these debts out of his own pocket. That some of the crew were drunk as some writers have

---

12 James, *Naval History*, vol 6, p 207.

stated is highly unlikely. Given how long had elapsed since *Chesapeake* had left her berth at the Long Wharf in Boston (where the majority of shore leave must have ended) and her subsequent spell at anchor behind Spectacle Island, it is impossible to believe that any of the crew were still drunk when she finally met *Shannon*.

The one aspect of *Chesapeake*'s supposed manning deficiency which does hold up under close examination is the inexperience and subsequent conduct of some of her junior officers. Of those who had served during her last cruise, the two senior lieutenants were unavailable through illness and only former third officer, Augustus Ludlow, was available for duty. Ludlow was appointed as first lieutenant, although he was barely twenty-one years of age and had never held that position before. George Budd, an officer of even less experience, was made second lieutenant, while two young midshipmen, Edward Ballard and William Cox, were given acting commissions as third and fourth lieutenants respectively. It was Cox who took Lawrence below after he sustained his second (mortal) wound and was subsequently court-martialled for failing to return to the deck afterwards, charged with cowardice, disobedience of orders, desertion from quarters, neglect of duty and un-officer-like conduct. He was exonerated on the first four charges and only found guilty of un-officer-like conduct, for which he was 'cashiered, and rendered forever incapable of serving the navy'.[13]

It is perhaps surprising that a substantially intact and powerful warship can be captured when a considerable proportion of her crew are unharmed and in a fit condition to continue the fight. However, once *Chesapeake*'s crew were contained below decks, they were virtually helpless. With the weather deck secured, *Shannon*'s boarders had total command of the vessel, including steerage via the helm, albeit disabled. The ship's means of propulsion, the sails, were managed solely from topside. This scenario was quite common in actions decided by boarding and there are countless other examples, not least that of Nelson himself when he took the mighty Spanish battleships *San Josef* and *San Nicolas* at the Battle of Cape St Vincent. In this case, *Shannon*'s precise gunnery had so devastated

---

13 Cox died in 1837. After a long campaign by his descendants, his conviction was overturned by Congress in 1952.

the *Chesapeake*'s command structure that in their disorder her crew were unable to mount serious resistance.

The only option for the remaining officers and crew of *Chesapeake*, imprisoned below decks, was to scuttle the vessel or blow her up. In fact, Lawrence, lying mortally wounded in the wardroom below, gave orders for the latter, but fortunately for the large body of men on board still alive (both American and English), these were ignored.

It has been argued that had Lawrence reduced the way on *Chesapeake* sufficiently early enough, without luffing as he came up with *Shannon*, the resulting gunnery exchange could well have resulted in a much closer outcome. I believe this would have only postponed the inevitable. *Shannon* was so well prepared in all respects that, barring some catastrophic accident, she would have achieved a comprehensive victory in any case, even if Broke had been unable to conclude the encounter as quickly as he did with his opportunistic boarding.

The following extract comes from the report on the action addressed to Captain the Hon Bladen Capel, Senior Naval Officer at Halifax, dated 6 June 1813 in Broke's name but almost certainly composed by another:

> No expressions . . . can do justice to my brave officers and crew; the calm courage they displayed during the cannonade, and the tremendous precision of their fire, could only be equalled by their ardour with which they rushed to the assault.

Broke's legacy

Victory is what counts in war and in a country brought up on a diet of near unbroken naval success in the Napoleonic conflict, Broke's remarkable victory over the Americans after the British Navy's three frigate defeats, counted for even more. Broke was made famous overnight and a grateful nation bestowed on him a hereditary baronetcy. Both immediately and later it was recognised that his success was largely due the care, forethought and planning he had put into his ship's preparation as well as his own skill and courage. As Mahan observed, 'no more thoroughly efficient ship of her class had been seen in the British Navy during twenty years war with France'.[14]

---

14 Mahan, *Sea Power in the War of 1812*, vol 2, p 133.

Interested parties began to look in detail at the ideas and methods Broke had developed on board *Shannon,* and the skilled breed of gunners he had trained. As her reputation for exceptional gunnery spread Broke was even ordered to exchange men from his gun crews into other ships to share their skill.

The achievement of Broke and his followers was to convince the service that a whole new order of accuracy was possible at sea using techniques derived from his methods and other officers soon began to imitate them. His ideas had clearly influenced his brother officers on the Halifax station. In October 1815 Admiral Codrington wrote: 'The *Tenedos* is quite in the Shannon style, and it is thought Captain Hyde Parker, who commands her, would on a similar occasion acquit himself *à la Broke'.*[15]

Broke's friend, brother officer on the Halifax station and fellow gunnery enthusiast Sir John Pechell adopted *Shannon'*s systematic exercise and target practice, and recommended that such methods should be adopted throughout the fleet. Such enthusiasm, however, was not universal, and in the post-war years St Vincent lamented the lack of attention to this vital aspect of naval skill: 'I hear the exercise of the great guns is laid aside, and is succeeded by a foolish frippery and useless ornament.'[16] Nonetheless Broke was recognised as the doyen of all matters relating to artillery at sea, and when Sir Howard Douglas was writing a treatise on naval gunnery in 1819, Broke responded generously and provided Douglas with invaluable material during a prolonged correspondence. The finished work was published in 1820 and large tracts of the text quoted Broke's words verbatim. It was a seminal work on naval gunnery and, even with the rapid technological advances in gun design, manufacture and ballistics in the nineteenth century, it remained relevant, continuing to be published with later amendments until the 1850s.

[Sir H Douglas's] treatise on naval gunnery will form an excellent code of instruction for our young officers in those sciences which so materially distinguish the Captain of a ship of War from the mere <u>intelligent navigator,</u> the <u>humane commander,</u> the <u>Pilot,</u> the

15 Gardiner, *The Naval War of 1812,* p 61.
16 Quoted in Bartlett, *Great Britain & Sea Power, 1815–1853.*

Astronomer & the <u>Accountant</u>, who is qualified to command a <u>large</u> <u>rich</u> <u>Merchant</u> <u>ship</u>.[17]

Even with the superb example Broke had set, as late as the third decade of the nineteenth century the Navy had no official policy regarding gunnery, no coordinated system for testing new techniques or weapons, and none for disseminating information about developments in gunnery science.

In January 1828, Broke was invited by the Admiralty to make suggestions with regard to gunnery practice and there was some discussion about using a guard-ship for the more intensive training of two or three hundred seamen gunners. Here was a faint anticipation of a naval gunnery training establishment. Sir Howard Douglas with his treatise had ignited the discussion about the need for such a facility of which Broke was a keen advocate. It was a project dear to his heart, and he had received much encouragement from those in a position to share his enthusiasm. Inevitably, not all were in favour. Writing to Pechell on 7 June 1819, he said:

much of the opposition . . . will be soon [be] overcome when <u>officers</u> <u>themselves will</u> <u>earnestly</u> instruct our men in a new system – the difficulty is to urge their zeal and attention & <u>to give them</u> the eager interest we feel in this important pursuit & which many of them in the triumphant state of our navy have deemed needless . . . [often] the <u>Gunner himself</u> has not an idea of <u>Gunnery beyond loading his guns</u> <u>& securing them in a gale of wind</u> . . . Our young students at the College should be most assiduously practiced in the proposed system [of gunnery] & taught that it is so important a branch of their study as navigation or astronomy.[18]

In 1829, a junior naval officer, Commander George Smith, presented detailed proposals for the very gunnery school that Broke and others had long been advocating and in June 1830 the Navy Board authorised the creation of just such a school with Smith himself as its first superintendent. The school was very aptly established in the venerable old hulk of *Excellent* in Portsmouth harbour. Formerly a 74-gun third

17 SRO HA93/9/311.
18 SRO HA93 9/301.

rate she had had a distinguished career, and had been commanded at the Battle of Cape St Vincent by Collingwood, one of the great gunnery enthusiasts of the Napoleonic War.

Under Smith's able leadership the school quickly established an excellent reputation for its professional tuition of seamen gunners and officers, and became recognised for its important role in the experimental testing of prototype guns. Later the school became established as a permanent shore-based facility on Whale Island. The training aboard *Excellent* was highly successful. The system created a permanent and highly trained corps of professional gunners, with the possibility of advancement by merit and a permanent career. These developments were truly revolutionary and laid the foundations for a far more modern and progressive navy.

In 1840, however, events occurred which confirmed the value of the school for even the most sceptical of older officers. In November of that year during the Syrian campaign British, Austrian and French squadrons were involved in the attack on a well-defended fortress at Acre. After a successful bombardment from the British ships one *Excellent*-trained officer observed:

> The very first broadsides were murderous . . . It is also an historical fact that for guns of that period, in wooden ships, something like perfection had been attained. Officers and men had been thoroughly trained under the newest system; and all matters connected with gunnery worked with the regularity of clocks.[19]

Broke died in January 1841 but he lived just long enough to be aware of the impressive British gunnery at Acre and he must have taken considerable satisfaction in the fulfilment of something he had worked so hard to achieve during his lifetime. Truly, Philip Broke was the godfather of the gunnery school at *Excellent*, and its creation and achievements stand as perhaps his greatest legacy.

Suggested Further Reading
Poolman, Kenneth, *Guns off Cape Ann* (1961).
Gardiner, Robert (ed), *The Naval War of 1812* (1998).

---

19 Lambert, *Trincomalee*, pp 63–4.

II

Broke's 'Miraculous' Recovery

Peter H Schurr

It is unfortunate that the description of Broke's wounds in the *Memoir of Admiral Broke* written in 1864 by Revd J G Brighton is inaccurate, for many later historians have based their comments on one of the few published accounts, accepting it as correct. It is therefore necessary to assemble the reliable facts and put others on one side.

May I take you back to the action in which two rolling-broadsides had been fired by the *Shannon* which now had the captured American frigate grappled to its side. 'Brave Broke', as he was later to be named, was leading a boarding party; they had reached the deck of the *Chesapeake* and were involved in close hand-to-hand fighting. The American Captain Lawrence, suffered two severe injuries, one of which later proved mortal, and had been carried below. Captain Broke was attacked 'from behind' by three men armed with a pike, a cutlass and a musket. He managed to parry the pike, which must therefore have been to one or other side; this upset his balance and he could not recover his guard before a cutlass was brought down on his head. This was followed by blows from the butt of a musket on both sides. Broke lost consciousness for a short time and was carried across the deck away from the fray; here a temporary dressing was put over his bleeding wounds before he was carefully taken back to his own ship. The surgeon of the *Shannon*, Mr Alexander Jack, would have known that quite severe bleeding from the scalp can readily be stopped by finger pressure on the sides of the wound, but much blood had been lost already. This turned to Broke's advantage since 'therapeutic bleeding', so prevalent at that time, was deemed unnecessary.

There is a fanciful description by Brighton of how 'the third American, having clubbed his musket, drave home his comrade's weapon until a large surface of the skull was cloven entirely away, the brain left bare'. This would have been after the manner of the expert egg-eater at breakfast who can slice off the top of a boiled egg with a single blow of his knife, exposing the yolk. I can say categorically that it did not happen. Fortunately, we have a factual description of the wound, represented by the healed scar nine years after the injury, from Sir Astley Cooper, the eminent surgeon from Guy's Hospital, who, consulted by Broke on account of another head injury, examined him in November 1822. Sir Astley describes how 'On the left side of the head the sabre cut has depressed the bone and compressed the brain' and he then explains how the edges of the broken bone had united to the skull. A corroborative and contemporary account by the ship's surgeon also reports a 'deep cut on the parietal bone, extending from the top of the head in a direction towards the ear, [the bone having been] penetrated for at least three inches in length' (see Figure 11.1).

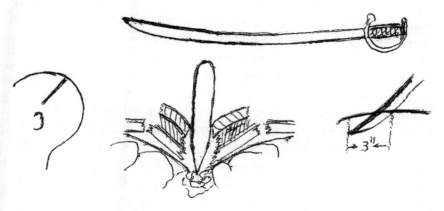

Fig 11.1 A cutlass and three aspects of Broke's head wound. (Sketch by the author).

We now have a comprehensible picture. As the cutlass (sabre) descended on the strong convex surface of the left side of the skull, between the ear and the top of the head, the bone would have shattered on both sides of the blade into fragments about the size of a twopence piece or less, creating a valley roughly three inches long. The sharp edges of the broken bone and the edge of the blade as well, would have cut into the coverings of the brain and breached its surface. As the cutlass was withdrawn, the fragments of bone probably closed in the depths of the wound, trapping some brain and membranes which might have been visible, though obscured by blood. The amount of brain exposed would have been very small (see Figure 11.1). Given the length of the scar, and by estimating the curvature of the weapon, we can guess the depth of the cut (see Figure 11.1). It cannot have been more than about an inch below the surface at its deepest part. However, the extent of the damage to the brain also depends on the amount of bleeding and bruising associated with the blow and torn tissues. A guide to the severity of the injury is the shortness of Broke's loss of consciousness and the relatively rapid recovery he made, which was almost complete apart from residual diminished sensation in his right hand and arm. In the early part of the nineteenth century it was known that damage to one hemisphere of the brain affected the opposite side of the body, but the localisation and mapping of brain function did not begin to take place until much later in the century. The wound overlay the part of the brain concerned with sensation, hence the permanent, though lessened, loss of feeling demonstrated by Sir Astley Cooper. The simple dressings that were applied were appropriate treatment for the time; today one might attempt to elevate or remove the in-driven bone and to explore the wound further, but the final result would not have been very different. The wound was severe but recoverable.

There is no suggestion that the wound became infected and the slow healing recorded was probably due to partial separation of the scalp edges, despite the adhesive strips used to bring them together, and we do not know if there was a subsequent leakage of fluid. Contemporary notes record that some powdered lime, possibly used to clean the decks, may have entered the wound. I think this is not likely and, far from being beneficial, it would have been a source of further injury to the tissues. We can surely presume that the wound had healed sufficiently for Broke to give up the use of a bandage when he wrote that he wore his hat at the end of August. Surely, too, he was bare-headed for the conferment of his baronetcy later in the same year.

Although Broke never returned to active service in the Navy, it is clear that he managed to live a fairly full life until he fell from his horse in early August 1820, seven years after the fight on the *Chesapeake*. The cause of this mishap is unknown. When Broke fell, his foot remained caught in the stirrup, so that he was dragged for a short distance before he could free himself. The side on which he fell is not stated but the right side of his face was grazed, so he may have fallen to his right. He was briefly 'stunned', but then able to walk a quarter of a mile to his mother's house. He subsequently remembered nothing of the walk; this was a consequence of concussion from the fall. He was bled by his local doctor and made a good recovery, apart from a new alteration of sensation on the *left* side of the body. Sir Astley Cooper attributed this to blood on the brain or its membranes on the right side – opposite to the old head injury, with which it does not appear to have been associated – and Sir Astley did not find any detectable sign of another fracture. It is also possible that the sensory disturbance came from a neck injury when he was being dragged by his horse, for the side of his face was pulled along the ground and, with his foot raised high in the stirrup, his neck must have been flexed strongly to the left. We cannot know exactly what happened and there is little point in speculating. Apart from the disturbance of sensation, he seems to have been well for about two years until he developed other unrelated problems.

In 1840, twenty years after the fall and twenty-seven years after the cutlass injury, we find him being prepared for an unspecified operation. We do not know its nature or his symptoms, but it might have been for difficulty in passing water or the presence of stones. His letters speak of a series of operations, none of which produced the promised cure, and sadly he died a month later on 2 January 1841.

Was his recovery after the cutlass injury 'miraculous'? I hope I have been able to show that, though serious, it was less damaging than had been thought at the time. Perhaps the miracle was that his clinicians put their faith in *Vis Medicatrix Naturae* – the healing power of Mother Nature, which is a frequent source of miracles even today.

OLD AGE

'When I came to reside here I found Sir Philip Broke living in great retirement, and almost entirely devoted to the care of your invalid mother, still suffering from his wounds, but always cheerful and with a smile upon his countenance, and a friendly greeting which set one at ease with him at once. He seemed very regardless of what are generally considered the comforts of life, and entirely so of its luxuries; but I knew that his hand was always open to those in need, of whatever class or calling they might be. . . . On coming into this part of Suffolk, I was pleased to observe the great affection with which he was regarded, and the enthusiasm with which my parishioners and others would speak of him, whom they justly regarded as their hero. I trust we shall long remember the example of his fortitude and resignation in suffering, his great cheerfulness, peaceableness, and constant endeavours to promote the welfare and happiness of all around him.'

Revd H Edgell (Rector of Nacton 1835–94) to Broke's eldest son, Rear Admiral Sir George Broke-Middleton, Bart (10 March 1864)

12

Representing Nations: Caricature and the Naval War of 1812

James Davey

For many British contemporaries the War of 1812 was distant and remote. Fought thousands of miles away, the conflict paled in comparison to the great struggle against Napoleonic France. And yet, a glance through the newspapers, pamphlets and parliamentary reports of the time suggests that the war gained an important place in the popular consciousness. In particular, it was the naval war that attracted British interest. The frigate defeats of 1812, covered elsewhere in this volume, brought shock and even panic to British observers accustomed to considering the Royal Navy an invincible institution, subsequent naval victories also garnered widespread attention. The *Shannon–Chesapeake* action of 1813, which re-established British naval confidence, was an important turning point in the way that the war was reported back home. Speaking in the aftermath of the victory, the radical writer William Cobbett observed that 'there is more boasting about this defeat of one American frigate than there used to be about the defeat of whole fleets'.[1] While the unprecedented naval mastery achieved after the Battle of Trafalgar had eliminated the need for large set-piece decisive battles, the British nation took solace in smaller, though no less important victories.

For the United States, the war holds a more prominent place in the annals of its national history. Often termed a 'Second War of Independence', the conflict was turbulent and threatening: American territory was invaded, and the presidential mansion burned. The war had many legacies, not least the creation of a national anthem and a century of westward expansion. For many American citizens, particularly those

---

1 *Political Register*, vol 24, p 73.

who inhabited the east coast, the course of the conflict was marked by events at sea. What had begun as a continental war for control of North America was quickly transformed into a maritime conflict. The American invasion of Canada soon became bogged down, and was ultimately repulsed. Instead, victories at sea were used by the United States government to maintain support for a war that had been met only with defeat and embarrassment on land. Americans turned to their navy, and its heroic commanders, for national icons. During the first year of the conflict, the only battles the United States won were at sea, despite a long-standing neglect of their navy.

For both nations, then, the naval war was increasingly prominent, reflected in ballads, newspapers, medals, paintings and prints. One type of visual culture was particularly well-suited to communicate the complexities of the conflict: caricature. Bringing together a journalistic concern for current affairs with highly sophisticated satirical imagery, caricatures were sometimes published within days of the events they depicted. They intervened directly in the formation of public opinion, and dealt with national stereotypes, government policy, and emerging notions of celebrity and heroism. Caricatures thus speak volumes about the attitudes and debates prevalent at the time, profoundly reflecting and affecting those who saw them.[2] Between 1770 and 1830, the golden age of graphic satire, there were approximately 20,000 satirical prints produced in Britain.[3] Each print could be produced in large numbers, and some of the most popular caricatures were printed in their thousands. Caricature developed as a pastime of politically literate, fashionable classes; print shops on the Strand, Oxford Street and Bond Street became centres of satirical print-selling. Cheaper, cruder caricatures, such as those produced by Thomas Tegg in Cheapside, catered for the lower end of the market and opened them up to a larger audience. As H Viztelly recorded in his memoirs:

> The shop windows of the London printsellers were the people's real picture galleries at this period, and always had their gaping crowds before them. The caricaturists of the day, representations of famous prize-fights, and Cruikshank's and Seymour's comic scetches [sic]

---

2 Donald, *The Age of Caricature*, pp 2, 7.
3 Gatrell, *City of Laughter*, p 9.

were most to the taste of the cognoscenti of the pavement . . . the only cheap prints people then had an opportunity of purchasing.[4]

Whether expensive or cheap, caricatures presented satirical images to a market, predominantly urban, and politically conscious. By relying on image, symbolism and allegory to communicate a message, caricatures were virtually immune to prosecution for sedition, libel or obscenity. Consequently, they convey much about the unspoken attitudes and fears of British people in a way that books, pamphlets or newspapers could not.

Caricatures were also exported overseas, not least to America, where a tradition of print satire began to develop. In the formative years of the American Republic, political caricature remained rare. Frank Weitenkampf counted only seventy-eight political caricatures issued before 1828. Newsprint was expensive and scarce, while engraving remained a difficult and time-consuming practice. The War of 1812, though, would witness a growing demand for print satire, with artists such as Amos Doolittle and William Charles becoming very popular. These colourful, immediate reactions to events of national importance helped shape an early sense of American national identity. In Britain too, the war gained considerable prominence in the minds of the British population. The country's most famous satirists, particularly George Cruikshank (who after the retirement of James Gillray in 1811 became the pre-eminent satirist in London) paid particular attention to the conflict. On both sides of the Atlantic caricatures were produced about the war that touched on broader issues: the importance of naval power, ideas about the nascent United States and democratic politics, the rules of warfare, and notions of patriotism and national character.

In Britain, the Navy and its exploits had long been a recurring and popular theme in caricature. Whether celebrating the Navy's senior commanders, or the complex figure of the British sailor 'Jack Tar', naval caricature flourished during the war against French Revolutionary and Napoleonic France.[5] It took time for the War of 1812 to capture the public imagination. *A Sketch for the REGENTS speech on MAD-ASS-SON'S insanity*, produced by George Cruikshank

4 Viztelly, *Glances Back Through Seventy Years*, vol 1, p 38.
5 Davey and Johns, *Broadsides*, p 3.

towards the end of 1812 (see Plate 7), made a rare mention of the war. In this print the angel Gabriel is shown blowing the message 'bad news for you' at the American President James Madison, who stands between Napoleon and the devil. The print focuses on General Hull's surrender of Detroit to the British commander, Sir Isaac Brock, on 16 August 1812. The caricature shows Britannia, ably assisted by a fearsome English lion that stands triumphantly, looking on while Madison tears his hair out in frustration. The crude pun on Madison's name in the title only emphasises British contempt for the American president. At the same time, the personification of America at the centre of the print appears to be reaching out for Britannia's shield, taking the form of 'Columbia'. In this, the 'true' America is making a plea for protection from Britain. The faint seascape in the background, and the symbolic presence of Britannia, are the only suggestions that the war of 1812 was also being fought on the waves.

Throughout 1812, the British public were given many reasons to doubt the competence and continuing relevance of the Navy. That year, the Royal Navy suffered a number of reverses in single-ship actions, news of which shocked many across the country. The first – the defeat of the British frigate *Guerrière* by the USS *Constitution* under Captain Isaac Hull – occurred on 19 August 1812 only three days after his uncle General Hull had surrendered. *The Times* of 10 October 1812 noted pointedly 'Never before in the history of the world did an English frigate strike to an American'. As news of further defeats arrived, newspapers bewailed 'Another British Frigate Taken by the Americans!' Following the subsequent loss of the frigate *Java*, *The Times* of 20 March 1813 grew more scornful, and detailed how the American victories had made them boastful and arrogant:

The public will learn with sentiments we shall not presume to anticipate, that a third British frigate has struck to an American . . . down to this moment not a single American frigate has struck her flag. They insult and laugh at our want of enterprise and vigour. They leave their ports when they please and return to them when it suits their convenience; they traverse the Atlantic; they beset the West India Islands; they advance to the very chops of the channel; they parade along the coast of South America: nothing chases, nothing intercepts, nothing engages them but to yield them triumph.

The former Foreign Secretary, George Canning, noted that 'the sacred spell of invincibility of the British navy was broken by those unfortunate captures'.[6]

It did not take long for the naval war in America to become the subject of parliamentary dispute. During the early months of 1813 both Whigs and Radicals urged for a public inquiry into the management of the war. On 4 May, the Earl of Darnley contrasted 'the success of our arms' on land with the nation's recent 'naval disasters'. Referring to reports of an action between the *Peacock* and the American *Hornet*, Darnley bemoaned the 'fresh disaster'. Two months later, in July 1813, the radical and unpredictable Lord Cochrane, a naval officer himself, made the firmest accusation yet, asserting that, 'during the present war with the United States of America, his Majesty's naval service has, in several instances, experienced defeat, in a manner and to a degree unexpected by this House, by the Admiralty, and by the Country at large'.[7] While this political opposition stood little chance of parliamentary success due to the Tory majority, disappointment and concern for the Navy abounded.

The news of the *Shannon*'s striking victory over the *Chesapeake* on 1 June 1813 therefore proved a considerable tonic, and saw the resurrection of support for the Navy. In the months that followed, newspapers rejoiced in the news. The *Liverpool Mercury* on 16 July 1813 noted the 'glorious retrieval of our naval reputation':

We do not recollect any naval occurrence which has excited so much expression of general congratulation, as the recent capture of one of the American ships of war. Compared with many other engagements between single vessels, it would, indeed, be ranked among the most distinguished for skill and intrepidity.

The newspaper noted with relish that the news of the victory came at the same time as Lord Cochrane's resolutions were brought to the public. Caricaturists seized the moment to produce patriotic satires that celebrated British achievement, and mocked American hubris.

In *British Valour and Yankee Boasting or, Shannon versus Chesapeake* (see Plate 6), Captain Broke and his boarding party of

6 *Hansard*, vol 24, cc 643, 18 February 1813.
7 *Hansard*, vol 26, cc 1102, 5 July 1813.

sailors and marines are shown on the deck of the *Chesapeake*. While the speed and intensity of the fighting is captured vividly by Cruikshank, the battle is used to make a broader point about national character. Broke is shown prominently, seizing an American sailor by the hair, demanding his surrender. On the far left, a young officer runs forward brandishing a Union Jack. British sailors are shown fighting, and defeating, all who stand in their way. One sailor takes Captain Lawrence round the neck and lifts him from the ground, squeezing him up against the mainmast. Another holds an American seaman by the pigtail and the seat of his trousers, preparing to throw 'these Lubberly Yankee Doodles' overboard. By contrast, the American sailors are shown running away, kneeling in surrender, being kicked into the sea, or being stabbed gruesomely with a bayonet.

The print's placement of British 'valour' in notable contrast to the 'Yankee Boasting' refers directly to the accusations of American arrogance that had so enraged *The Times* (and other commentators) months before. On 11 July 1813, in the radical newspaper *Examiner*, James Henry Leigh Hunt had described how the American nation was no longer thought of affectionately, but as uncouth and boorish:

> We do not think well of our former behaviour to the United States, and are inclined to think as highly as possible of the skill and gallantry of their sailors . . . but the Americans, on the strength of succeeding against a few vessels of inferior strength, have lately shewn a little too much of their nation's bad taste, by their vulgar and noisy boasting, and we are heartily glad to see this wholesome lesson afforded them.

The *Shannon–Chesapeake* action, then, was a turning point not only in the war itself, but in the way the war was represented back home. For the first time the conflict off the American coast was seen in a positive light by the British population. From that point on, Broke's action would be regularly referred to in caricatures, a constant reminder of a famous naval victory.

The increased prominence of the naval war is evident in the 1813 print *Preparing John Bull for General Congress* (see Plate 20) which satirised the failed 'Congress of Prague' that took place during the summer of 1813. This attempt to secure a peace in Europe was unsuccessful, and provoked considerable criticism in Britain. In this caricature the representative figure of the British people, John Bull, is shown as a latter-day Gulliver, attacked from different directions by a variety of different threats. His arm, representing Hanover, is carried off to Napoleon on the far right of the picture, leaving a gushing wound symbolising the vast subsidies paid by Britain to foreign nations. John Bull is notably distressed: 'Have mercy on me & do not send me thus maimed to congress', he cries with no apparent likelihood of rescue, 'I can hardly distinguish Friend from Foe in the severity of my sufferings'.

The War of 1812 is given a prominent position in the print, as is the recent victory of the *Shannon*. John Bull's right leg, labelled 'West Indies', is attacked by an American vessel, shrouded in smoke. An American naval officer cries: 'D—n that Bull Dog the Shannon he has gored the Cheesapeak. if the English Ministers will but keep him out of our way we'll pepper this leg'. A bulldog, representing the 'British Navy', is shown leaping towards the American vessel. He wears a muzzle, and demands for it to be taken off. These references refer to the opprobrium that was heaped upon the British ministry in the first half of 1813 for not reinforcing the American station. Darnley's May 1813 motion to the House of Lords had emphasised the small size of the British fleet stationed off the American coast, and argued that a larger force would have blockaded all of the Unites States' warships in port. This, he stated, 'might have prevented the disasters we now had to lament'. In his eyes, 'the heavy responsibility for the late disasters [rested] upon ministers'. Similarly, the government was attacked for not conducting the war strongly enough; admirals were sent to negotiate rather than make war. *The Times* had noted on 2 January: 'when Mr Madison's mad proclamation of war seemed to invite them to crush the American navy at a blow, they did not eagerly embrace the offer . . . no formal order to sink, burn and destroy was given to our Admiral.'

This vast and complex caricature is both patriotic and anxious. John Bull's position is precarious, attacked from all sides. What is also notable, though, is the prominence given to the naval aspects of the War of 1812, and the detailed and complex references to recent political events. This sophisticated print was designed to be viewed by a population who acknowledged and understood the potential threat Britain faced across the Atlantic. While the reference to the *Shannon–Chesapeake* was an easy nod to a recent triumph, John Bull's perilous position suggested a more concerning present reality.

Other caricatures would use the *Shannon*'s victory in a more straightforward manner. There is little ambiguity in *The Yankey Torpedo*, which was published towards the end of 1813 (see Plate 8). Cruder and more immediate than *Preparing John Bull for General Congress*, William Elmes' imaginative and violent caricature shows Jack Tar presenting his posterior to an American cannon-spewing sea monster. 'I'll give you a taste of the Shannon and send you down to old Davy,' he threatens. The print was inspired by a new invention devised by the American engineer Robert Fulton: a sloop was filled with gunpowder, ignited by clockwork, taking the form of a primitive torpedo. It was used in 1813 during the defence of New York, and its attack on the accepted rules of naval engagement caused great indignation in Britain. Elmes represents the new threat of Fulton's invention, and brings together the weapons of conventional warfare with a terrifying sea monster, the Devil and Death.[8] Once again, the print calls into question the character of Americans, here shown to be devious and ruthless, rather than the vulgar boasters of *British Valour and Yankee Boasting or, Shannon versus Chesapeake*.

Nowhere was the denigration of American national character made more obvious than in the representation of the United States' president, James Madison. The vilification of a foreign leader was nothing new. Over the previous decade, Napoleon Bonaparte had emerged as a figure of hate and fun in Britain. Shown as a diminutive character, dwarfed by his hat (and often by his wife), Napoleon was a particular focus of patriotic British satire. Caricaturists saw in Madison another figure who could be lampooned at will. In the 1814 print *Boney and Maddy Gone to Pot* (see Plate 9), Napoleon and Madison are shown together, comparing their respective fortunes. Napoleon is noticeably shorter, and angrily clutches papers ordering his immediate exile to Elba, a consequence of his battlefield defeat in 1814. He is saying, 'you See its all dicky with me. They have sent me to Pot.' Madison fears the worst, knowing that the full might of the British armed forces would shortly be coming his way. As he comments, 'soon I fear it will be all dicky with me. they will send me to pot too'. Madison is shown aping Napoleon's posture and angry gesture in a way that makes him appear

---

8 Davey and Johns, *Broadsides*, p 63.

even more ridiculous. Both individuals are seated on a commode made under 'John Bull Patent'. The toilet humour lowered the tone, and emphasised the reality of the two leaders' situation.

Months later, the British raid on Washington presented another opportunity to mock the American president. During the attack, the capital was temporarily occupied by British troops and a series of government buildings, including the presidential mansion, were burnt. *The Fall of Washington – Or Maddy in full flight* (see Plate 21), delighted in the story – circulated widely at the time – that the raid on the capital had forced President Madison to abandon a celebratory dinner, laid out in honour for an expected American victory. The irony of this reverse, and his apparent inability to prevent the raid, is brought forth to great comic effect. Madison and one of his ministers are shown fleeing from the burning ruins of Washington. They carry strategic plans in their hands, but many fall to the ground, demonstrating (as if the burning of the capital was not enough) the disastrous course of the war. Madison's partner, possibly Armstrong, the Secretary of War, holds papers inscribed with plans that had come to nought, not least the 'Project for the conquest of Canada'. He looks at Madison, forlornly concerned about his missed supper. More pertinently, the fleeing minister notes that 'the people won't stand any thing after This'. Following the raid on Washington, Armstrong was forced to resign.

This print shows Madison, again, as a vassal of Napoleon. In the left background, American spectators nonchalantly predict that he will soon be rushing off to join Napoleon in Elba, repeating the theme of *Boney and Maddy Gone to Pot*. Madison is portrayed in stark contrast to his heroic predecessors as president. One onlooker remarks: 'The great Washington fought for Liberty, but we are fighting for shadows.' Madison is also contrasted with the American citizens standing in the background, depicted as Quakers, with lank hair and broad-brimmed hats.[9] One, stood behind, points to the flames, saying, 'I suppose this is what Maddis [sic] calls benefiting his Country!' The other responds: 'Why it will throw such a light on affairs that we shall find it necessary to change both men and measures.' It was well known in Britain that many Americans, especially in New England, were

---

9 George, *Catalogue of Political and Personal Satires in the British Museum*, vol IX (1949).

opposed to the war. Madison is shown opposing the true interests of America and Americans.

The representation of the United States in British political caricature had changed dramatically during the last years of the eighteenth century. British caricaturists – from whom American artists of the time lifted almost all of their symbols, figures, and even whole caricatures – had in the past preferred to depict the United States as an Indian warrior or maiden, 'Columbia'. Increasingly though, during the 1770s 'Brother Jonathan' appeared as a second representation of the American people. As early as 1776 an English political cartoon had depicted 'Brother Jonathan' defending the breastworks at Bunker Hill. This figure was initially identified with the disruptive, politically radical elements in American society. However, he was very different from the aggressive, xenophobic representations of Frenchmen that emerged in the 1790s. Generally shown as emaciated, treasonous and anarchic individuals, there was nothing subtle, or indeed friendly, about the way the French were shown in British caricature. By contrast, 'Brother Jonathan' was drawn as a 'son' of John Bull; he was part of the British family.[10]

As America developed its own line of political caricature, 'Brother Jonathan' was reimagined. This became particularly true during the War of 1812, when the virtuous Yankee, embodied by the rustic Brother Jonathan, was shown resisting the corpulent and corrupt John Bull.[11] In *Brother Jonathan Administering a Salutary Cordial to John Bull* (see Plate 10), a spritely American is shown pouring Perry down the throat of a British army officer: 'Take it, Johnny – take it I say – why can't you take it?' he cries, to John Bull's consternation, while naval ships fire in the background. The print, produced by the American artist Amos Doolittle, commemorated Captain Perry's success against the British on the Great Lakes. While the punning wordplay and patriotic message were typical of British political caricature, the artist reinvents these themes in a fundamentally American context. Brother Jonathan is shown as a republican figure, a model citizen of virtuous restraint, and the young and vigorous embodiment of America.[12]

The War of 1812 presented a slew of opportunities to refine and disseminate an idea of American character, departing from its British

---

10 Morgan, *An American Icon*, pp 65–8.
11 Conforti, *Imagining New England*, p 153.
12 Morgan, *An American Icon*, pp 69–70.

genealogy. It also gave American caricaturists the rhetorical space to begin developing their own tradition of visual satire. William Charles, a Scottish immigrant to the United States, was the most prominent draughtsman making satirical prints about the war. Having emigrated to New York in 1806, he then moved to Philadelphia, and published a series of caricatures that brought him fame as the first American political cartoonist. While his debt to the British artists Gillray and Rowlandson is obvious, his 'earthy humour' was distinctive and very popular. Almost all of Charles' two or three dozen caricatures dealt with the War of 1812.[13] In *Bruin become Mediator or Negociation for Peace* (see Plate 22), a bear, representing Russia, seeks agreement between John Bull and Columbia. Columbia rejects peace, since John Bull has not withdrawn his horns, labelled 'Orders-in-Council', a direct reference to the supposed cause of the war. In response, John Bull complains of the stings of 'Wasps and Hornets', references to the *Hornet*'s defeat of the British vessel *Peacock* in February 1813, and the *Wasp*'s fight with the British sloop *Frolic* in October 1812. The ships' fortuitous names prompted an outpouring of patriotic American satire, showing discomforted British figures being attacked by huge, outsize insects.[14] In a nation increasingly imbued with a sense of its maritime prowess, it mattered little that the *Frolic* had been almost immediately re-captured, and the *Wasp* ultimately forced to surrender.

While often rude and sometimes shocking, the caricatures produced on both sides of the Atlantic during the War of 1812 were not as hostile as others made at the time. American caricaturists, almost without exception, reserved their harshest criticism for George III, rather than Parliament or the British population. British caricaturists, too, refrained from promoting a representation of America that was uniformly offensive; they saved their revulsion for the enemy across the English Channel. Instead, pictorial satire of the period reveals much more about the way each nation saw itself. In the United States, the growth of print satire symbolised characteristics intrinsic to the new nation. Based around the figures of 'Columbia' and 'Brother Jonathan', or his

---

13 Hess and Kaplan, *The Ungentlemanly Art*, p 63.
14 See also *Wasp Taking A Frolic, John Bull stung to agony by the Wasp and Hornet; John Bull threatened by insects from all quarters*; and *The Hornet and Peacock, or, John Bull in distress*.

later relation 'Uncle Sam', the country's naval exploits would create an ideal of American identity. In this, caricature made an important and lasting contribution to the process of nation-building.

For Britain, national character would be depicted directly through its naval personnel. While officers such as Broke achieved great fame, increasingly the British sailor was used to show fundamental British values. In the *Liverpool Mercury*'s account on 16 July 1813 of the *Shannon–Chesapeake* action, it was the men of the lower deck that had gained the most fulsome praise:

> The combat was begun with calm and deliberate determination; and when it was suddenly decided by the British seamen boarding their adversary, the manly and collected spirit of British valour and discipline was particularly distinguished. It was in this, that the real superiority of our navy over that of America, or of any other country is chiefly conspicuous.

The brave, unbending character of the British seaman became a powerful example of British identity. Shorn of grace or intellectualism, the sailor stood for valour, stubbornness, manliness – characteristics that were considered essential for national security and well-being. The British sailor at the centre of *The Yankey Torpedo* is brash and simple: his importance to British prospects in the face of new and unpleasant dangers is evident. Looking at *The fall of Washington – or Maddy in full flight*, it is not Admiral Cockburn shown raiding the city, but two British sailors, prominent in their blue coats. Madison's cowardice and incompetence are watched in unrestrained glee, as they mock the abortive American attempts to undermine British power.

Caricature, then, helped shape how both American and British people saw themselves and their place in the world. It also played a crucial role in spreading news and opinions about the War of 1812 across both nations. These prints demonstrate a high level of familiarity with the key events of the war. When caricaturists spoke of the 'Shannon', or the 'Chesapeake', or even the 'Wasp' and 'Hornet', they used words in the public domain, easily recognisable to those that read them. It was this widespread comprehension that allowed artists on both sides of the Atlantic to use to the naval war to forward their own ideas about national character.

Suggested Further Reading

Davey, James and Johns, Richard, *Broadsides: Caricature and the Navy 1756–1815* (2012).
Donald, Diana, *The Age of Caricature* (1996).
Hess, Stephen and Kaplan, Milton, *The Ungentlemanly Art: A History of American Political Cartoons* (1968).
Morgan, Winfred, *An American Icon: Brother Jonathan and American Identity* (1988).

I would like to thank Martin Salmon, Richard Johns and Joshua Newton for their helpful suggestions and comments when writing this piece.

13
Halifax and its Naval Yard

Julian Gwyn

The Halifax naval yard, with which Captain Philip Broke became familiar, had served as the base for the North American Squadron since construction began in 1758 during the Seven Years War. It was built cheaply by 1763 for £8,000, which was less than the cost of building a small frigate at the time. The yard became extremely useful following the violent incident between the *Chesapeake* and Royal Navy *Leopard* in 1807, which ushered in a period of heightened tension. War with the United States was not expected by the Admiralty while Napoleon dominated most of Europe. Nor were there forces available for a strategy of deterrence to overawe the hostile American administration. With no substantial addition made to the strength of the squadron, there was little need to augment the size of the workforce in the Halifax yard. President Madison's declaration of war in June 1812 at first changed surprisingly little, until the full scope of Napoleon's disastrous March on Moscow and Russia's re-entry into the European war was grasped in London. Britain's Baltic Fleet, her second largest, could then be stood down and British troops and ships be released from Europe to make the slow passage across the Atlantic to Halifax. Even after Wellington's great victory at Vitoria that same June, the famous Duke was complaining to the Admiralty of a lack of naval support and an admiral had to be sent out to Spain to mollify him.

At the outbreak of war with the United States the yard consisted of thirty-three major buildings and a dozen more minor structures, all of which were surrounded by two kilometres of ten-foot stone walls. Included within the walls were a mansion and stables for the resident commissioner, begun in 1785, where Broke came to recuperate in 1813. In addition, there was an array of large storehouses, two built of stone, a stone capstan house, a mast house, a boathouse and offices. Handsome houses for the naval officer, master attendant and master shipwright were erected in 1793. The yard lacked a chapel, common in British naval yards elsewhere. There was, however, a hospital with three wings built in 1783 of wood, and nearby a fine residence for the hospital's agent, surgeon and dispenser built in 1815. The burial ground nearby had to be enlarged by one-third in 1813 because of the war. On the yard's waterside there were nine wharves, among them were two for careening, an anchor wharf, a watering wharf and a hospital wharf. There were two mast ponds at the north and south ends of the yard. A powder magazine for the Navy was built in 1813 at the north end of the yard by the royal engineers. In the beginning the yard was more than a kilometre beyond the northerly limits of Halifax, a small town first established in 1749. By Philip Broke's day the town's northern suburbs had reached the yard, bringing with them a number of grog shops and houses of ill repute, as well as the homes of some of the yard workers. During the war with the United States, Halifax was home to perhaps 12,000 civilians, besides the military and naval personnel. By 1815 the town was growing uncomfortably close to the southern boundary of the yard and a 150-foot lot was purchased as a firebreak against 'the great increase in building there, which is entirely of wood'.

Halifax, besides being the seat of government, boasted a new residence for the lieutenant governor, a House of Assembly also in a new stone building, a supreme court, and a vice-admiralty court. Its principal business was overseas commerce but the colony's exports were annually dwarfed by the value of her imports. This unfavourable trade balance was largely offset by British government spending in the colony. For the war years, 1793 through 1815, this averaged annually about £250,000. During the American war, on average 530 merchant vessels entered Halifax harbour annually, totalling 73,500 tons. This represented a doubling of tonnage when compared to 1808–10. So successful were the Navy and Nova Scotia's privateers in capturing American vessels that there was a dampening effect on shipbuilding. Only 2,650 tons were launched annually in Nova Scotia in 1812–15. These boom years were remembered a quarter-century later when a legislative committee wrote: 'Halifax may yet become in peace, what it was in the years 1812 to 1815, during the American War'. This did not happen until the late 1850s and part of the 1860s.

In 1812 the Halifax yard was the only fully operational site in North

America where British warships could refit and resupply. The work of refitting at Halifax focused on external hull repairs 'limited to what could be tackled on the careen'. This meant careening, caulking, repairs to the ship's keel and rudder, and replacing damaged masts, bowsprits, yards, spars, plank, copper, rigging and sails. The Halifax yard, like those built in the 1730s and 1740s on Jamaica and Antigua, was not intended for shipbuilding, and hence no dry dock was established. This remained the work of the home yards in England, which also carried out major rebuilding of heavily damaged or worn-out warships. Nevertheless, two small vessels were built at the Halifax careening yard: sloop *Halifax* (22 guns) launched in 1806 and gun brig *Plumper* (12 guns) in 1807.

At its busiest during the American War the Halifax yard employed fewer than 270 men, five of them officers, not counting the hospital staff. If this was the largest industrial site in British North America, it remained one of the smallest of Britain's overseas bases, with far fewer workers than Antigua, Jamaica, Gibraltar, Madras, Malta and Trincomalee. The only smaller ones were the new bases at the Cape of Good Hope and Kingston in Upper Canada.

The Admiralty Board's decision to erect a major yard at Ireland Island in Bermuda cast a shadow over the Halifax naval yard. The deep-water passage there had been discovered in 1794 during the survey of the Bermuda islands ordered by the Admiralty Board. In 1809 Admiral Warren successfully urged the Admiralty to build a new large naval yard at Ireland Island by pointing out that, compared to Halifax, it was 'so much nearer the cruising ground of the enemy and Halifax so difficult of access during the winter'. Though built against the French, the new yard was used, when still under construction, against the Americans. While the war lasted it increased pressure on the Halifax yard, all sorts of supplies having to be shipped there, for Bermuda was deficient in almost all the necessary building materials. Among other items, the Halifax yard shipped oak timber for the careening pits as well as several prefabricated buildings. It also sent a transport ship to freight hemlock piles from Miramichi in New Brunswick for the wharf, and pine timber and deals for the capstan house and other buildings.

The yard, since 1775, had a naval officer for its Resident Commissioner. In 1812 this was Captain John Inglefield, who had served in

Halifax since 1803. Earlier he had been commissioner in the Corsica, Malta and Gibraltar yards. Earl St Vincent had described him as 'honest and sufficiently intelligent, but pompous, flowery, indolent and wrapped up in official forms, staytape and buckram'. Inglefield retired in 1812 as a senior captain. His replacement was Captain Philip Wodehouse, the younger son of John, First Baron Wodehouse. Promoted rear admiral when the yard was closed in 1819, Wodehouse was the most popular commissioner among those who held that office, if the farewell messages he received at his departure from Halifax are any indication.

This intelligent, warm and kind-hearted man held a special place in the affections of his officers, clerks, artificers and ordinary labourers, while he admired the 'zeal, attention and ability' of the workforce dominated by native Nova Scotians. Nevertheless, the rapid inflation in Halifax, which characterised the American war, led Wodehouse to believe that he was 'very inadequately paid'. Still, his income as commissioner was equivalent to that of the Bishop of Nova Scotia.

Perhaps three-quarters of the labour force and six of the seven foremen were the direct responsibility of the master shipwright, who oversaw the repair of ships and the building and maintenance of the yard buildings, wharves, walls and breastwork. The veteran master shipwright in 1812 was Welsh-born William Hughes. Brought up in Deptford Yard, in 1775 he had volunteered to work in Halifax, where he spent the rest of his life. He died in office in 1813. His replacement, who carried a heavier burden of work than any previous master shipwright, was Thomas Hawkes who was promoted from Deptford, where he acted as foreman of the yard.

Responsible for the smooth management of the paperwork was the naval officer, also known by his former title of naval storekeeper. Not only did he submit ten monthly, nine quarterly and eight annual reports, his principal task was the efficient handling of naval stores sent to the yard by the Navy Board and the timely submission of requisitions for replacement stores. He kept the cash chest to pay the yard workers and local suppliers. He drafted advertisements for newspapers when tenders were announced to secure locally available supplies not provided by the Navy Board. He prepared and oversaw the contracts which resulted. During the extreme hurry of the years 1812–15, the office was filled by Daniel Dawes, who had arrived in Halifax in 1803, having served as purser of *Dreadnought*.

With the threat of war with the United States in the spring of 1812 the admiral ordered yard personnel to form a yard battalion. From the beginning of May, part of every afternoon was spent in military training. The battalion volunteers were outfitted in blue jackets, white pantaloons or trousers, round hat, cockade and white feathers, black neckerchief and quarter gaiters. When inspected by the admiral and the lieutenant governor the parade was congratulated on their 'regularity and good conduct'. Their training was never put to the test.

When President Madison declared war in June 1812 not only was the fleet based in Halifax greatly augmented, though not for many months, but simultaneously there was an increased demand for skilled workers. Wage rates paid in the yard could not compete with those current on the Halifax commercial waterfront. Shipwrights and caulkers, as an example of the best paid, by 1814 received a daily wage of ten to twelve shillings from commercial ship owners, while Nova Scotians working in the yard received only five shillings. In the last year of the war, some forty artificers, mainly scarce shipwrights, left the yard, some of them even departing for the United States.

In the twelve months before the outbreak of hostilities with the United States, on average 199 men were at work in the yard. During the thirty months of war the monthly average rose to 241, a 21 per cent increase. In case the war should continue into 1815, Commissioner Wodehouse requested an additional fifty shipwright-caulkers from Britain to handle the anticipated increased workload. The size of the fleet – squadron is hardly a suitable description at that moment – rose to more than 120 ships of all sizes. Before the war, the average time to refit a ship was a month; with two careening wharves, this meant perhaps twenty-four ships per year.

There were other duties undertaken by the yard during 1812 and 1813. Heavy use of the naval hospital during the war with the United States caused constant demands for a wide range of repairs and improvements. As another example, transports fitted out to carry soldiers to Halifax had to be converted into cattle boats to ship bullocks and hay for the use of the Bermuda careening yard. Moreover, among the hundreds of American vessels captured by the fleet, some were commissioned into the Navy and had to be valued. Among these was *Chesapeake*. Valued at £19,183 2s 9d, she underwent necessary repairs for a summer's crossing to Portsmouth. To this evaluation the

Navy Board took exception, as they did with a number of other captured American vessels – though the difference between the Halifax estimates and those made at Portsmouth was rarely more than 1 per cent, hardly worth the Board's trouble and vindicating the valuers in the Halifax yard.

Some six warships a month in the Halifax yard could be loaded for a six months' voyage under normal conditions. Unloading storeships from England as well as provisioning warships before sailing could not be undertaken by the 'people of the yard' without considerable outside help. Working parties of seamen were regularly recruited to help. The pay scale since 1806 was determined by the Navy Board. A sailor could earn sixpence a day, a boatswain's mate ninepence, a midshipman one shilling, and a lieutenant two shillings and sixpence, to be paid by the yard's naval storekeeper.

During the war few repairs were undertaken on yard structures, as priority was given to warships. In 1815 the commissioner described the yard buildings, especially the storehouses and wharves, as 'in the most defective state'. Some of the beams in the slop loft had given way and the joists and floors of the principal storehouses needed repairs. The yard's storehouses were then bursting from the enormous quantities of supplies needed by the much-expanded North American fleet. Already part of both the cavernous mast house and boathouse had been converted to storehouses. To respond to the emergency, it was decided to raise the roof of the storehouse built in 1771, so as to add a ten-foot high storey.

In addition, many of the wharves were in poor shape. Hawkes reported that the North Wharf which formed part of the north mast pond, was 'so settled in one part that the high spring tides flow over it', and allowed spars to escape into the harbour. Similarly, the anchor wharf was partly awash in a ruinous state by 1814, while the anchor wharf's wooden crane, acquired in 1783, was in little better condition. He recommended that the crane be replaced by a modern one similar to those then common in the English naval yards. The Navy Board's authorisation to undertake their repair was delayed until 1816.

Instead, despite the wartime pressure on the yard, two new buildings were planned. The first was a modest house for the boatswain, an officer who was generally employed afloat and frequently at night. As the Navy Board had authorised a similar request from the yard at the

Cape of Good Hope, approval was promptly given and the house was built as the war raged. The second was a mansion for the admiral, built without the benefit of an architectural design. The Admiralty was keen to spend the money since the £3,000 had been allocated by Parliament in 1811, though tenders were called for only late in 1814. Construction began in 1815 on an eight-acre site on the hillside above the hospital and at some distance from the burial ground.

In conclusion, from late 1813 to the war's end in the spring of 1815, the undermanned Halifax yard was almost overwhelmed. With the help of the naval base in Bermuda, then still under construction, the Halifax naval yard dealt effectively with most of the fleet's problems of refitting, repair and supply. The Admiral's House survives today as a handsome museum, while some of the yard's early structures were badly damaged in the 1917 Halifax harbour explosion. The rest of the eighteenth-century buildings were demolished by the Royal Canadian Navy in 1941 in the midst of the Battle of the Atlantic in the 1939–1945 war.

Suggested Further Reading

Gwyn, Julian, *Excessive Expectations: Maritime Commerce and the Economic Development of Nova Scotia* (1998).

Gwyn, Julian, *Ashore and Afloat: The British Navy and the Halifax Naval Yard to 1820* (2004).

WICKEDNESS!

'Our armies have prospered so much in Canada; had <u>we</u> done as well, these spiteful renegades would be cringing for peace; but our blockades are forming, and they will soon learn who commands the ocean. It will be a pious work to chastise them for it for it will soon lead to peace; and, after tasting the miseries of war they will recollect that they are <u>the only people</u> who might have enjoyed the blessing of peace without danger or dishonour. They are most absurdly wicked. <u>God</u> mend them.'

Broke to Loo (20 May 1813)

14

HMS *Shannon*'s Later Commissions

Martin Salmon

The immediate aftermath of the battle left both the *Shannon* and *Chesapeake* damaged and vulnerable. Having sent away the *Tenedos*, it was fortunate that Broke's bid to bring the *Chesapeake* out of Boston did not also bring the arrival of Broke's long anticipated meeting with Commodore Rodgers and his squadron. They had left Boston three weeks earlier hoping to intercept a West Indies convoy. Broke would learn only later that the *Shannon*'s victory was just one part of a day that saw a third of the US frigates put out of action as the *United States* and *Macedonian* were chased into New London and would not get to sea again for the rest of the war. The return to Halifax took five days, where the *Shannon*'s log records that as she entered the harbour she 'received several cheers from inhabitants as likewise from HM ships & vessels'.[1] After landing the wounded, including her captain, repair work on the ship began almost immediately and over the following six weeks stores, masts, yards, bowsprit, anchors and ballast were all removed while the ship was moored alongside the dockyard. Parties were frequently sent on board the *Chesapeake* where similar work continued.

The work on both vessels continued and HMS *Chesapeake* was commissioned into the Royal Navy on 14 July. Throughout August, while Broke convalesced, the *Shannon*'s damaged masts were replaced and the frigate was recaulked, as fifty-seven shipwrights and caulkers arrived on board to begin the process of refitting. On 19 August, the work was nearing completion and the log records 126 gallons of spruce beer were taken on board.

On 5 September, the *Shannon* left on a short cruise under the temporary command of Captain Humphrey Senhouse. In part a

---

1 Captain's Log, HMS *Shannon*, 6 June 1813: ADM 51/2861.

shakedown cruise to ensure the 158 rounds of shot the *Chesapeake* had hurled at the *Shannon* had done no deeper damage, this was also a reminder that the war went on and would not wait for convalescing captains. Broke observed to Loo, in a letter dated 5 September: '*Shannon* has just gone to sea; success to her for Senhouse and my old crew's sake'. Three weeks later he wrote: 'Senhouse is just going to sea on a good cruising ground and he always takes prizes.' Broke's confidence was not misplaced. On 15 September they had boarded a brig and two ships. The log records 'allowed the brig to proceed; detained the two ships, sending officers and men on board'. Three days later on the return to Halifax, they captured an even greater prize, the American privateer *Elbridge Gary*, together with the schooner *Queen Charlotte*, which had been captured by the privateer.

The voyage had been a success and preparations were made for the return to England. On 4 October, the *Shannon* sailed with Broke and a convoy of thirteen merchant ships. Designed to protect merchant shipping from American privateers, the convoy could only proceed at the speed of the slowest ship. Despite the significant penalties for speeding on ahead at risk of capture, some of the merchantmen had no intention of waiting for the slower sailers. Three days later the log records only '8 sail of convoy in sight, the others having kept way . . . at a greater rate of sailing they must have parted company intentionally'. In poor weather and low visibility, shepherding the convoy was thankless work with repeated entries in the log such as 'made the signal to make more sail; not the least attended to by the ship *Meteorite*'. Despite the headaches caused by his wound, Broke's regime of exercising the main-deck guns continued almost daily. On 19 October, they chased a strange sail which turned out to be a brig en route from Poole to Newfoundland who had lost her own convoy. A week later nearing British waters they met another brig, this time heading from Gibraltar to Greenock. Two days later land was sighted and the signal was made for the merchantmen bound for Greenock and the Bristol Channel to separate. On 2 November, the *Shannon* finally arrived at Spithead after a passage of twenty-six days. Broke's own correspondence shows that the first thing he did was to write to Loo: 'I am finally here'. But the log was not the place for his thoughts on leaving the *Shannon*, his home for virtually seven years and a stage for the fight of his life. Three days later the log recorded that the *Shannon* fired her last 'salute of 21 guns in commemoration of [the] gunpowder plot'. The following day the powder hoy came alongside and the powder was removed.

Much as at Halifax in June, the following month was occupied removing the stores, masts, yards, sails, anchors and ballast. On 17 November, the ship's company were mustered and the Articles of War read. As the last stores and ballast were unloaded, the final log entry reads 'came alongside two tenders to transport the ship's company to HM ship *Prince*. At noon light breezes and cloudy. Hauled the colours down. [signed] PBV Broke, Captain.'[2] Like so many other ships after the peace of 1815, the *Shannon* was laid up 'in ordinary' for many years. Between 1815 and 1817 she underwent a 'middling to large' repair at Chatham costing £26,328, perhaps correcting the last of the damage of June 1813 and again a 'very small repair' (costing £4,969) at Chatham in 1826.

Then in 1828, after almost fifteen years of inactivity, the *Shannon* was again prepared for sea. Recommissioned under Captain Benjamin Clements, she was sent to the Caribbean (see Figure 14.1). The station's main concern was the suppression of piracy and anti-slavery operations. There she spent the next three years before finally returning

Fig 14.1 The *Shannon* at Curaçao, by George Pechell Mends.

---

2 Captain's Log, 29 November.

in 1831. Her sailing days over, she was fitted as a receiving ship and hulk at Sheerness. In 1841 Broke himself died and a few years later the *Shannon* suffered the final indignity of being stripped of her name. While little more than a floating warehouse, the old *Shannon* rode at anchor on the Medway and her name still had a powerful and inspiring aura the Navy needed. In 1844 a new screw frigate was ordered. It was to be christened *Shannon*, so the decaying wooden frigate on the Medway became the *St Lawrence* (see Figure 14.2). As a new name it at least recalled a river and a shallow allusion to the North American waters she had made her own. What she could never be separated from was her reputation. In this and another drawing from on board the ship, the artist George Pechell Mends refers to her as 'old Shannon', despite her new name. To the end of her days the frigate built at Brindley's yard in 1806 remained inextricably linked with 'an Irish river and an English Broke', the famous naval toast.

The *Shannon*'s end finally came in 1859 when, as the *St Lawrence*, she was broken up at Chatham. Throughout the year the *Illustrated London News* was bursting with news of Victorian enterprise and endeavour. After fourteen years news finally came of the fate of Sir John Franklin's lost expedition for the Northwest Passage. At Portsmouth, the three-decker *Victoria* was launched, watched by the Queen, the royal family and an immense crowd. While the *Victoria* was fitted with a screw propeller and steam engines, no one could have known she would be the last wooden warship to carry an admiral's flag. At the

Fig 14.2 The *Shannon* as the *St Lawrence*, a hulk at Sheerness, 4 September 1844.

Thames Ironworks, the finishing touches were being put to Britain's first ironclad, the *Warrior*. The new era was defined further by the giant new steamship *Great Eastern*, larger than any vessel ever seen. Amid these developments no mention was made of the final passing of one of the vessels that had helped to establish British maritime supremacy. Only the *Chatham News* of 19 November thought it worth notice: 'The St Lawrence, formerly the renowned Shannon, has been completely broken up.'

While the *Shannon* enjoyed a long and successful career spanning over half a century, her breaking up was not the last link with the frigates of Nelson's time. Restored and still afloat in 2013 in Hartlepool (see Plate 23), the Bombay-built teak frigate *Trincomalee* was built in 1817. Based on the captured French *Hebe* of 1796, both the *Trincomalee* and Broke's *Shannon* were built to the same *Leda*-class design. A visit to Hartlepool and a walk onboard the *Trincomalee* is as near as we can get to sharing Broke's long years with his 'wooden wife' and those fifteen crucial minutes off Boston, two hundred years ago.

15

Chesapeake Mill

John Wain

In April 2002, fourteen individuals paid a visit to the Chesapeake Mill in an attempt to investigate the lack of progress in preserving this historic building which incorporates the timbers of HMS *Chesapeake*, the former US frigate. The meeting gave birth to the Britannia Naval Research Association which has become closely identified with the promotion of interest in the history of this remarkable watermill which lies upon the river Meon in the village of Wickham in Hampshire, England. Two years earlier, in May 2000, Dr Alan Flanders, a US naval historian, and I arrived in Wickham on a common quest to identify the building that had been referred to in various books and even mentioned on the back of an old cigarette card. We found local people to be ignorant of the Chesapeake Mill and its significant naval history.

Nestled on the Meon mill stream this square, symmetrical building sits under a red-tiled mansard roof. Closed though it was on the day of our first visit, and in a disused state, we peered through dirty windows and could see at once the very timbers that we had come to find. They were recognisably ship's deck beams exhibiting joint housings just begging to be measured and recorded!

The mill owner, Bruce Tappenden, gave us an impromptu tour of the building and we were soon under the spell of the 'Unlucky Chesapeake', as it has become known down two centuries.

The ships' timbers retained in the mill are historically important as so much primary evidence supports their provenance. The incorporation of ships' timbers in buildings of many periods is not uncommon, but these timbers can rarely be tied to any named ship.

A quick count and survey of the timbers in the mill and reference to Bruce Tappenden's researches confirmed that these were indeed likely to be the *Chesapeake*'s timbers. The scientific confirmation investigations to identify species and their origins were carried out later by

St Andrews University and its associates. The origin and condition of the timbers were of particular interest to Alan whose ancestors had been shipwrights in the naval yard that built *Chesapeake* in Gosport, Virginia. Our findings pointed to the possibility that even the USS *Constitution,* which still sails as the oldest commissioned naval vessel afloat, does not contain as much original material as survives in the Chesapeake Mill. Furthermore, the timbers in the mill have been ashore and protected from the elements for nearly two hundred years.

After *Chesapeake's* capture on 1 June 1812 she had been repaired at Halifax, then sailed to England, measured and assessed for her sailing qualities on a voyage to the Cape of Good Hope and judged of no special value to the Royal Navy as a warship – hence her reduction to hulk status. She was the first of the large American frigates to be captured by the Royal Navy in the War of 1812, albeit a 38-gun smaller variant. She was designated to be recycled as building material but her detailed lines and measurements were first recorded for the Admiralty archives.

When the *Chesapeake* was sold out of the Royal Navy on 18 August 1819 to Joshua Holmes for £3,450 she had been lying at Pesthouse Quay, Portsea, in her final maritime role as a hospital ship. Holmes subsequently advertised the sale of the timbers in the *Hampshire Telegraph* on 15 November 1819 and again in the following year.

The advertisement placed in the *Telegraph and Sussex Chronicle* for 17 April 1820 was headed 'Superior Ship Timber'. Offered for sale were:

The hulls of his majesty's late ships Chesapeake and Cherub are now breaking up at Pesthouse, Portsea, where there is for sale, a very large quantity of oak and fir timber of most excellent quality and well worth the attention of any person; consisting of 150 oak and fir beams of the following sizes 5 by 7, 7 by 9, 8 by 10, 12 by 15 from 20 to 40 feet long; Oak and Fir plank 2¼, 3, 4, 5, 6 and 7 inches of long lengths from 40 to 70 feet, floors, futticks [sic], top timbers, knees, carlins, ledges, cabin fittings and a larger and more superior assortment of ship timber than was ever before offered to the public.

Also an excellent double capstan, about 30 tons of Swedish iron, spikes, bolts and about 30 iron knees.

The above may be shipped free of expense being close to the water – for particulars enquire of Joseph Pushman and Co. on the premises.

John Prior who owned the old watermill on the Meon at Wickham was at that time intending to rebuild this structure. It seems that 300 lots of the original offering from *Chesapeake* and *Cherub* were still available and were sold by auction at the same premises of Pushman and Co on 17 August 1820. It is known from bills of sale that this is the origin of the material that John Prior bought for his new mill.

Comparing the two advertisements and the extra information that the second conveys provides even more evidence about the timber and other material which finally found its way into the structure of the mill:

> To be sold by auction on Monday 14th August 1820 at 11.00 o'clock at the old established timber yard Pesthouse, Portsea. About 300 lots of fir and oak timber taken from his majesty's late ships Chesapeake and Cherub consisting of oak and pitch-pine beams of long lengths, three, four, five, and six inch oak and pine plank, two sets of fine floors and first futticks [sic], a large quantity of live oak timbers from 10 to 18 feet long, about 12 inch square, a large assortment of white oak knees, top timbers, carlings, ledges, ladders, hatches, gratings, stanchions etc, three pumps complete with brass chambers, one double capstan, one small mast, sundry topmasts etc, etc.

A good portion of her timber was bought at auction by Prior to be used in the erection of his new watermill. This red brick structure replacing the earlier mill was much larger, its breadth being governed by the length of deck beams (32 feet) recovered from the dismantled frigate. In the mill, fourteen gun deck and berth deck beams are readily identified as ship's timbers. Others exist in much modified form in various parts of the mill. At least 165 deck ledges are used as carlings in conjunction with the beams to support the three floors. The planks covering these have been much altered but it is possible that some material here is in its original form. Bruce Tappenden, the mill's last operator, was sceptical about this, believing that the heavily used mill floors must have been replaced several times.

Most of the timber is American southern long leaf pine (ref US Forestry Commission laboratories); however, at least one lintel over a window has been shown to be white oak and from a futtock, part of the ship's framing also mentioned in the above advertisements. The beams are marked with cuts from a race tool to indicate which part of the ship they were destined for as well as other marks thought to identify ship repairs at Halifax after the battle. There are also grapeshot scars created during the encounter with *Shannon*, powder burns, traces of original paint and even a small remnant of canvas screening attached to a beam. Trenails and bolts are evidenced but most valuable of all are the actual joint housings cut into the deck beams and the footprints left by original jointing of other structural parts of the hull. By direct measurement and comparison with existing Admiralty records, these beams can be placed accurately into the overall structure of the vessel. One large beam retains the mast partner housings whose dimensions are known, so placing that beam in a precise location.

Planking has been identified as coming from the ceiling from within the ship and also from its exterior. Much of the planking lining the mansard roof of the mill appears to be refashioned timber, evidenced by serial bolt holes.

A stone tablet on the facade of the mill declares 'Erected AD 1820 I Prior'. The mill is known to have had in 1826 'a pair of breast shot wheels driving five pairs of stones, two flour machines, bolting mill, smutt and winnowing machines capable of grinding and clearing 40 loads of wheat a week'. It was built when the post-wartime economy was on the wane. The local demand to process flour and feeds had slumped and it seems unlikely that the mill ever operated to its full capacity.

In 1866, the Revd Brighton visited the mill and wrote of its atmosphere particularly in respect of its naval history and the significance of the *Shannon–Chesapeake* action of 1813. He was engaged in writing the biographies of Captain Sir Philip Broke and his lieutenant in *Shannon*, Provo Wallis. It is clear that the mill had become by this time identified with the Chesapeake name.

By 1913 the mill was powered by an Armfield water turbine and the Chesapeake Roller Flour Mills had become a widely known name in milling. The last mill stones were removed in 1948, but from 1978 the mill started producing animal feedstuffs, using electrical power for the roller and crusher and turbine power for the mixer and hoist.

Since the publication in 1866 of Brighton's biography of Broke put the mill on the historical map, Wickham has witnessed numerous visitors. Probably boosted by Teddy Roosevelt's book *The Naval War of 1812* and the works of Alfred Mahan, Americans found their way to this site to sense the special atmosphere of the Chesapeake Mill's timbers and decks that were witness to heroism and devastation in an uncharacteristic sharp defeat for their nascent US Navy. More recent American naval captains have walked the same deck where Captain Lawrence was struck down and have heard the echoes of his gallant words, 'Don't give up the ship', as he was carried below mortally wounded; a saying destined to become the motto of the US Fleet.

In 1952, the mill was listed as an historic building and was sold in 1998 to Hampshire County Council. The current leaseholders have restored the roof and preserved the timbers in their original condition. They open the building to the public on most days.

Until recently there was no memorial in Britain to the War of 1812 other than individual graves and tablets in churches and cemeteries: Broke's at Nacton, Provo Wallis's at Funtington, Falkiner's at Brighton. At Abingdon, seventy miles from the sea, there is in Spring Lane cemetery the headstone of Commander George Raymond who served in Broke's *Shannon* on 1 June 1813 and carried to his grave, lodged in his arm, a musket ball fired from the *Chesapeake*, this fact being recorded on his tombstone. Exactly 200 years after the battle, a memorial to the fallen of both sides, dressed with the blue ensign and the US 15-star ensign of that time, has been unveiled at Chesapeake Mill in the presence of Commander Raymond's great-great-granddaughter.

A MODEST RETIREMENT

'Buy nothing for us abroad, except it be those trifles of native curiosity, which cost hardly anything, whether of natural production or the ingenious work of the savage, or a few pounds of arrowroot; so you see my commissions are very humble. I assure you, my dear, that my utmost hope is to be able to keep on at the old Hall, so that if I can afford nothing else there may be always a warm, hospitable home for all the old family, when the chances of life bring them there, that the old BADGERS may always have the old earth to bear up for when they want a home; and this I shall try to do, however humble my establishment – Broke Hall – if there is even nothing there but brown bread, and beef, and ale, and a blazing log on the fire, where we may sit when we meet to talk of old times and enjoy whatever we have got left.'

Philip Broke to his son Rear Admiral Sir George Broke-Middleton, Bart (20 March 1834)

16

Ballads and Broadsides:
The Poetic and Musical Legacy of the
Shannon and the *Chesapeake*

Richard Wilson

In July 1813 Broke was recuperating in Halifax, Nova Scotia when he began leafing through some letters from his beloved Louisa, 'Loo': 'Among the last of your letters which reached me was that enclosing the verses so prophetic, about *Shannon*. I dare say the poet will be very vain of his prediction coming true.'[1] These 'prophetic' verses, the first to feature Broke, had been printed in the previous autumn's *Naval Chronicle* (pp 421–2) bearing the title 'The Retort Courteous'. They were a rejoinder by 'Nauticus' to a poem from 1811 entitled 'Rodgers and Decatur. Tit for Tat; *Or the Chesapeake paid for in British blood!!!*' which had extolled American success in the *President–Little Belt* Affair. Like that original piece, the verses that Loo sent to Broke were to be sung to the tune 'Yankee Doodle':

> The boaster Rodgers is gone out,
>   Who fought the *LITTLE BELT*, Sir;
> And very brave it was, no doubt,
>   So small a craft to pelt, sir.
>   Yankee doodle, &c.

> But if brave BROKE he chance to meet,
>   He'll drub him for his trouble;
> And every British heart will beat,
>   To pay the bully double.
>   Yankee doodle, &c....

---

1 Brighton, *Broke Memoir*, p 273.

And as the War they did provoke,
  We'll pay them with our cannon.
The first to do it will be BROKE
  In his gallant ship, the *SHANNON*.
    Yankee doodle, &c.

Many of Broke's letters to Loo in the years leading up to the battle reveal his driving desire not for glory but 'honour', and this yearning for the esteem of the nation governed much that he did at sea. Now he felt that this had been achieved: 'It is high time I should come home, lest I should become too vain. A lady (I don't know who yet) sent me a new velvet cap on Sunday, with some poetical compliments; but I will be modest when I get into Suffolk, and turn farmer, and renounce vanity with my laced coat.'[2] In the eighteenth and nineteenth centuries it was not uncommon for victories such as the *Shannon*'s to garner such 'poetical compliments'. Poetry had long helped focus national pride. In times when few people could read, versifiers and minstrels were part of a monarch's entourage charged with relaying 'good news' (we might call it 'spin') to the populace. In classical times the laurel was associated with victory, and Richard I's *versificator regis* became in seventeenth-century Britain the Poet Laureate whose job was to produce works at moments of great national rejoicing or import. Despite his modesty, Broke might have thought his victory an appropriate subject for an 'official' poem from Henry Pye, the Laureate of the day (though with Pye being dubbed 'the worst Poet Laureate in English history',[3] missing out might not have been such a bad thing). But Pye died just days after news of the engagement reached England and, with Walter Scott then refusing the post, Broke's victory went poetically unrecognised.

Officially at least . . . But, as Broke's biographer the Revd Brighton commented in 1866, 'It has been noticed, in all times, that any deed of tried and acknowledged heroism has found its bard. There was a general stringing of lyres, in either land, on this occasion.' Although he went on to say that, following the bloody battle, 'the feeling between the countries was too bitter for either to produce a poem likely to endure',[4] many attempted to prove him wrong, though sometimes with

---

2 Brighton, *Broke Memoir*, p 286.
3 Blake, *Disraeli* (New York, 1966), p 110.
4 Brighton, *Broke Memoir*, p 318.

what was simply doggerel. *The Naval Chronicle* in December 1813 printed this *Impromptu* headed: 'On the Dinner bespoken by the crew of the *Chesapeake*, who pledged themselves, in the course of a few hours, to bring the *Shannon* into port':

> The bold *Chesapeake*
> Came out on a freak,
> And swore she'd soon silence our cannon;
> While the *Yankees*, in port,
> Stood to laugh at the sport,
> And see her tow in the brave *Shannon*.

> Quite sure of the game,
> As from harbour they came,
> A dinner and wine they bespoke;
> But for *meat* they got *balls*
> From our staunch wooden walls,
> And the dinner *Engagement* was – BROKE.

In his native Suffolk the pronunciation of Broke's name usually agrees with the toast 'An *English Broke* and an *Irish* river'[5] but, perhaps mostly for poetic reasons, verses of the day often rhymed the victorious captain's name thus:

> Who has broken the charm that hung over the fleet,
> The charm that occasion'd dismay and defeat?
> Too many have vainly attempted the stroke,
> But thanks to the Shannon – at last it is BROKE.[6]

Poems such as the above from *The Public Ledger* for 12 July 1813 were penned very soon after news of the famous victory reached England via the *Nova Scotia* brig on 7 July, which coincided with the announcement of Wellington's victory at Vitoria (attended by Broke's younger brother Charles). Wellington's own reception of Britain's naval victory, as communicated in writing to Lord William Bentinck on 20

---

5 Brighton, *Wallis Memoir*, p 91.
6 This and a number of the following poems were reprinted in *The Spirit of the Public Journals for 1813.*

July, appears somewhat muted: 'The *Shannon*, Captain Broke, has taken the *Chesapeake*, which I consider a most fortunate event.' Nevertheless, he did toast Broke and the *Shannon* at the first anniversary dinner of the Battle of Salamanca. Others, such as *The Morning Chronicle* of 9 July, were more effusive: 'There requires no panegyric to be passed on Captain Broke and his crew, for the exemplary manner in which they have vindicated the character of the British Navy. A more gallant exploit was never achieved at any period of our naval glory.' On 14 July, the *Morning Herald* presented 'A Fact v. a Speech':

> 'The Yankees beat our men; and my advice
> Must rule, or else this still will come to pass.'
> Lord Patriot bolts out this; and, in a trice,
> Despatches came, and prov'd my Lord an — !

The following day they printed 'A Yankee Eclogue':

Doodle Sam:
> The *Chesapeake* frigate, with forty-nine cannon,
> Is gone out to capture, and bring in, the *Shannon*.
> Our frigate is largest, and as for the crew,
> The Yankees are many, the English but few.
> St George he is for England; Napoleon is for us:
> Napoleon is a great man, who tried to beat the Russ.

Doodle Tim:
> I see the *Chesapeake*; I see her in the fight:
> I see her colours fly; I see them – out of sight.
> There's nothing on the mast; there's no sound of cannon;
> I tremble for the news of the *Chesapeake* and *Shannon*.
> St George he is for England; Napoleon – whom is he for?
> Our Ruler is for France; but whom the deuce are we for?

Doodle Sam:
> 'Tis but a random shot has brought our colours low;
> They'll soon be up again; ay, up I see them go.
> But what's that besides? There something goes up blue;
> 'Tis the old British flag, and the highest of the two!

St George he is for England; Napoleon's for himself:
America's the dupe, and our Ruler gets his pelf.[7]

On 23 July the *Morning Post* presented an 'Epigram, inscribed (without permission) to the crew of the *Chesapeake*, by an Hibernian', whilst this 'Impromptu on the circumstance of the captain of the *Shannon*, which took the *Chesapeake*, being named "Broke"', from the same publication of 2 August, shows that the (mis)pronunciation of his name provoked some amusement:

How strange, on our nautical records 't will seem,
And even still stranger whenever 't is spoke,
That the hero who first gain'd old England's esteem
In the second American warfare was 'Broke!'

'Select Poetry, for August 1813' from *The Gentleman's Magazine* had a more considered offering from Lieutenant Edward Stewart RN, son of another published poet, the Revd Charles Edward Stewart, Rector of Rede in Suffolk:

THREE fatal fights Britannia saw
With mix'd surprize and woe;
For thrice she saw her Union flag
By hostile hands laid low.

Then, casting round an anxious eye
Amongst her naval men,
Her choice she made, that choice was Broke
To raise her flag again.

'Command,' she cries, 'yon gallant ship,
And form her chosen crew,
And bid my flag victorious fly,
Where it was wont to do.'. . .

---

7 'Pelf' is a word for money or wealth, especially when gained dishonestly or dishonourably.

Hail, Suffolk's pride! such fame may I,
A son of Suffolk, share;
Or, if I fall, like glorious Watt,
To fall, what hour so fair?

Lead on, where'er your Country calls.
And Glory points the way,
Wherever Ocean rolls his tides,
Your conquering flag display;

And prove, tho' thrice superior force
Might transient trophies gain,
Britannia rules the wat'ry world,
Sole Empress of the Main.

In late 1813, *The Monthly Review or Literary Journal* (vol 72, p 212) reviewed an anonymous poem entitled 'The *Shannon* and the *Chesapeake*' thus:

Though Homer has given a catalogue of the ships which conveyed troops to the siege of Troy, he does not appear to have been acquainted with the language of sailors; and the same assertion may be extended to the generality of poets of all ages and nations. The Muses, it will be said, delight more in woods, mountains, and streams of fresh water, than in 'Neptune's salt wash.' Here, however, is a poet who appears to be well versed in the naval nomenclature, and is qualified for describing in appropriate terms the gallant action between the *Shannon* and the *Chesapeake* frigates, which gloriously terminated in the capture of the American . . . The writer exults in our dominion of the main, and predicts its perpetuity.

The Antijacobin Review and True Churchman's Magazine (vol 45, pp 317–20) agreed with this assessment of this poem: 'It is a source of great satisfaction to us that, at length, the naval achievements of British sailors have found bards worthy of them . . . [Broke's] gallant action with the *Chesapeake* is here sung in suitable strains, and all particulars of the hard-fought contest are preserved without injury to the beauty of the verse':

Thus, Britons! On the watery field
   Our matchless fathers fought;
Thus BLAKE his arms were wont to wield,
   And thus his conquests bought;
Thus was the haughty Moor subdued,
Thus tamed the Belgian fierce and rude;
And thus we won Iberia's gold
That braved our strength in days of old. –
Such was the flame your NELSON breath'd
   When DENMARK hung her head;
And such his brows with laurels wreath'd,
   When his high spirit fled;
This flame shall ever blast your foes
   In contest hand to hand,
As BROKE on ocean nobly shews,
   And WELLINGTON by land.
And GEORGE! If ceaseless round thy shore
Infuriate war is doom'd to roar,
   Its wrath shall burst in vain: –
'BRITONS strike home!' be this our spell
Columbia's erring rage to quell;
Or dared the world her impious cause sustain,
This to 'the world in arms' should proudly tell,
BRITONS *still* rule, and aye *shall* rule the main!

Despite these jingoistic assertions of British naval superiority, it was
Lawrence who was notably feted both before and after his fateful
meeting with Broke: 'The brave, the noble Lawrence is no more. He
who added the last brilliant trophy to our triumphal diadem [with the
defeat of *Peacock*], the bed of glory has received.'[8] Lawrence's death
received more poetic attention than Broke's victory. (The latter may
have made the mistake of not dying in action when, perhaps, his fame
would have been assured.) While others of *Chesapeake*'s crew were
court-martialled and excoriated, Lawrence was virtually canonised by
contemporary and later writers, including the noted 'Poet of the

---

8 *Annapolis Maryland Republican*, reprinted in *Washington National Intelligencer*, 2 July
   1813.

American Revolution', Philip Freneau, and Thomas Tracy Bouvé of Hingham, Massachusetts.

Broke's modest funeral was held privately in London where he died in January 1841, although his body was later carried through the streets of Ipswich to the tolling of the muted bells of St Mary-le-Tower church before interment in his native village of Nacton. In death Lawrence was treated with rather more pomp and circumstance: 'On the proudest page of American history, among the achievements of valour by her sons, the name of our lamented Lawrence will be conspicuously recorded. Although the last act of his life brought misfortune to his country, it has entailed no dishonour; it has rather shed a new ray of glory on our already brilliant naval character.' At Halifax, on 8 June 1813:

His funeral obsequies were celebrated with appropriate ceremonials and an affecting solemnity. His pall was supported by the oldest captains in the British service that were in Halifax; and the naval officers crowded to yield the last sad honours to a man who was late their foe, but now their foe no longer. There is a sympathy between gallant souls that knows no distinction of clime or nation. They honour in each other what they feel proud of in themselves. The group that gathered around the grave of Lawrence, presented a scene worthy of the heroic days of chivalry. It was a complete triumph of the nobler feelings over the savage passion of war.[9]

Despite the solemnity of this occasion, various inhabitants of Salem, Massachusetts, wanted the bodies of Lawrence and his second in command, Lieutenant Ludlow, brought back to America, which was soon done under a flag of truce and with the permission of the President of the United States. Alongside the eulogies in Belcher's *Account of the funeral honours bestowed on the remains of Capt. Lawrence...* are fascinating descriptions of the battle and its aftermath, including Lawrence's burial in Halifax and his subsequent reinterment at Salem on 23 August. There are a number of 'Poetical Notices', tributes to

---

9 Details of Lawrence's funerals are taken from *An account of the funeral honours bestowed on the remains of Capt. Lawrence and Lieut. Ludlow: with the eulogy pronounced at Salem on the occasion by Hon. Joseph Story*, printed by Joshua Belcher, Boston, 28 August 1813.

Lawrence, Ludlow and William White, Sailing Master, alongside (perhaps surprisingly for such an avowedly 'Yankee' publication) an 'English account' of the engagement. Despite being an allegedly English poem, even this goes on to praise '*Brave Lawrence*, fam'd for other deeds':

> The minute guns are heard afar,
> But bear not *now* the sound of war.
> The minute stroke the sailor rows,
> And pity's tear-drop nobly flows. –
> And now the mournful sailor weeps,
> Where still in peace the Hero sleeps.

Salem would not be Lawrence's final resting place, however. Once more he would be moved, this time to New York where, on 16 September 1813, his body was placed in Trinity Church Cemetery just off Broadway, a resting place that has inspired more verses, even into the twentieth century, such as these by Clinton Scollard:

> . . . Out from Trinity's dim portal floats the chanting choir;
> Matchless midst the girdling granite lifts the graceful spire.
> Many slumberers around him, men of Church and State;
> Here he sleeps, our sailor hero, great among the great!
> Simple lines to mark his slumber; how the letters speak!
> 'Lawrence' (hark, ye money-getters!) 'of the Chesapeake!'
>
> Stone may call in clearer accents than the loudest lip
> Just a name! What does it cry you? 'Don't give up the ship!'
> Aye, there's something more than millions, – a far nobler aim!
> Here he sleeps, our sailor hero, nothing but a name!
> Yet (and who can pierce the future?) this may one day be
> As a burning inspiration both on land and sea![10]

American publications of the day celebrated all those killed or wounded on board the *Chesapeake*, such as the so-called 'broadside' printed by Nathaniel Coverly in Boston (see Figure 16.1). With the

---

10 From 'The Grave of Lawrence (Trinity churchyard)', in Gleaves, *James Lawrence*, p 258.

CHESAPEAKE AND SHANNON :

A LIST OF THE KILLED AND WOUNDED ON BOARD THE CHESAPEAKE, FURNISHED BY LIEUT. CHEW, LATE PURSER OF THE CHESAPEAKE.

OFFICERS.—Edw. J Ballard, acting lieutenant ; James Broome, 1st lt. of Marines ; Wm. A White, sailing master ; Pollard Hopewell, midshipman ; John Evans, do. Courtland Livingston, do.

Daniel Burnham, quarter-master ; James Woodbury, do. ; Michael Kelly, quarter-gunner ; John Carter, boatswain's mate.

SEAMEN.—Henry H. Monroe, Abraham Cox, Sterling Clerk, Alex. Marine, Thos. Evans, John Miller, Daniel Martin, Robert Bates, Wm. Russell, Harris Ball, Andrew Williams, Joseph Simmons, John W. Duggan, David Bias, Josiah Shatfield, Jno. Philips, Benj. Esday, John Reed 2d, Samuel Mullin, Michael Sawyer, James Betten, John Crab, Samuel M. Purkins, Joseph Judith, John Jones, Christopher Houstan, George Crayton, boy.

MARINES—Thos Wheaton, Benj. Morrison, John Mulligan, John German, John Huntress, James Trainor, Jacob Preston,

Phillip Bryant, Redman Barry, Robert Standley, Delany Ward.

WOUNDED.

OFFICERS.—JAMES LAWRENCE, Esq.— Captain, since deceased ; Augustus C. Ludlow, lt. since deceased ; George Budd, lt. ; Wm. Cox, acting do. ; Sm'l. Livermore, acting chaplain ; Francis Nichols, Walter Abbott, Wm. A. Weaver, Edmund M. Russell, Wm. Berry, midshipmen.

Peter Adams, boatswain, since dead ; Jefferson Griffith, quarter-master ; James A. Lewis, quarter-master ; Forbes Dela, quarter-gunner, since dead ; Sm'l. Hudson, sail maker's mate ; Thm. Finnagan, gunner's yeoman ; Thomas Smith 2d, quarter-gunner ; John Veazy, do ; John Giles, do. ; Thomas Rouse, do. ; and Thomas Jackson, 2d. quarter-master.

SEAMEN.—James Sprout, Sylvester Stacy, John Appleton, Peter Quantin, James Butler, John Johnson, John Peterson, Th.

Sterling, Peter John, John Smith, Joseph Weyland, Francis Symonds, since dead ; John Brice, Eliphalet Carr, Thom. Flanagan, John Hodgman, since dead ; Francis Franklin, Henry Hyde, Alex. Grant, Enoch Hackett, And. Mercer, John Tallman, James Parker, Eben. Day, Giles Cone, since dead ; And. Vandesnau, Derby Lee, since dead ; John Hunt, do. ; Rolla Peters, Rob. May. Joseph Vaughan, John Davo, since dead ; Noel Dearborn, John Rollins, Charles Sargent, Wm. Metcalf, Ch. Thompson, Abra. Richardson, Jas. Durfee, Lewis Hanscom, since dead ; Wm. Hubans, Benj. Sumner, Wm. M'Cofforty, Marcus Mansel, since dead ; John Dering, John Petuswing, Wm. Peterson, Wm. Stewart, Asa Newhall, Alex. Brown, Mathias Douglas, John M'Neal, since dead ; John Crutchott, Thom. Jones, 2d. John Caldwell, Wm. Cardiner, and John Kegan.

MARINES Sergeants, John Twis, Wm. Harris ; corporal Wm. Dixon, since dead ; privates Rich. Hoffman, Jas. Brown, Joseph Twis, George Upham, John Crippen, Sam. Jackson, John Johnson, John Wright, Miles Morris, Mathias Woolberry, Warren Fogg, Thomas Johnson, Geo. Clyne, Joseph Crane, Wm. Lewis John Lyre, and John Brady.

COLUMBIANS here behold the list,
Of those who met a glorious doom ;
They who in Freedom's cause have bled,
And sleep within a watery tomb.

Shall not one tribute then, be paid,
To the bold heroes of the wave ?
Yes ! ever will we bear in mind,
The freemen who have fought so brave.

Their country's honor was the Star,
By which those heroes, dauntless steer'd ;
And while the Eagle wav'd in air,
They neither toil nor danger fear'd.

Ardent they sought the hostile band,[1]
And o'er the blue and trackless deep,
They dar'd the foe in glorious fight,
And sunk in glory's arms to sleep.

But long the wave as they descry,
Shall freemen mourn for heroes brave,
And tears of fond regret shall fall,
And mingle with the briny wave.

Ye spirits, dauntless, who withstood,
The tempest of the battle-fray,
Your names remember'd e'er shall be,
When Freemen march to field away.

Long, long, the wave on which ye fought,
Shall meet the musing patriot's eyes,
And proudly boast, beneath that wave,
Full many a noble hero lies.

Heroes, farewell ! oft shall thy shades,
In fond remembrance, ever dear,
Receive the grateful sacrifice,
Of holy Freedom's choicest tear.

Printed by NATHANIEL COVERLY, JUN. Milk-Street ; Corner Theatre-Alley, BOSTON.

Fig 16.1 'Chesapeake and Shannon: A list of the killed and wounded', a broadside printed by Nathaniel Coverly, Boston, 1813.

advent of the printing press, broadsides had taken over from the minstrels in Britain. A single sheet of paper, usually printed only on one side, broadsides (also known as 'roadsheets' or 'vulgars') were often decorated with woodcut illustrations. As Kate Van Winkle Keller writes:

> Broadsides were the best vehicles for fast-breaking news. It took only a few hours to set up a new sheet, print it and let it dry enough to send bundles out to the ballad sellers on the street-corners. When

news of a battle reached town, the broadside printer flew into action: the contract poet generated a new song, dramatic woodcuts were selected from the stock on hand or quickly ordered, the form set up, the introduction typeset, and as soon as the new song was ready, it was put into type. There was no time to waste.[11]

Posted on buildings or handed out on street corners, they were used by the authorities to publicise new laws or regulations but were also tools for the subversive – a cheap and easy means of disseminating information, and difficult to trace. Although broadsides as a source of information were gradually replaced by newspapers, the format was retained by poets who could make money when their works struck a chord with local or national sentiment. Here is an example that Everett Tomlinson, writing nearly a hundred years later, says 'speedily became very popular, even the schoolboys using it for their reading lessons':[12]

'Twas in the morning, the first day of June,
We weighed our anchors & sail'd about noon;
To meet a bold ship that hover'd quite nigh,
The force of our ship she seem'd to defy.

Our captain was brave, a man of high fame,
For taking the *Peacock*, he'd a great name,
We scarcely had pass'd Boston harbour's light
Before the *Shannon* was plain to our sight. . . .

The action commenc'd by the roar of the cannon,
We pour'd our broadside into the *Shannon*;
The *Shannon* she then returned the same,
And both were envelop'd in an ocean of flame.

The cannons did then incessantly roar,
And the decks all o'er encrimson'd with gore;
Yet our brave sailors they were not dismay'd,
No foes to our country can make them afraid.

11 Keller, *Ballads and Songs for Boston in the War of 1812*.
12 Tomlinson, *Stories of Colony and Nation*, p 175.

> Our brave commander a wound did receive,
> For which all our crew did very much grieve;
> Forty-eight brave seamen lay dead in their gore –
> Ninety-seven were wounded – their fate we deplore . . .
>
> Our glorious freedom we drew with our breath;
> The boon we'll keep unsullied till death.
> If wounded – 'tis our country's intention,
> For all that's disabl'd to give a good pension.[13]

When cut in half lengthways, broadsides became broadslips, or when folded they made chapbooks. Where these contained several poems or songs such collections were known as 'garlands'. *The Suffolk Garland or East Country Minstrel* was a rather grander version of this, produced in 1818 under the stewardship of the Revd James Ford of Ipswich. It contained a number of encomiums to Broke, including this short 'Epigram' by the Revd Lewis Blakeney:

> Gallant BROKE, (Men of Suffolk! your Hero exult in,)
>   Has redeem'd Britain's falsely-defam'd naval glory:
> For – he fought, beat, and captur'd a rival insulting,
>   In less time than was needful to write the proud story!

The *Garland* also mentions an 'elegant and spirited Poem' bearing the title 'Tributary Verses upon the Capture of the American Frigate *Chesapeake* by the British Frigate *Shannon*' by Lieutenant M Montagu of the Royal Navy. Broke's biographer Brighton, writing in 1866 (p 318), considered this 'probably the best' of all the poems celebrating the engagement but reprints a 'defective copy' of the full fifty-verse *England Victorious* that Montagu Montagu (1787–1863) had published himself in 1814 to 'supersede' one put out 'entirely without his sanction or knowledge'. Montagu had joined the Navy in 1799 and went on to be a noted author, translator and autograph-collector who bequeathed his manuscript collection to Oxford's Bodleian Library. His dedication to Broke is dated 26 November 1813 in Portsmouth, the

---

13 An original broadside in the collection of the American Antiquarian Society, also reprinted in Neeser, *American Naval Songs and Ballads*, 167–9.

city where, just twenty-four days earlier, the victorious sea captain had
first set foot back in Britain:

46
He comes, Illustrious Chief! Prepare
The splendid wreath, 't is his to wear,
Of never-fading bays:
Prepare the bright perennial crown,
While loud the trump of high renown
Resounds the victor's praise.

47
Brave Tars! what joy to you, returning,
With anxious hope your bosoms burning,
And wish no more to roam, –
To meet again each well-known face,
The cordial hand, and warm embrace,
The friendly welcome-home.

48
A grateful country too will greet
Your glad return, and ye shall meet
Her daughters' sweetest smiles;
And, as ye tell th' inspiring tale,
With conscious pride her sons will hail
'The Guardians of her Isles.'

The Suffolk Garland was subtitled 'A collection of poems, songs, tales,
ballads, sonnets and elegies, legendary and romantic, historical and
descriptive, relative to that County'. Its compiler singled out the ballad
as a distinctive form of popular verse and quoted Joseph Addison from
The Spectator of 1711, in his Preface:

An ordinary SONG or BALLAD that is the delight of the common
people cannot fail to please all such readers as are not unqualified for
the entertainment by their affectation or ignorance . . . I took a
particular delight in hearing the SONGS and FABLES that are come
from father to son, and are most in vogue among the common

people: for it is impossible that any thing should be universally tasted and approved of by a multitude, which hath not in it some peculiar aptness to please and gratify the mind of man.

Ballads, also defined as 'simply a folksong that tells a story',[14] were the first literary experience for many in the eighteenth and early nineteenth centuries. They were sung in taverns and inns, memorised and passed on to others. Most ballads were sold cheaply as single-sheet broadsides, and, although the heyday of broadsides had passed by the time of the engagement between the *Chesapeake* and the *Shannon*, they were still popular in New England. Though these ballads were intended to be sung, and could be about love, politics, religion or newsworthy events of the day, only the lyrics would be printed. Occasionally the name of a well-known tune might be given, but melodies were interchangeable, or might be improvised on the spot. The poetry of these songs (for that is what many of them were) may not have been of the highest order, and plagiarism was rife ('Columbia' for 'Britannia' was an easy substitution for ballads brought across the Atlantic), but they were filled with a patriotic fervour that fulfilled the requirements of the fledgling United States:

Written and Corrected by James Campbell, late of the Constitution; *in behalf of the brave Captain Lawrence and Lieutenant C Ludlow, of the* Chesapeake. *Tune:* Disconsolate Sailor

> YE sons of Columbia, O hail the great day,
>   Which burst your tyrannical chain,
> Which taught the opprest, how to spurn lawless sway,
>   And establish equality's reign.
> Yes, hail the blest moment when awfully grand,
>   Your Congress pronounc'd the decree;
> Which told the wide world, that your pine cover'd land,
>   In spite of Coration was free . . .
>
> How can you who have felt the oppressor's hard hand,
>   Who for freedom all perils did brave;

---

14 Darling, *The New American Songster*, p 3.

How can you enjoy ease, while one foot of your soil
   Is disgrac'd by the toil of a slave.
O rouse then in spite of a merciless few,
   And pronounce this immortal decree,
That 'whate'er be man's tenets, his fortune, his hue,
   He is man, and shall therefore be free.'[15]

There are various extant examples of the following ballad written by the British in imitation of the famous Yankee song about the *Constitution*'s defeat of the *Guerrière* in August 1812. It was sung to the tune 'Pretty Peggy of Darby' and was well known in Nova Scotia even into the last century:

   The *Chesapeake* so bold,
   Out of Boston, we've been told,
   Came to take a British frigate
      Neat and handy, O!
   All the people of the port
   They came out to see the sport,
   And the bands were playing
      'Yankee doodle dandy, O!'

   The British frigate's name,
   Which for the purpose came
   Of cooling Yankee courage
      Neat and handy, O!
   Was the *Shannon* – Captain Broke,
   All her crew were hearts of oak,
   And at fighting they're allowed to be
      The dandy, O! . . .

   Here's a health to Captain Broke,
   And all the hearts of oak,
   That took the Yankee frigate
      Neat and handy, O!
   And may we always prove

---

15 Neeser, *American Naval Songs and Ballads*, pp 160–1. In fact, the words were adapted from 'American Independency' by Edward Rushton (London, 1806).

That in fighting and in love,
The true British sailor
Is the dandy, O!

It is this ballad that features in chapter six of Thomas Hughes' *Tom Brown's School Days*: 'when they come to the words, "Brave Broke he waved his sword, crying, Now, my lads, aboard, / And we'll stop their playing Yankee-doodle-dandy oh!" you expect the roof to come down'. Hughes attended Rugby School from 1834 to 1842 and these may be his memories of how Broke's victory was being celebrated nearly thirty years after the event. Broke also features in a number of novels by Patrick O'Brian, as cousin of the fictional hero Jack Aubrey. In *The Fortunes of War*, which concludes with a description of the battle, Broke is even imagined reciting verse himself (albeit in Latin).

As is readily apparent, many of these popular ballads replaced accuracy with powerful imagery and poetic spirit. Some place the battle in the wrong month ('On board the *Shannon* frigate in the merry month of May / To watch the bold Americans, off Boston lights we lay . . .') whilst others describe Broke's demise in the encounter. Lawrence's famous last words feature in many New England broadsides, such as 'Come, messmates, cheerly lead the night' which was to be sung to the tune 'Jack at Greenwich':

> . . . When o'er Nantasket's fatal wave
> Our Lawrence fought the battle,
> And for a hero's crown or grave,
> Bade all his thunders rattle;
> Says he, 'my lads you know the way,
> While fights the foe, give slaughter,
> And, should our valour win the day,
> Then, give the vanquish'd quarter.'
> But, when capsized, the words that last
> Hung on his dying lips boys,
> Were, 'Let our flag still crown the mast,
> And don't give up the ship, boys.'
> *The ship, boys, &c.*

On hammock bloody, wet or dry,
We all must pay our score, boys;
But, death and danger's all my eye,
We've seen their face before, boys.
With Hull, we stood the Guerriere's force,
And doff'd the pride of Dacres,
Who swore he thought the joke too coarse
From modest Yankee quakers.
When Bainbridge too, the stout and brave,
Just spoil'd the Java's trip, boys,
We swore upon that crimson wave
We'd ne'er give up our ship, boys.
    The ship, boys, &c.

Now, what's the use to talk all night
'Bout Perry, Jones, Decatur?
The foe to beat as oft as fight,
God bless 'em, tis their nature.
And long before dishonour's shoal
Brings up our gallant navy,
There's many a noble Briton's soul
Must weigh for grim old Davy.
For all in Scripture lingo pat,
Our chaplain proves it glib, boys,
That 'pugnam bonam', and all that
Means, 'Don't give up the ship, boys.'
    The ship, boys, &c. . . .[16]

One version of a ballad may differ quite considerably from another. As Robert Neeser says, many ballads were never written down at all: 'They were the songs composed and sung by seamen themselves, always descriptive, generally very long, with innumerable verses and committed to memory and handed down from one generation of songsters to another . . . No trace of these songs remains today.'[17] Another ballad that lost historical accuracy with the passing of the

---

16 *The Rhode Island Literary Repository*, vol 1, April 1814 to April 1815, p 219.
17 Neeser, *American Naval Songs and Ballads*, p xvi.

years was this, sung in the summer of 1937 by Mrs Edward Gallagher, wife of the lighthouse keeper at Chebucto Head, Nova Scotia:

> 'Twas on the glorious fourth of June
> At ten o'clock in the forenoon
> That we sailed out of Boston Bay
> That we sailed out of Boston Bay
> For to fight the *Chesapeake* boys. [18]

But it wasn't just amateurs who sang about the battle. The Norwich-born composer James Hook (1746–1827) wrote 'The Chesapeake Prize to the Shannon: A New Song' ('At Boston one day, / As the *Chesapeake* lay'), which was 'sung with unbounded applause by Mr Dignum at Vauxhall Gardens'. 'The Review of New Musical Publications' in *The Monthly Magazine or British Register* for January 1814 contained this announcement:

> *The* Shannon *and* Chesapeake, *the Rival Frigates; sung with unbounded applause by Mr Sinclair, at the Theatre Royal Covent Garden and by Mr Cooke at the Lyceum Theatre. Written by Mr [T.G.] Ingall; composed by J. Whitaker*: 'The melody of "The *Shannon* and *Chesapeake*" does much credit to Mr Whitaker's talents and ardour of feeling. The expression is throughout as forcible as just, and will scarcely be listened to by any one without a prompt sensibility to the *amor patriae* of the author.'

Such were the verses in question (see Figure 16.2):

> . . . Swift flew the word, Britannia's sons
>   Spread death and terror where they came;
> The trembling foe forsook their guns,
>   And called aloud on Mercy's name.
> Brave BROKE led the way, but fell wounded and weak,
>   Yet exclaimed 'They've all fled from their cannon;
> Three cheers, my brave fellows, the proud *Chesapeake*
>   Has lower'd her flag to the *Shannon*.'

---

18 Creighton, *Traditional Songs from Nova Scotia*, p 226.

Fig 16.2 The first verse of 'Shannon and Chesapeake, the Rival Frigates', composed by John Whitaker (1776–1847) to words by T G Ingall, London, 1813.

The day was won, but Lawrence fell,
　　And clos'd his eyes in endless night;
And oft Columbia's sons will tell,
　　Their hopes all blighted in the fight.
But brave CAPTAIN BROKE, tho' yet wounded and weak,
　　Survives to again play his cannon,
And his name from the shores of the wide Chesapeake
　　Shall be prais'd to the banks of the Shannon.[19]

This particular song seems to have had an impact well beyond the Britain's shores. In *Twenty Years before the Mast* published in 1896, the American Charles Erskine, who circumnavigated the globe with Admiral Charles Wilkes, remembers an occasion in Rio de Janeiro harbour in 1838:

Among other vessels there was the English line-of-battle ship *Thunderer*, of ninety guns and a crew of one thousand men. They usually sang on board of her every night, and always wound up at eight bells by singing the first or second part of 'The Chesapeake and Shannon,' which was very aggravating to American patriotism. One night Commander Wilkes happened to appear on deck just as they were singing the obnoxious song, which seemed to annoy him extremely . . . One of the crew went aft and asked him if we might return that song next Saturday evening by giving them 'The Parliaments of England'. 'Yes, my man,' was the reply, 'and give it to them in thunderous tones, with plenty of Yankee lightning.' Fifty of the best singers began to practice, and on the next Saturday evening, just as the crew on board of the *Thunderer* had finished singing their usual song, our chorus commenced . . . It was sung with such a will that it re-echoed throughout the silent bay and made the welkin ring. We soon heard the call of the boatswain followed by his mates, calling all hands to cheer ship, and then we were given three times three, from the one thousand voices on board the ninety-gun ship.

It wasn't just songs that celebrated Broke's victory; composers for the piano also cashed in. Amongst these were 'The Engagement of the

---

19 *The Monthly Magazine or British Register* (London, 1 January 1814), p 541.

Shannon & *Chesapeake* frigates, a Characteristick Naval Divertimento for the Pianoforte, Composed & Dedicated to the Gallant Sir P B V Broke and his Brave Crew' by T H Butler, and 'The Glorious Victory of the *Shannon* over the *Chesapeake*, a Descriptive Battle Piece' by Thomas Howell (see Frontispiece). Both of these were aimed at the 'amateur' musician. (It must be remembered that piano playing was primarily a domestic pursuit – Broke's contemporary, Beethoven, had just two of his Sonatas played in public during his lifetime.) Whilst perhaps not of the highest musical inspiration, these take the player through the battle with descriptive headings such as 'Under easy sail off Boston Harbour' and 'After a furious cannonading and noble resistance on both sides, the *Chesapeake* is boarded', with musical instructions including 'Rifleshot from the Shrouds', 'Running fire from the Marines' and 'Heavy Cannonade'. Both pieces include settings of 'Rule, Britannia!', as does Beethoven's *Wellington's Victory*, composed to commemorate the Battle of Vitoria on 21 June 1813, which shows just how important this particular tune was in embodying Britain's naval vision of itself. (Incidentally, Thomas Arne wrote it in 1740 in the frenzy that followed the success at Porto Bello of the Broke family's Suffolk neighbour Admiral Edward Vernon.)

Why are all these poems, songs and ballads important to a historian of the War of 1812? It is because they tell us about how ordinary people responded to an event that *The Naval Chronicle* of 1813 (vol 30, p 41) called 'the most brilliant act of heroism ever performed'. In England they speak of the psyche of a seafaring people for whom salt water has always coursed through their veins. In America they served to unite a still disparate nation. Broke retired to lead a tranquil life in the Suffolk countryside, but he was not forgotten. When, on 26 February 1884, his daughter-in-law Lady Broke-Middleton laid the foundation stone of a swimming pool at Ipswich School (where Broke had once been a pupil), a 'neat block of Dumfries redstone'[20] bore an inscription to Broke's memory accompanied by a Latin verse that reads:[21]

---

20 *Ipswich Journal*, 1 March 1884.
21 Smart, *The Works of Horace*, vol I, p 237.

Should you sink it in the deep, it comes out more beautiful;
should you contend with it, with great glory will it overthrow the
conqueror unhurt before,
and will fight battles to be the talk of wives.

Suggested Further Reading

Laws, G Malcolm, *American Balladry from British Broadsides* (1957).
Neeser, Robert W (ed), *American Naval Songs and Ballads* (1938).
Simpson, Claude M, *The British Broadside Ballad and Its Music* (1966).

17

The Peace and its Outcome

Quotes selected by Colin Reid

'The English will end by subscribing to all that the Americans desire
. . . and in the future that country will be England's most powerful
adversary. Before thirty years have passed it will make her tremble.'

Napoleon (December 1812)

'Lord Gambier delivered to me the three British copies and I delivered
to him the three American copies of the treaty . . . and I told him that
I hoped it would be the last treaty of peace between Great Britain and
the United States.'

John Quincy Adams (diary for 24 December 1814)

'We have good officers coming forward . . . who would soon have
planted our standard on the walls of Quebec and Halifax . . . but in
finance we have suffered cruelly . . . we are begging daily bread at the
doors of our bankrupt banks.'

Thomas Jefferson (March 1815)

'We were all happy enough for we Peninsular soldiers saw that neither
fame nor any military distinction could be acquired in this species of
milito-nautico-guerrilla-plundering warfare.'

Sir Harry Smith on the news of peace reaching British forces off Mobile
(February 1815)

'If our first struggle was a war of our infancy, this last was that of our
youth; and the issue of both, wisely improved, may long postpone, if
not forever prevent a necessity for exerting the strength of our
Manhood.'

James Madison (1818)

'. . . it would be idle to say that, for either side, the war was not worth fighting. To Great Britain it was probably a necessary incident of the Napoleonic struggle, for neither British statesmen of that day, nor the people whom they governed, realised either the power or the rights of the United States. To America it was certainly a necessary prerequisite for attaining the dignity and self-respect of a free nation.'

Theodore Roosevelt (1882)

'The war was the national war of Canada. It did more than any other event or series of events could have done to reconcile the two rival races within Canada to each other. It was at once the supplement and the corrective of the American War of Independence.'

C P Lucas (1906)

'The lords of the ocean were so seriously annoyed by these reverses that when the tide turned and the *Chesapeake* was defeated in June 1813 by HMS *Shannon* outside Boston harbour, the event won a place in song and history out of all proportion to its importance . . . but a tradition of mutual respect was established between the two English-speaking navies that in later years developed into friendship.'

G M Trevelyan (1937)

'It has frequently been said that neither the War of 1812 nor the Peace of Ghent settled anything. This is far from being true. The four joint commissions set up by the treaty proved to be landmarks in the amicable adjustment of international disputes.'

Thomas A Bailey (1940)

'The results of the peace were solid and enduring. The war was a turning-point in the history of Canada . . . henceforward the world was to see a three-thousand-mile international frontier between Canada and the United States undefended by men or guns. On the oceans the British Navy ruled supreme for a century to come, and behind this shield the United States were free to fulfil their continental destiny.'

Winston Churchill (1957)

'Although the war of 1812 was the last armed conflict between Britain and the United States . . . the old animosities remained. England was, for Americans, the most hated nation, while the English upper class continued to denigrate all things American.'

W R Brock (1960)

'The War of 1812 was not a success for the United States. She had gone to war to oppose Great Britain's policies at sea. In particular she was concerned with the British Orders-in-Council, the impressment of American seamen, British violation of American territorial waters, and the blockade of her sea ports. Despite some naval successes on the Great Lakes, American attempts at invading Canada had been defeated. At sea there had been some outstanding victories against certain of HM ships, but the tide was turned by Captain Broke in HMS *Shannon*.'

Rear Admiral H F Pullen RCN (1970)

'In due course the War of 1812 would be seen as the foundation on which a dominion had arisen, an interpretation that owed almost everything to the consequent needs of a would-be Canadian nation situated at a safe distance from the events so celebrated . . . British America's existence had been confirmed but its future shape and prospects remained unclear.'

P J Marshall (1998)

'Had the negotiations failed, the growing strength of Great Britain meant that the situation of the United States – economic, diplomatic, military – might have remained fundamentally insecure for many decades in a nineteenth century world dominated by the British Empire . . . In that sense, the United States won its second War of Independence. It would encounter no further obstacles to its growth and prosperity as an independent nation.'

Nicholas Duggan (2010)

BROKE'S REWARDS

John Blatchly

Captain Philip Broke returned from his victory over the Chesapeake to find himself a public hero. For his brave conduct in that victorious fight he was created a baronet and given a gold medal by the Lords of the Admiralty. *The Times* of 20 May 1814 described the gold sword presented to him which he wore in his full-length portrait by Samuel Lane. Broke received the freedom of the City of London, and in January 1815 was nominated a Knight Commander of the Bath. The charger and the cup and cover were presented to him in Suffolk that year also. There was also a piece of plate, of the value of 100 guineas, from The Underwriters of Halifax in Nova Scotia. From Ipswich Corporation he received formal thanks but nothing tangible.

The Suffolk gentry, not all Tories, collected subscriptions for a silver-gilt charger almost a metre in diameter. The committee was chaired by Sir Thomas Gooch (Benacre Hall) and its members were from the great local families: Rowley (Tendryng Hall), Middleton (Shrubland Hall), Pettiward (Finborough Hall), Edgar (Red House, Ipswich), Kilderbee (Great Glemham Hall), Berners (Woolverstone Hall). The design included an embossed representation of the encounter and 'a chaste, unostentatious inscription'.

At a meeting at the Bear and Crown (the Whig headquarters at election times), members of the Ipswich Free and Easy Club (not all Whigs) voted to present Broke with a silver-gilt cup and cover costing 100 guineas. It has naval trophies and other decorative devices together with the Broke arms and crest, and is the only valuable artefact left to us in Suffolk; fortunately it was purchased by Ipswich Museum, while most of the other items were sold at the auction of the contents of Shrubland Hall and are now in private possession in the States.

One touching memorial of the sacrifice he made in the action, for his naval career was over and his active involvement in public life severely restricted, was from Mistress Caroline Acton, his mother's sister, so that he was a nephew rather than a brother-in-law. She lived at 12 Lower Brook Street in Ipswich (Knapton House today). Her garden was a green oasis behind the Georgian street frontage. There, sometime after Broke's promotion to rear admiral in 1830, she erected a monument to commemorate her brother-in-law's triumph, a column surmounted by a sphere, all in stone, with a bronze plaque. The column is long gone, but the plaque is Ipswich School Museum. It reads:

THIS COLUMN WAS ERECTED BY MISS CAROLINE
ACTON IN COMMEMORATION OF THE GALLANT
CONDUCT
OF HER BROTHER-IN-LAW, ADMIRAL SIR PHILIP VERE
BROKE, WHEN CAPTAIN OF H.M.S. SHANNON IN HIS
VICTORIOUS ACTION WITH THE AMERICAN FRIGATE
CHESAPEAKE JUNE 1 1814

Selected Bibliography

Adams, H (ed), *The Writings of Albert Gallatin* (Philadelphia, 1879).

Arthur, B, *How Britain Won the War of 1812* (Woodbridge, 2011).

Barbuto, Richard V, *Niagara 1814: America Invades Canada* (Lawrence, KS: University Press of Kansas, 2000).

Bartlett, C J, *Great Britain and Seapower, 1815–1853* (Oxford, 1963).

Baynham, Henry, *From the Lower Deck: The Navy 1700–1840* (London, 1969).

Bennett, Geoffrey, *The Battle of Jutland* (London, 1964).

Bew, John, *Castlereagh*, vol 2 (London, 2011).

Bickham, Troy, *Weight of Vengeance* (Oxford, 2012).

Bourguignon, Henry J, *Sir William Scott, Lord Stowell, Judge of the High Court of Admiralty, 1798–1828* (Cambridge, 1987).

Brighton, Revd J G, *Admiral Sir P B V Broke . . .: A Memoir* (London, 1866).

Brighton, Revd J G, *Admiral of the Fleet, Sir Provo W P Wallis: A Memoir* (London, 1892).

Castlereagh: *see* Shoberl.

Conforti, Joseph A, *Imagining New England: Explorations of Regional Identity from the Pilgrims to the Mid-Twentieth Century* (Chapel Hill, NC, 2001).

Conway, Sir Martin, *No Man's Land: A History of Spitsbergen* (Cambridge, 1906).

Craton, Michael, 'The Caribbean Vice Admiralty Courts, 1763–1815. Indispensable Agents of an Imperial System' (PhD thesis, McMaster University, 1968).

Creighton, Helen, *Traditional Songs from Nova Scotia* (Toronto, 1950).

Darling, Charles W (ed), *The New American Songster: Traditional Ballads and Songs of North America* (Lanham, MD, 1983).

Davey, James and Johns, Richard, *Broadsides: Caricature and the Navy 1756–1815* (Barnsley, 2012).

Dickinson, H W, *Educating the Royal Navy: 18th and 19th Century Education for Officers* (New York, 2007).

Donald, Diana, *The Age of Caricature: Satirical Prints in the Reign of George III* (New Haven, 1996).

Douglas, Sir H, *Treatise of Naval Gunnery* (1820; 4th rev edn, 1855; reprinted London, 1982).

Dudley, Wade G, *Splintering the Wooden Wall: The British Blockade of the United States, 1812–1815* (Annapolis, MD, 2003).

Dudley, W S and Crawford, M J (eds), *The Naval War of 1812: A documentary history*, vol 1, 1812 (Washington, 1985); vol 2, 1813 (1992); vol 3, 1814–15, (2002); vol 4 (forthcoming 2014).

Eustace, N, *1812: War and the Passions of Patriotism* (Philadelphia, 2012).

Ford, James (ed), *The Suffolk Garland or East Country Minstrel* (Ipswich and London, 1818).

Ford, Worthington Chauncey, *Broadsides, ballads, &c printed in Massachusetts 1639–1800* (Boston, 1922).

Forester, C S, *The Naval War of 1812* (London, 1957).

Gardiner, Robert (ed), *The Naval War of 1812* (London, 1998).

Garitee, J R, *The Republic's Private Navy: The American Privateering Business as Practiced by Baltimore during the War of 1812* (Middletown, CT, 1977).

Gatrell, Vic, *City of Laughter: Sex and Satire in Eighteenth-Century London* (London, 2006).

George, M Dorothy, *Catalogue of Political and Personal Satires in the British Museum*, vol 9 (London, 1949).

Gilje, Paul A, *Free Trade and Sailors' Rights in the War of 1812* (Cambridge, 2013).

Gilkerson, William, *Boarders Away II: Firearms in the Age of Fighting Sail* (Lincoln, RI, 1993).

Gleaves, A, *James Lawrence* (New York, 1904).

Green, Jack P, 'Colonial History and National History: Reflections on a Continuing Problem', *William and Mary Quarterly*, 3rd ser, 64 (2007), pp 235–50.

Gwyn, Julian, *Excessive Expectations: Maritime Commerce and the Economic Development of Nova Scotia* (Montreal, 1998).

Gwyn, Julian, *Ashore and Afloat: the British Navy Yard and the Halifax Naval Yard to 1820* (Ottawa, 2004).

Hansard Parliamentary Debates at: www.parliament.uk.

Hattendorf, John B, 'The Third Alan Villiers Memorial Lecture: The Naval War of 1812 in International Perspective', *Mariner's Mirror*, 99.1 (February 2013), pp 5–22.

Hattendorf, John B, 'The US Navy and the "Freedom of the Seas", 1775–1917', in Rolf Hobson and Tom Kristiansen (eds), *Navies in Northern Waters 1721-2000* (London and Portland, OR, 2004), pp 151–74.

Hess, Stephen and Kaplan, Milton, *The Ungentlemanly Art: A History of American Political Cartoons* (London, 1968).

Hickey, Donald R, *The War of 1812: A Forgotten Conflict*, Bicentennial edition (Urbana, Illinois, 2012).

Hill, J Richard, *The Prizes of War: The Naval Prize System in the Napoleonic Wars, 1793–1815* (Stroud, 1998).

Hitsman, J Mackay, *The Incredible War of 1812: A Military History* (Toronto, 1965).

Irving, Washington, 'Biography of Lawrence', *Analectic Magazine*, II (Philadelphia, 1813), pp 137–242.

James, William, *Naval Occurrences of the War of 1812* (London, 1817; reprinted 2004)

James, William, *The Naval History of Great Britain*, vols 1 & 6 (London, 1837; reprinted 2002).

Jenkins, M C and Taylor, D A, *Yardarm to Yardarm: How the War of 1812 Created America's Navy* (Boston, 2012).

Keller, Kate van Winkle, *Ballads and Songs for Boston in the War of 1812 – The Isaiah Collection*, at: ww.1812music,org/ITCEssayR1.

Knight, Roger, *Britain against Napoleon: The Organisation of Victory, 1793–1815* (London, 2013), Chapter 15: The American War, 1812–14: The Manpower Emergency.

Lambert, Andrew, *The Challenge: Britain against America in the Naval War of 1812* (London, 2012).

Lambert, Andrew, *Trincomalee: The Last of Nelson's Frigates* (London, 2002).

Latimer, Jon, *1812: War with America* (London, 2007).

Lavery, Brian, *Nelson's Navy: The Ships, Men and Organisation, 1793–1815* (London, 1988).

Lavery, Brian (ed), *Shipboard Life and Organisation, 1731–1815* (Aldershot, 1998).

Laws, G Malcolm, *American Balladry from British Broadsides* (Philadelphia, 1957).

Laws, G Malcolm, *Native American Balladry* (Philadelphia, 1964).

Leech, Samuel, *A Voice from the Main Deck* (London, 1844).

Liverpool: *see* Yonge.

Madison, James, *An Examination of the British Doctrine which Subjects to Capture a Neutral Trade not Open in Time of Peace* (Washington, 1806; reprint London, 1990).

Mahan, Alfred T, *Sea Power and its Relation to the War of 1812*, 2 vols (Boston, 1905).

Malcomson, Robert, *Lords of the Lake: The Naval War on Lake Ontario, 1812–1814* (Toronto 1998).

Marshall, P J, *Remaking the British Atlantic: The United States and the British Empire after American Independence* (Oxford, 2012).

Martin, T, *A Most Fortunate Ship: A Narrative History of 'Old Ironsides'* (Chester, CT, 1980).

Marryat, Captain F, *Frank Mildmay; or, The Naval Officer* (London, 1828).

McCranie, Kevin D, *Utmost Gallantry: The US and Royal Navies at Sea in the War of 1812* (Annapolis, MD, 2011).

Morgan, Winfred, *An American Icon: Brother Jonathan and American Identity* (London, 1988).

Muir, Rory, *Britain and the Defeat of Napoleon* (London, 1996).

Neeser, Robert W (ed), *American Naval Songs and Ballads* (New Haven, 1938).

Padfield, Peter, *Guns at Sea* (London, 1973).

Padfield, Peter, *Broke and the Shannon* (London, 1968).

Pellew, G, *Sidmouth*, vol 3 (London, 1847).

Poolman, Kenneth, *Guns Off Cape Ann* (London, 1961).

Pullen, H F, *The Shannon and the Chesapeake* (Toronto, 1970).

Rodger, N A M, *The Command of the Ocean: A Naval History of Britain 1649–1815* (London, 2004).

Rushton, Edward, *American Independency* (London, 1806).

Savage, Carlton, *Policy of the United States toward Maritime Commerce in War*, 2 vols (Washington DC, 1934).

Schroeder, P W, *The Transformation of European Politics, 1763–1848* (Oxford, 1994).

Shoberl, W (ed), *Memoirs and Correspondence of Viscount Castle-reagh*, vol 2 (London, 1848–53).

Simpson, Claude M, *The British Broadside Ballad and Its Music* (New Brunswick, NJ, 1966).

Smart, C, *The Works of Horace, Translated Literally into English Prose* (New York, 1821).

Smith, Carleton Sprague, 'Broadsides and their Music in Colonial America', in *Music in Colonial Massachusetts, 1630–1820* (Boston, 1980).

Smith, J M, *Borderland Smuggling: Patriots, Loyalists and Illicit Trade in the North-West, 1783–1820* (Miami, 2006).

Snider, C H J, *Under the Red Jack: Privateers of the Maritime Provinces of Canada in the War of 1812* (London, 1928).

Spavens, William, *The Narrative of William Spavens, a Chatham Pensioner* (London, 1998).

Stagg, J C A, *The War of 1812: Conflict for a Continent* (Cambridge, 2012).

Steel, David, *The Greenland Pilot, being three Charts for the Fisheries of Greenland and Davis Strait* (1790?).

Symonds, C L, *Navalists and Antinavalists: The Naval Policy Debate in the United States, 1785–1827* (Newark DE, 1980).

The Spirit of the Public Journals for 1813, being an impartial selection of the most ingenious essays and jeux d'esprits that appear in the newspapers and other publications, vol 17 (London, 1814).

Tomlinson, Everett, *Stories of Colony and Nation: The War of 1812* (New York, 1906).

Turner, Wesley B, *British Generals in the War of 1812: High Command in the Canadas* (Montreal and Kingston, 1999).

Viztelly, H, *Glances back through Seventy Years: Autobiographical and other Reminiscences*, 2 vols (London,1893).

Voelcker, Tim, *Admiral Saumarez versus Napoleon: The Baltic, 1807–12* (Woodbridge, 2008)

Weitenkampf, Frank, *Political Caricature in the United States* (New York, 1953).

Wheaton, Henry, *A Digest of the Law of Maritime Captures and Prizes* (New York, 1815).

Wood, Gordon S, *Empire of Liberty: A History of the Early American Republic, 1789–1815* (Oxford, 2009).

Yonge, C D, *Life and Administration of the Second Earl of Liverpool*, vol 2 (London, 1868).

Index